Independent Component Analysis

Independent Component Analysis

A Tutorial Introduction

James V. Stone

A Bradford Book
The MIT Press
Cambridge, Massachusetts
London, England

Typeset by the author using LATEX∂ 2$_\varepsilon$.

Printed and bound in the United States of America.

Library of Congress Cataloging-in-Publication Data

Stone, James V.
  Independent component analysis : a tutorial introduction / James V. Stone.
      p.   cm.
  "A Bradford book"
  Includes bibliographical references and index.
  ISBN 0-262-69315-1 (pbk.: alk. paper)
  1. Neural networks (Computer science) 2. Multivariate analysis. I. Title.

QA76.87.S78   2004
006.3'2—dc22
                                                                              2004042589

10 9 8 7 6 5 4 3 2 1

To Nikki, Sebastian, and Teleri

Contents

Preface

This book is intended to provide the essentials of independent component analysis (ICA) using intuitive examples described in simple geometric terms. The tutorial style adopted should make this book suitable for readers of varying mathematical sophistication, from the almost innumerate enthusiast to the research scientist.

In writing this book, I have not been overly concerned with much in the way of mathematical proofs, nor with unnecessary mathematical notation. This approach can be justified to some extent because the rapidly expanding field of independent component analysis is replete with such formal accounts. More generally, formal mathematical proofs require assumptions which are often physically untenable, as noted by Einstein,

> As far as the laws of mathematics refer to reality, they are not certain; and as far as they are certain, they do not refer to reality.

Most importantly, disregarding all but the most important mathematical proofs leaves the reader free to explore the fundamental characteristics of independent component analysis without constantly tripping up the many caveats usually associated with highly mathematical treatments. The resultant tutorial account of independent component analysis is essentially true, even though such essential truths may not include certain technical details and caveats.

The tutorial approach adopted in this book has two consequences. First, important facts are repeated as appropriate in different sections of the book. I make no apology for this. What is obvious to the trained mathematician often bears a degree of repetition to the novice. Second, new topics are usually introduced on a "need to know" basis. This strategy of introducing new topics only when they are required ensures that the account of each new topic is well motivated by the problem at hand, and can be described in terms of relevant examples.

In attempting to understand the details of a particular method, it is often helpful to examine computer code which implements that method. This allows the reader to examine how a given mathematical method described in the text translates into working computer code. With this in mind, basic demonstration computer code is provided in appendices. This code, and more complete versions of it, can be obtained from my web site: http://www.shef.ac.uk/~pc1jvs.

Finally, my intention has been to cut through the distracting issues that inevitably accompany any new method (e.g., variants of independent component analysis methods that are smaller, faster, or cheaper), and to describe the essential core of independent component analysis in relation to a few intuitive examples. However, it must be acknowledged that there are a small number of variants of independent component analysis which, while not essential for understanding the principles of the method, are of considerable interest, and these are described briefly.

Readers are encouraged to send me comments at the following address: Dr JV Stone, Department of Psychology, Sheffield University, Western Bank, Sheffield, S10 2UR, England. Email: j.v.stone@sheffield.ac.uk

Acknowledgments

The inspiration for this book was a workshop on "Information Theory and the Brain" in September 1995, where Anthony Bell presented a paper (by Bell and Sejnowski) on independent component analysis. During subsequent years my enthusiasm for this research area increased as I came to realize that many problems can be usefully reformulated in terms of independent component analysis. My ongoing education in such matters was facilitated during visits to two laboratories in North America. At the University of Toronto, Zoubin Ghahramani, Geoffrey Hinton, and Mike Revow provided a brief but intensive education in linear models. At the Salk Institute in San Diego, discussions with numerous members of Terry Sejnowski's laboratory provided insights into the potential of independent component analysis. These visits were funded by a Wellcome Mathematical Biology Fellowship.

I would like to thank the people who read early drafts of this book: Alistair Bray, Stephen Eglen, John Frisby, Pasha Parpia, Nikos Papadakis, Ying Zheng, and three reviewers: Martin McKeown plus two anonymous reviewers. Stephen Isard deserves special mention for his meticulous comments on several drafts of the book. I would also like to thank John Porrill for discussions of independent component analysis, and Barbara Murphy at The MIT Press for much valuable advice.

Finally, and mostly, I would like to thank my wife Nikki Hunkin for her support and encouragement in writing this book.

J.V. Stone   April 2004
Department of Psychology
Sheffield University
England.

Abbreviations

BSS	blind source separation
cdf	cumulative density function
CLM	central limit theorem
ICA	independent component analysis
PCA	principal component analysis
pdf	probability density function
SVD	singular value decompositoin

Mathematical Symbols

The terms *signal* and *variable* are used interchangeably. Methods particularly relevant to symbols are given in parentheses.

$\lvert . \rvert$	vector length, absolute value of matrix determinant
$.$	dot product of vectors, also known as inner and scalar product
$\mathbf{A}$	mixing matrix
a, b, c, d	elements of mixing matrix $\mathbf{A}$
$\alpha, \beta, \gamma, \delta$	(alpha, beta, gamma, delta), elements of unmixing matrix $\mathbf{W}$
$\overline{C}$	matrix of long-term covariances between signal mixtures
$\hat{C}$	matrix of short-term covariances between signal mixtures
D	diagonal matrix of singular values (SVD)
$\tilde{D}$	truncated version of matrix D (SVD)
$E[.]$	expected value
η	(eta) learning rate constant
F	measure of predictability (1/complexity)
$g(.)$	cumulative density function (univariate or multivariate)
$g'(.)$	first derivative of g, pdf corresponding to cdf g
$g''(.)$	second derivative of g
$H(.)$	entropy
$\mathbf{J}$	Jacobian matrix of derivatives (ICA)
J	Jacobian (scalar, determinant of Jacobian matrix)
K	kurtosis
λ	(lambda) eigenvalue (PCA), factor loading (FA), temporal weighting
M	number of signal mixtures
n	number of possible outcomes (e.g. two for a coin)
∇f_K	(nabla) vector-valued gradient of function f_K
N	number of observed values in a signal (e.g. $s_1 = (s_1^1, \ldots, s_1^N)$)
$p(x^t)$	probability that variable x has value x^t
p_i	probability of ith out of n possible outcomes
$p_s(.)$	pdf of signal s
$p_x(.)$	pdf of variable x
$p_{xy}(.)$	joint pdf of variables x and y
$p_y(.)$	pdf of extracted signal y
$p_Y(.)$	pdf of variable Y
$p_Z(.)$	pdf of variable Z
$\rho(x, y)$	(rho) correlation between signals x and y

s_i^t	tth value of ith source signal
$\mathbf{s}$	vector variable of source signals (extracted by $\mathbf{W}^*$)
σ	(sigma) standard deviation
S	source signal space
S_i	ith axis in source signal space S
S_i'	ith transformed axis, $S_i' = \mathbf{A}S_i$
ψ	(psi) unmixing coefficient
T	superscript (^{T}) denotes transpose operator
$\mathbf{v}_1$	vector of mixing coefficients, $\mathbf{v}_1^T = (a, b)$
$\mathbf{v}_2$	vector of mixing coefficients, $\mathbf{v}_2^T = (c, d)$
U	matrix of short-term covariances (complexity pursuit), set of eigenvectors (SVD)
U_i	short term variance of ith signal (complexity pursuit)
$\tilde{U}$	approximation to eigenvectors U (SVD)
V	matrix of long-term covariances (complexity pursuit), set of eigenvectors (SVD)
V_i	long term variance of ith signal (complexity pursuit)
$\tilde{V}$	approximation to eigenvectors V (SVD)
$\mathbf{w}_i$	ith weight vector for extracting ith source signal from $\mathbf{x}$
$\mathbf{W}$	unmixing matrix, $\mathbf{y} = \mathbf{W}\mathbf{x}$
$\mathbf{W}^*$	optimal unmixing matrix, $\mathbf{s} = \mathbf{W}^*\mathbf{x}$
X	signal mixture space
X_i	ith axis in signal mixture space X
$\overline{x}$	mean value of signal x
x_i^t	tth value of ith signal mixture
$\mathbf{x}$	vector variable of signal mixtures
$\tilde{\mathbf{x}}$	SVD approximation to $\mathbf{x}$
y_i	signal extracted from $\mathbf{x}$ by $\mathbf{w}_i$
$\mathbf{y}$	vector variable of signals extracted by matrix $\mathbf{W}$
$Y = g(y)$	cdf, integral of pdf $p_s(y)$
$\mathbf{Y}$	vector variable, $\mathbf{Y} = g(\mathbf{y})$
$\mathbf{z}$	vector variable of sphered mixtures (complexity pursuit)
z_i	ith scalar variable
Z	variable
$\mathbf{Z}$	vector variable.

I INDEPENDENT COMPONENT ANALYSIS AND BLIND SOURCE SEPARATION

What is essential is invisible to the eye.

—The Little Prince, Antoine De Saint-Exupéry, 1943

1 Overview of Independent Component Analysis

Every problem becomes very childish when once it is explained to you.
— Sherlock Holmes (The Dancing Men, A.C. Doyle, 1905)

1.1 Introduction

It is often said that we suffer from "information overload," whereas we actually suffer from "data overload." The problem is that we have access to large amounts of data containing relatively small amounts of useful information. This is true both in our daily lives, and within many scientific disciplines. Independent component analysis (ICA) is essentially a method for extracting useful information from data.

ICA is of interest to a wide variety of scientists and engineers because it promises to reveal the driving forces which underlie a set of observed phenomena. These phenomena include the firing of a set of neurons, mobile phone signals, brain images (e.g., functional magnetic resonance imaging, fMRI), stock prices, and voices (see figure 1.1). In each case, a large set of signals are measured, and it is known that each measured signal depends on several distinct underlying factors, which provide the driving forces behind the changes in the measured signals. In other words, each measured signal is essentially a *mixture* of these underlying factors.

For example, the 100 stock prices in the London FTSE index represent a set of 100 time-varying measurements, each of which depends on a relatively small number of distinct time-varying causal factors (e.g., the latest retail sales figures, unemployment rates, and weather conditions). Thus each stock price can be viewed as a different mixture of these factors. If these factors could be extracted from the 100 measured signals then they could (in principle) be used to predict future movements of those 100 stock prices.

Similarly, if the time-varying outputs of 100 neurons in the visual cortex of the brain were measured then ICA could be used to test the extent to which all 100 neurons depend on a small set of causal factors, corresponding (for example) to luminance and the orientation of contrast edges. Having identified these factors, it would then be possible to estimate the extent to which each individual neuron depended on each factor, so that neurons could be classified as coding for luminance or edge orientation.

In every case, it is these factors or *source signals* that are of primary interest, but they are buried within a large set of measured signals, or *signal mixtures*. ICA can be used to extract the source signals underlying a set of measured signal mixtures.

1.2 Independent Component Analysis: What Is It?

ICA belongs to a class of *blind source separation* (BSS) methods for separating data into underlying informational components, where such data can take the form of images, sounds, telecommunication channels or stock market prices. The term "blind" is intended

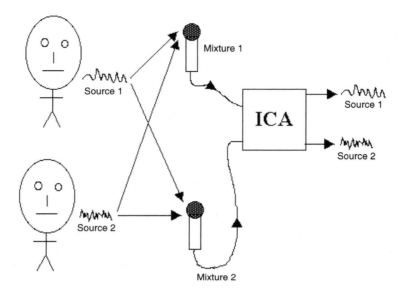

Figure 1.1
ICA in a nutshell. If two people speak at the same time in a room containing two microphones then
the output of each microphone is a *mixture* of two voice signals. Given these two *signal mixtures*,
ICA can recover the two original voices or *source signals*. This example uses speech, but ICA can
extract source signals from any set of two or more measured signal mixtures, where each signal
mixture is assumed to consist of a mixture of source signals (see text).

to imply that such methods can separate data into source signals even if very little is known
about the nature of those source signals.

As an example, imagine there are two people speaking at the same time in a room
containing two microphones, as depicted in figure 1.1. If each voice signal is examined at
a fine time scale then it becomes apparent that the amplitude of one voice at any given point
in time is unrelated to the amplitude of the other voice at that time (see figure 1.2). The
reason that the amplitudes of the two voices are unrelated is that they are generated by two
unrelated physical processes (i.e., by two different people). If we know that the voices are
unrelated then one key strategy for separating voice mixtures into their constituent voice
components is to look for unrelated time-varying signals within these mixtures. Using this
strategy, the extracted signals are unrelated, just as the voices are unrelated, and it follows
that the extracted signals are the voices. So, simply knowing that each voice is unrelated
to the others suggests a strategy for separating individual voices from mixtures of voices.
This apparently mundane observation is a necessary prerequisite for understanding how

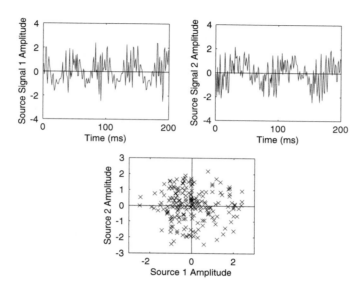

Figure 1.2
ICA exploits the fact that two signals, such as voices, from different physical sources are independent. This implies that, if the two different source voice signals shown in the top panels are examined at a fine time scale then the amplitude of one voice (top left) at any given time provides no information regarding the amplitude of the other voice (top right) at that time. This can be confirmed graphically by plotting the amplitude of one voice at each time point against the corresponding amplitude of the other voice (bottom panel). The resultant distribution of points does not indicate any obvious pattern, suggesting that the two voice signals are independent.

ICA works. The property of being unrelated is of fundamental importance, because it can be used to separate not only mixtures of sounds, but mixtures of almost any type (e.g., images as in figure 1.4, radio).[1]

While it is true that two voice signals are unrelated, this informal notion can be captured in terms of *statistical independence*.[2] If two or more signals are statistically independent of each other then the value of one signal provides no information regarding the value of the other signals.

---

1. In fact, sounds present a harder separation problem than electromagnetic signals, such as radio. This is because sound travels sufficiently slowly that it arrives at different sensors (microphones) at different times. This differential delay can be overcome in practice (e.g., Lee *et al.*, 1997). For simplicity, we will assume there is no such delay in the speech examples considered here.

2. For brevity, we will usually use the term *independence*.

Before considering how ICA works, we need to introduce some terminology. As its name suggests, independent component analysis separates a set of *signal mixtures* into a corresponding set of statistically independent component signals or *source signals*. The mixtures can be sounds, electrical signals, e.g., electroencephalographic (EEG) signals, or images (e.g., faces, fMRI data). The defining feature of the extracted signals is that each extracted signal is *statistically independent* of all the other extracted signals.

1.3   How Independent Component Analysis Works

ICA is based on the simple, generic and physically realistic assumption that if different signals are from different physical processes (e.g., different people speaking) then those signals are statistically independent. ICA takes advantage of the fact that the implication of this assumption can be reversed, leading to a new assumption which is logically unwarranted but which works in practice, namely: if statistically independent signals can be extracted from signal mixtures then these extracted signals must be from different physical processes (e.g., different people speaking). Accordingly, ICA separates signal mixtures into statistically independent signals. If the assumption of statistical independence is valid then each of the signals extracted by independent component analysis will have been generated by a different physical process, and will therefore be a desired signal.

The preceding description represents the high-level strategy implicit in ICA. The mathematical nuts and bolts of precisely how ICA works are described in subsequent chapters. While the nuts and bolts are necessary, grasping the essential physically motivated underpinnings of independent component analysis is the key to understanding these nuts and bolts.

1.4   Independent Component Analysis and Perception

The problem of blind source separation solved by independent component analysis is analogous to the problem encountered by every newborn animal: how to decompose perceptual inputs into their underlying physical causes. For example, if an animal looks at an object then each retinal receptor has an output which is a function of several physical causes, including the luminance, reflectance, slant, tilt, and motion of the object's surface. ICA methods have the potential to provide a rigorous model of how the decomposition of perceptual inputs can be learned by making use of generic and physically plausible constraints, such as statistical independence and spatiotemporal continuity (see chapter 11 for an example using stereo disparity). This is not intended to suggest that the brain implements ICA, but simply that ICA and neuronal computation are based on a common set of underlying principles (see Barlow, 1981) for a classic and lucid account of this type of approach with respect to uncorrelatedness rather than independence).

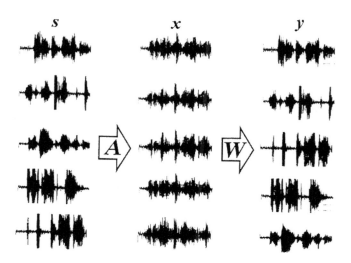

Figure 1.3

Speech Separation.

Left: Each of five people speaking simultaneously generates an independent voice *source signal*. The set of source signals is denoted **s**.

Middle: If there are five microphones present then the output of each microphone is a mixture of five independent source signals (i.e., voices). The (unknown) speaker-microphone distances are represented by the mixing process labeled **A**. The set of signal mixtures is denoted **x**.

Right: ICA extracts five independent components from the set of signal mixtures, where each extracted signal is an estimate of one of the original source signals (i.e. single voices). The unmixing process identified by ICA is denoted **W**, and the estimated source signals are denoted **y**. Note that ICA re-orders signals, so that an extracted signal y_i and its source signal s_i are not necessarily on the same row. From (Bell & Sejnowski, 1995).

1.5   Principal Component Analysis and Factor Analysis

ICA is related to conventional methods for analyzing large data sets, such as *principal component analysis* (PCA) and *factor analysis* (FA) (see chapter 10 and appendix F). Whereas ICA finds a set of independent source signals, PCA and FA find a set of signals with a much weaker property than independence. Specifically, PCA and FA find a set of signals which are *uncorrelated* with each other. This is a crucial distinction, to which we will return later. For example, PCA would extract a set of uncorrelated signals from a set of mixtures. If these mixtures were microphone outputs then the extracted signals would simply be a new set of voice mixtures. In contrast, ICA would extract a set of independent signals from this set of mixtures, so that the extracted signals would be a set of single voices.

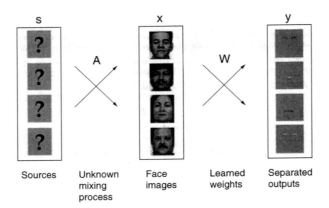

Figure 1.4
Face Recognition.
Left: Each of four prototypical unknown faces is a (spatial) independent source signal. The set of four source signals is labeled **s**.
Middle: The faces of four people are each assumed to be a different mixture of underlying prototypical faces (left), where the mixing process is labeled **A**. The set of four signal mixtures is labeled **x**.
Right: ICA extracts a set of signals, each of which is an estimate of one of the unknown spatial source signals. This unmixing process is labeled **W**, and the set of four estimated source signals is labeled **y**. Note how the estimated source signals contain spatially localized features corresponding to perceptually salient features, such as mouth and eyes. From (Bartlett, 2001).

The "forward" assumption that signals from different physical processes are uncorrelated still holds, but the "reverse" assumption that uncorrelated signals are from different physical processes does not. This is because lack of correlation is a weaker property than independence. In summary, independence implies a lack of correlation, but a lack of correlation does not imply independence.

1.6   Independent Component Analysis: What Is It Good For?

ICA has been applied to problems in fields as diverse as speech processing, brain imaging (e.g., fMRI and optical imaging), electrical brain signals (e.g., EEG signals), telecommunications, and stock market prediction. However, because independent component analysis is an evolving method which is being actively researched around the world, the limits of what ICA may be good for have yet to be fully explored.

Two contemporary applications of ICA are presented in figures 1.3– 1.4. Note that ICA can be used to find independent components which can take the form of speech, electrical signals or images.

In conclusion, ICA is based on a single physically realistic assumption: namely, that different physical processes generate outputs that are independent of each other. In the following chapters it will be shown how this assumption not only provides an intuitive insight into how ICA works but also how it provides insight into how the physical world works.

2 Strategies for Blind Source Separation

The world is full of obvious things which nobody by any chance ever observes.
— Sherlock Holmes (The Hound of the Baskervilles, A.C. Doyle, 1902).

2.1 Introduction

It should be apparent by now that, for our purposes, the world is full of mixtures of source signals, and that most problems can be reduced to unmixing a set of mixtures into their underlying source signals. The problem of unmixing signals is known as *blind source separation* (BSS), and independent component analysis (ICA) is a specific method for performing BSS.

In this chapter, we explore the basic concepts required for understanding BSS and the basic strategies which underwrite BSS methods, such as ICA. We begin by examining the generic effects of mixing signals together, and how these effects can be used as a starting point for unmixing signals. For the present, we consider two signals only, and restrict the examples to speech signals.

Before embarking on this informal account of mixing and unmixing, it should be noted that we will not concern ourselves with much in the way of mathematical precision, nor mathematical notation, in this chapter. This leaves us free to explore the fundamental characteristics of mixing and unmixing without constantly tripping up the many caveats usually associated with mathematical treatments. In short, the following account is essentially true, and the omitted "ifs" and "buts" can wait for the more formal account given later.

As a reminder, recall that we use the term *source signal* to refer to an unmixed signal (e.g., a single voice), and *signal mixture*, or simply *mixture*, to refer to a mixture of source signals.

2.2 Mixing Signals

When two speech source signals are mixed to make two signal mixtures, as shown in figure 2.1, three effects follow. Each of these effects can be used as a basis for unmixing (but only two of these are used by ICA).

Independence: Whereas speech source signals are statistically independent, their signal mixtures are not. This is because each source signal is shared between both mixtures such that the resultant commonality between signal mixtures ensures that they cannot be independent. See figure 2.2.

Normality: If the values in a speech source signal are plotted as a histogram then a "peaky" structure emerges, whereas a corresponding histogram of a sawtooth signal yields a flat histogram. Crucially, a histogram of a signal mixture that is the sum of these two signals

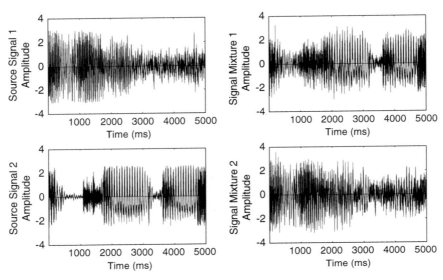

Figure 2.1
Two voice source signals (left) sampled every millisecond (ms) for 5 seconds, and two different mixtures of these voice signals (right). Each mixture could be the output of one microphone placed at different locations in a room with two people speaking at the same time, as depicted in figure 1.1. The different locations of microphones ensure that the two mixtures contain different proportions of each voice signal.

yields a more bell-shaped structure, as shown in figure 2.3. These bell-shaped histograms are referred to as *normal* or *gaussian*.

Complexity. The temporal complexity of any mixture is greater than (or equal to) that of its simplest (i.e., least complex) constituent source signal. This ensures that extracting the least complex signal from a set of signal mixtures yields a source signal. While this conjecture appears to be true in general, it can be observed directly if the source signals are pure tones (sine waves), as shown in figure 2.4.

2.3 Unmixing Signals

The above informal descriptions of three effects of mixing source signals are sufficient to establish basic principles for recovering these source signals from several sets of signal mixtures. In each case, the line of reasoning is the same, and goes something like this:

If the signals we happen to extract from a set of mixtures are independent like source signals, or have non-gaussian (e.g., peaky) histograms like source

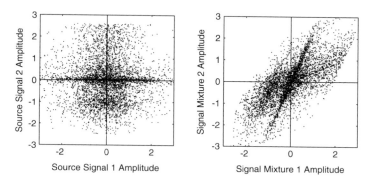

Figure 2.2
Independence.
Amplitude values in two different signal mixtures are more highly correlated than amplitude values in the source signals that contribute to each mixture, because each mixture contains a proportion of each source signal. A graph (left) of values of one voice *source* signal versus corresponding values of the other voice source signal from figure 2.1 therefore has very little structure, suggesting that the two voice signals are unrelated (i.e., independent). In contrast, a graph (right) of values of one voice signal *mixture* versus corresponding values of the other voice signal mixture from figure 2.1 shows that, as one mixture amplitude increases, the other mixture amplitude also increases. Thus the amplitudes of the two mixtures, but not the voice source signals, are correlated.

signals, or have low complexity like source signals, then they must be source signals.

By analogy, if it looks like a duck, walks like a duck, and quacks like a duck, then it must be a duck. In general, this type of strategy can be summarized as follows:

If source signals have some property X and signal mixtures do not then given a set of signal mixtures we should attempt to extract signals with as much X as possible, on the understanding that these extracted signals will be the required source signals.

Now, we can substitute "independence," "normality," and "complexity" for X to yield three principles for unmixing, as follows.

Independence. If source signals are independent and signal mixtures are not then extracting independent signals from a set of signal mixtures should recover the required source signals (as discussed in chapter 1).

Normality. If source signals have non-gaussian (e.g., peaky) histograms and

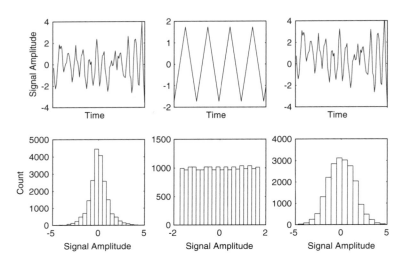

Figure 2.3
Normality.
Signal mixtures have gaussian or normal histograms.
Left: A speech source signal (top) and a histogram of amplitude values in that signal (bottom). A histogram is a graphical representation of the number of times each signal amplitude occurs. Speech signals tend to have amplitudes close to zero, so that the amplitude value with the largest count in the histogram is at zero.
Middle: A sawtooth source signal (top) and its histogram (bottom).
Right: A signal mixture (top) which is the sum of the source signals on the left and middle, and its histogram (bottom).
Any mixture of source signals has a histogram that tends to be more bell-shaped (normal or gaussian) than that of any of its constituent source signals, even if the source signals have very different histograms. For clarity, the top panels display only a small time interval of the signals used to construct the histograms in the bottom panels.

signal mixtures do not then extracting signals with non-gaussian histograms from a set of signal mixtures should recover the required signals.

Complexity. If source signals have low complexity (i.e., simple) structure and signal mixtures do not then extracting signals with low complexity from a set of signal mixtures should recover the required signals.

Although this general type of strategy is not *guaranteed* to work, it sounds highly plausible, and is very effective in practice. All we need now is a method for extracting signals with as much X (e.g., independence) as possible from a set of signal mixtures. In order to examine such methods, we first need to define a notation for mixing and unmixing

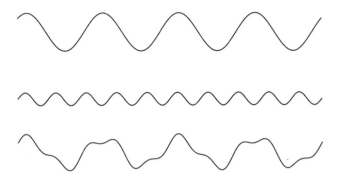

Figure 2.4
Complexity.
The complexity of a signal mixture (bottom) is greater than (or equal to) that of the simplest (i.e., least complex) of its constituent source signals (top). This *complexity conjecture* can be used as a basis for blind source separation. The bottom signal mixture is the sum of the top two source signals. Pure tones (sine waves) have been used in this example to emphasize the effects of mixing on signal waveforms.

signals (see chapters 3 and 4), and then use this notation to construct formal definitions of normality, independence, and complexity.

2.4   The Number of Sources and Mixtures

One important fact about standard BSS methods such as ICA is often not appreciated until some experience with the methods has been gained. Basically, there must be at least as many different mixtures of a set of source signals as there are source signals. For the example of speech signals this implies that there must be at least as many microphones (different voice mixtures) as there are voices (source signals).

If there are more source signals than signal mixtures then BSS methods cannot easily extract these source signals, although there are exceptions, e.g., see (Lewicki & Sejnowski, 2000). In practice, the number of signal mixtures is often larger than the number of source signals. For example, with electroencephalography (EEG) the number of different signal mixtures of a single set of source signals is equal to the number of electrodes on the head (usually greater than 10), and the number of sources is typically less than 10. If the number of source signals is known to be less than the number of signal mixtures then the number of signals extracted by ICA can be reduced either by preprocessing signal mixtures using *principal component analysis* (see section 6.8, chapter 10 and appendix F), or by specifying the exact number of source signals to be extracted (Porrill & Stone, 1997, Amari, 1999, Penny et al., 2001) (see end of subsection 7.7.4).

The reason for the above restriction on the relative numbers of source signals and their mixtures is analogous to the problem of seeing the full shape of a complex object from a set of snapshots. If a series of snapshots are taken from different viewpoints then each snapshot provides new information regarding the three-dimensional structure of the complex object. Similarly, for a given set of source signals, each signal mixture provides a different snapshot of each source signal, and many snapshots are required in order to estimate each individual source signal.

2.5   Comparing Strategies

It is striking that there are several strategies for extracting source signals from signal mixtures, where each strategy has spawned several distinct methods. Surely, if one of these methods is better than the rest, then why bother with the rest? First, because some methods have practical advantages for large data sets. Second, and more importantly, because *any method stands or falls according to the assumptions implicit in that method.* The assumptions associated with every method imply a specific *model* of the mixing process and of the source signals to be extracted. The precise nature of this model may not always be obvious, but it is always present. For example, a method's assumptions may imply a source signal model in which the source signals are independent, or non-gaussian, or have low complexity. Most methods give identical and perfect results for perfect (e.g., noise-free) data. However, if noise is present (and it always is in practical applications), or if the source signals severely violate the assumptions on which a method is based then that method would fail. It is therefore important to have a range of methods available, so that the method chosen is appropriate for the particular problem under consideration.

2.6   Summary

If a set of source signals are mixed to make a corresponding set of signal mixtures then three effects follow:

- the source signals are independent, whereas the signal mixtures are not;

- the histogram of each source signal is more non-gaussian (e.g., peaky) than the histogram of any signal mixture, which tends to have a gaussian histogram;

- the complexity of the simplest (i.e., least complex) source signal is less than (or equal to) that of any signal mixture containing that source signal.

A general strategy for how each of these effects can form the basis of a method for extracting source signals from a given set of signal mixtures was described.

II THE GEOMETRY OF MIXTURES

3 Mixing and Unmixing

3.1 Introduction

In this chapter, we introduce notation necessary for a formal understanding of the nuts and bolts of ICA and other blind separation methods. This notation will allow us to specify precisely what it means to "extract" a signal from a set of signal mixtures.

We begin with a notation for sets of signals like speech, and use this notation to describe how such signals are combined to form signal mixtures. We describe how the mixing process is specified in terms of a set of constants or *mixing coefficients*. We show that if these are known then they can be used to derive a set of *unmixing coefficients*, which can be used to extract source signals from signal mixtures. We then show how these unmixing coefficients can be derived from a set of known mixing coefficients. This will lead to an account (in subsequent chapters) of how ICA works by estimating the unmixing coefficients, even if the mixing coefficients are not known.

3.2 Signals, Variables, and Scalars

So far we have considered ICA in the context of voices, each of which is simply a speech signal varying over time. In order to broaden the discussion beyond speech, we need to define a general notation for signals.

Consider a signal which varies in amplitude from moment to moment, as shown in figure 3.1. For the sake of providing a physical example we will assume that a new signal amplitude is recorded every millisecond. Such a signal can be denoted by

$$s = (s^1, s^2, \ldots, s^N), \tag{3.1}$$

where s is a time-varying signal which takes amplitudes s^1, then s^2, then s^3, and so on (denoted as dots in equation 3.1), for N time steps (milliseconds), and ending with amplitude s^N. (The reason for writing successive signal amplitudes in a horizontal row will become apparent later.) A quantity such as s is usually known as a signal in engineering, and as a *scalar variable* in mathematics.

3.2.1 Images as Signals

Note that the amplitude of s does not have to vary over time, instead it could vary over space, as shown in figure 3.2. For example, if a line is drawn over a picture then the gray-level of the ink beneath that line from point to point along the line; and if many closely spaced lines are drawn in parallel then the entire picture is captured as a series of short signals each of which represents the gray-level variation along a single line (in fact, this is how a TV picture is constructed). This syntactic equivalence between time-varying signals

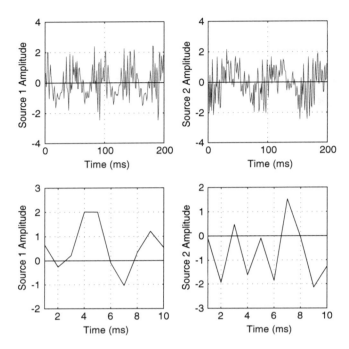

Figure 3.1
Top: Two different speech signals, sampled every millisecond for 200 milliseconds.
Bottom: Close up of speech signals, showing amplitude values over first 10 milliseconds.
Left: $(s_1^1, s_1^2, \ldots, s_1^{10}) =$(0.65 -0.26 0.21 2.01 2.00 -0.10 -1.05 0.32 1.21 0.53).
Right: $(s_2^1, s_2^2, \ldots, s_2^{10}) =$(-0.09 -1.94 0.48 -1.62 -0.09 -1.86 1.52 -0.05 -2.14 -1.26).

(like speech) and space-varying signals (like a TV image) ensures that ICA can be applied to either type of signal, although there will inevitably be some cost in ignoring the intrinsic two-dimensional structure of images. While we make use of temporal (i.e., time-varying) signals in the examples given here, it should be borne in mind that these can also be spatial.

3.2.2   Representing Signals: Vectors and Vector Variables

As we will be considering how to mix and unmix a *set* of two or more signals, we need a succinct notation to represent such sets. To return to the speech example, a set of two time-varying speech signals s_1 and s_2 can be represented as

$$s_1 \quad = \quad (s_1^1, s_1^2, \ldots, s_1^N) \tag{3.2}$$

$$s_2 \quad = \quad (s_2^1, s_2^2, \ldots, s_2^N), \tag{3.3}$$

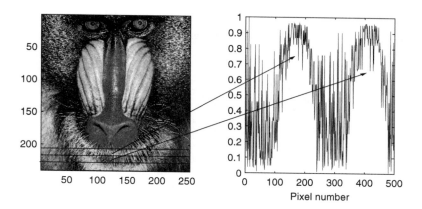

Figure 3.2
Independent component analysis (ICA) of images. As far as ICA is concerned an image (left) is just a signal (right) that has been sliced up into chunks of equal length, where each chunk corresponds to one row (or column) of an image. In this case, the signal formed by concatenating the pixel values of two consecutive rows of the image is shown on the right where the vertical axis indicated pixel brightness, as indicated by the arrows. Treating a two-dimensional (2D) image as if it were a one-dimensional signal ignores the fundamental 2D structure of that image. Despite this, useful results can be obtained using this method (e.g., chapter 11).

where the superscripts specify time, and the subscripts specify signal identity. For example, the amplitude of the second signal s_2 during the third millisecond is denoted s_2^3. Now the amplitude of both signals at this time can be represented as a pair of numbers (which will be written in a single column for reasons that will become apparent later),

$$\begin{pmatrix} s_1^3 \\ s_2^3 \end{pmatrix}. \tag{3.4}$$

Two or more associated scalar variables represented in this way define a *vector*. In this case, the vector $\mathbf{s}^t$ varies over time, and therefore defines a single *vector variable*, $\mathbf{s}$ (usually written in bold typeface). Thus, the third element of the vector variable $\mathbf{s}$ (i.e., the pair of amplitudes during the third millisecond) is a vector,

$$\mathbf{s}^3 = \begin{pmatrix} s_1^3 \\ s_2^3 \end{pmatrix} \tag{3.5}$$

$$= (s_1^3, s_2^3)^T, \tag{3.6}$$

where T is the *transpose operator*. The transpose operator is simply a convenient notation for converting *row vectors* to *column vectors*, and vice versa (see appendix A).

Now the amplitudes of both signals over N milliseconds can be written succinctly as a vector variable $\mathbf{s}$, which can be rewritten in one of several mathematically equivalent forms, as follows,

$$\mathbf{s} = \begin{pmatrix} s_1 \\ s_2 \end{pmatrix} \tag{3.7}$$

$$= \begin{pmatrix} (s_1^1, & s_1^2, & \ldots, & s_1^N) \\ (s_2^1, & s_2^2, & \ldots, & s_2^N) \end{pmatrix} \tag{3.8}$$

$$= (\mathbf{s}^1, \mathbf{s}^2, \ldots, \mathbf{s}^N). \tag{3.9}$$

Although we have used two variables above, any number of signals can be represented by a single vector variable such as $\mathbf{s}$.

3.3   The Geometry of Signals

A geometric interpretation of a set of two signals can be obtained by plotting consecutive amplitudes in s_1 against corresponding amplitudes in s_2, as shown in figure 3.3. This looks messy if we insist on drawing a line between successive data points. These lines indicate the temporal order of signal amplitudes, and as we are going to ignore temporal ordering for now, the line will be omitted, as shown in figure 3.3.

Each data point in figure 3.3 represents the amplitude of both signals at a single point in time. The amplitude of each signal corresponding to a given data point (i.e., at a given point in time) can therefore be obtained by drawing a line from that data point onto each of the axes. In this case, amplitudes of s_1 are obtained by drawing a line from each data point onto the horizontal axis S_1, and s_2 amplitudes are obtained by drawing a line from each data point onto the vertical S_2 axis, as shown in figure 3.3. Note that these lines are drawn at right angles to the desired axis. As two lines at right angles are said to be *orthogonal*, the amplitude obtained by drawing an orthogonal line from one data point to an axis is the length of the *orthogonal projection* of that data point onto that axis.

3.3.1   Mixing Signals

Now that we have a decent representation for a set of source signals, we can specify how such signals become signal mixtures, and then how source signals can be extracted from these mixtures.

As usual, we begin by considering two speech signals s_1 and s_2. When two such speech signals are recorded by a single microphone its output is a signal mixture which is a simple sum of the two signals, as shown in figure 3.4. We define a signal mixture as x_1 (we need the subscript because we will consider many mixtures below). The relative proportion of

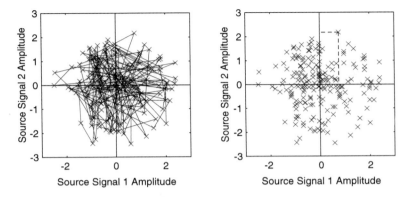

Figure 3.3
Left: Graph of speech source signal s_1 versus speech source signal s_2. Each plotted point represents the amplitudes of both speech signals at one point in time, with successive time points joined by lines.
Right: The same points plotted without lines. The amplitude of signal s_1 at a given time can be obtained by drawing a vertical line from one plotted cross onto the horizontal (S_1) axis, as shown. The corresponding amplitude of signal s_2 at that time is obtained by drawing a horizontal line from the same plotted cross onto the vertical (S_2) axis.

each signal in the mixture x_1 depends on the loudness of each speech sound at its source, and the distance of each source from the microphone. For simplicity, we assume the two sound sources are equally loud.

The different distance of each source from the microphone ensures that each source contributes a different amount to the microphone's output x_1. Let us assume that the microphone-source distances are such that one quarter of the mixture is from source s_1 and three quarters are from source s_2. In other words the mixture x_1 can be specified as a weighted sum of the two source signals, as shown in figure 3.5. Thus the mixture amplitude x_1^t at a given time t is the weighted sum of the source signals s_1^t and s_2^t at that time

$$x_1^t = a \times s_1^t + b \times s_2^t, \tag{3.10}$$

where the weighting or *mixing coefficients* a and b are given by $a = 1/4$ and $b = 3/4$. If we consider x over all N time indices then we have

$$(x_1^1, x_1^2, \ldots, x_1^N) = a \times (s_1^1, s_1^2, \ldots, s_1^N) + b \times (s_2^1, s_2^2, \ldots, s_2^N). \tag{3.11}$$

This can be written more succinctly as

$$x_1 = a \times s_1 + b \times s_2. \tag{3.12}$$

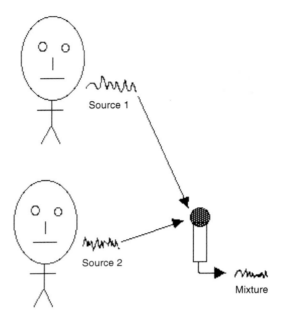

Figure 3.4
The output of a single microphone is a mixture x_1 of two speech source signals s_1 and s_2. If the two voice source signals are equally loud then the relative proportion of each source signal in the signal mixture depends only on the distance from the microphone to each speaker.

For the sake of brevity, we usually omit the symbol ($\times$) for multiplication:

$$x_1 = as_1 + bs_2. \tag{3.13}$$

As we are concerned here with unmixing a set of two signal mixtures (see figure 1.1), we need another microphone in a different location from the first. Again, the different distances of the sources from the microphone ensure that each source contributes a different amount to the microphone's output x_2 such that

$$x_2 = cs_1 + ds_2, \tag{3.14}$$

where the mixing coefficients c and d are different from a and b because the two microphones are in different locations.

Notice that the pair of signal mixtures (x_1, x_2) is analogous to the pair of source signals $\mathbf{s} = (s_1, s_2)^T$, and (x_1, x_2) can therefore be represented as a vector variable $\mathbf{x} = (x_1, x_2)^T$. The mixing process, represented by the four mixing coefficients (a, b, c, d), therefore

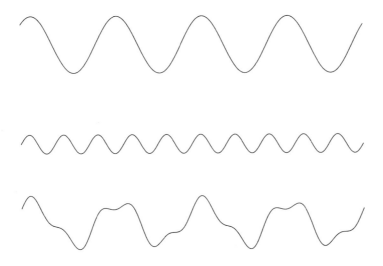

Figure 3.5
A signal mixture x_1 (bottom) is obtained as a *weighted sum* of two source signals s_1 and s_2 (top and middle). The weights or mixing coefficients a and b are determined by the distance of each source from the microphone, so that $x_1 = as_1 + bs_2$, where or $a = 1/4$ and $b = 3/4$ here. Pure tones (sine waves) have been used in this example to emphasize the effects of mixing on signal waveforms.

transforms one vector variable $\mathbf{s}$ to another vector variable $\mathbf{x}$. This implies that each source signal data point $\mathbf{s}^t = (s_1^t, s_2^t)^T$ at a given time t is transformed to a corresponding signal mixture data point $\mathbf{x}^t = (x_1^t, x_2^t)^T$, denoted as $\mathbf{s}^t \rightarrow \mathbf{x}^t$. This transformation has can be represented geometrically, as illustrated in figure 3.6.

3.3.2 Unmixing Signals

Now that we know how signals are combined to form signal mixtures, we can consider how to set about unmixing or extracting signals from their mixtures. For the present we assume the source signals are two speech signals and that the mixing coefficients (a, b, c, d) are known.

First, we need a slightly more formal definition of the problem. We know that each microphone output is a combination of source signals. The precise nature of this combination is determined by the mixing coefficients (a, b, c, d) (which, in turn, are determined by the source-microphone distances),

$$x_1 = as_1 + bs_2 \tag{3.15}$$
$$x_2 = cs_1 + ds_2. \tag{3.16}$$

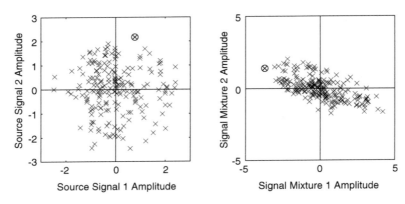

Figure 3.6
Geometric transformation of source signals into signal mixtures. A graph of speech source signal s_1 versus speech source signal s_2 is shown on the left, where each data point represents the amplitudes of both speech signals at one point in time, as in previous figures. Each pair of speech signal amplitudes is represented by a single data point (s_1^t, s_2^t) which is transformed to a corresponding pair of signal mixture amplitudes represented by a mixture data point (x_1^t, x_2^t) (right) (i.e., $(s_1^t, s_2^t) \rightarrow (x_1^t, x_2^t)$). As an example, the circled source signal data point on the left maps to the corresponding circled mixture data point on the right.

Generating mixtures from source signals in this linear manner ensures that each source signal can be recovered by recombining signal mixtures. The precise nature of this recombination is determined by a set of *unmixing coefficients* $(\alpha, \beta, \gamma, \delta)$,[1]

$$s_1 = \alpha x_1 + \beta x_2 \tag{3.17}$$

$$s_2 = \gamma x_1 + \delta x_2. \tag{3.18}$$

Thus the problem solved by all blind source separation methods consists of finding values for these unmixing coefficients. In geometric terms, this consists of finding the spatial transformation which maps a set of mixtures to a set of source signals (see figure 3.6).

We have seen that, just as there is a geometric interpretation for a set of two source signals, so there is a similar interpretation for a set of two signal mixtures x_1 and x_2. In figure 3.7, each data point represents the amplitude of both signal mixtures $\mathbf{x}^t = (x_1^t, x_2^t)^T$ at a single point in time t. The amplitude of each signal mixture corresponding to a given data point (i.e., at a given point in time) can therefore be recovered by orthogonal projection of that point onto each of the axes, as shown in figure 3.7. However, recovering

---

1. These Greek letters are alpha (α), beta (β), gamma (γ), and delta (δ), respectively.

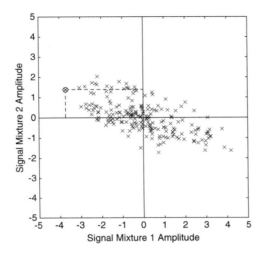

Figure 3.7
Graph of mixture x_1 and corresponding amplitudes of mixture x_2 (this is a copy of the figure on the right hand side of figure 3.6). Each data point represents the amplitudes of both signal mixtures at one point in time. The amplitude of signal mixture x_1 at a given time can be obtained by drawing a vertical line from one plotted cross onto the horizontal (X_1) axis, as shown. The corresponding amplitude of signal mixture x_2 at that time is obtained by drawing a horizontal line from the same plotted cross onto the vertical (X_2) axis.

the amplitude of each mixture is not very interesting because we already know the signal mixture amplitudes. On the other hand, if *source signals* could be recovered from a graph of *signal mixtures* then that would be a different matter. Precisely how this is achieved is the topic of the next chapter.

3.4   Summary

A notation for describing each signal as a scalar variable, and a set of signals as a vector variable, was introduced. The process of obtaining signal mixtures from signal sources using a set of mixing coefficients was introduced, and the reverse process was described in terms of a set of corresponding unmixing coefficients.

It was shown how a set of source signals can be represented as a scattergram in which each point corresponds to the values of the signals at one time, and that a set of mixing coefficients can be used to implement a geometric transformation of each point. The resultant set of "mixture" points can be transformed back to the original set of "source signal" points using a set of unmixing coefficients, which reverse the effects of the original geometric transformation from source signals to signal mixtures.

4 Unmixing Using the Inner Product

4.1 Introduction

In this chapter we describe how source signals can be extracted from a set of signal mixtures given that the mixing process (i.e., the set of mixing coefficients) is known.

The basic strategy is based on the following observation. In a graph of signal mixture x_1 vs. signal mixture x_2, each source signal is associated with a unique *source signal orientation*, as depicted in figure 4.1. Somewhat counterintuitively, this observation can be used to ensure that the source signals associated with all source signal orientations *except one* are excluded from a signal extracted from the set of signal mixtures. In the case of two source signals considered here, this implies that if the source signal orientation of s_2 is excluded from a signal extracted from the mixtures then the extracted signal can only be the source signal s_1.

This extraction process is fairly straightforward once the required source signal orientation is known, and extraction can then be implemented by *orthogonal projection*. The hard task is finding such orientations, and it is this task which is executed by blind source separation (BSS), as described in subsequent chapters.

In order to simplify matters, let us call the space defined by the source signal axes S_1 and S_2 as S, and the space defined by the mixture axes X_1 and X_2 as X, as depicted in figure 4.1. A pair of source signal values $\mathbf{s}_1^t = (s_1^t, s_2^t)$ defines a single point in S, such that a change Δs_2 in the value of only one signal s_2 is associated with a corresponding change in position along a line *parallel* to the axis S_2 in S, as shown in figure 4.1. Now the particular form of transformation induced by the mixing process maps parallel lines in S to parallel lines in X (although line orientations and lengths are usually altered during the transformation). This is known as a *linear transformation*. Therefore, the line defined by Δs_2 in S is transformed to an oriented line $\Delta s_2'$ in X, as shown in figure 4.1. (As might be suspected, the orientation of this line is not random, but is determined by the mixing coefficients (a, b, c, d)).

Now consider what happens to another line in S which is parallel to Δs_2, the vertical axis S_2 (see figure 4.2). This is transformed to an oriented line S_2' in X just like any other line. Note that Δs_2 is parallel to S_2. Now, we know that parallel lines in S map to parallel lines in X, therefore the parallel lines Δs_2 and S_2 in S map to corresponding parallel lines $\Delta s_2'$ and S_2' in X. Moreover, all changes in s_2 are associated with lines parallel to each other and to S_2 in S, and these parallel lines map to a set of lines parallel to each other and to S_2' in X.

A source signal can therefore be extracted from a set of signal mixtures by selecting signal changes associated only with the orientation of the transformed axis S_1' in X. Somewhat counter-intuitively, this is achieved by ignoring changes in X *not* associated with the orientation of the transformed axis S_2'. The logic of this is that, if the signal extracted from

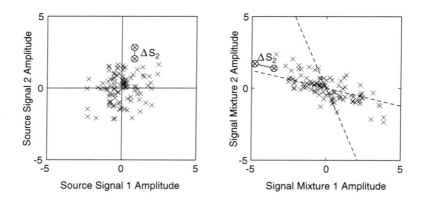

Figure 4.1

Left: A change Δs_2 in the value of signal s_2 induces a change in the position of the plotted point (s_1^t, s_2^t) that is parallel to the vertical axis S_2.

Right: A change Δs_2 in the value of signal s_2 induces a corresponding change $\Delta s_2'$ in the position of the transformed point (x_1, x_2) which is parallel to the projected or transformed axis S_2'.

The space defined by the axes S_1 and S_2 is defined as S (left), and the space defined by the axes X_1 and X_2 is defined as X (right).

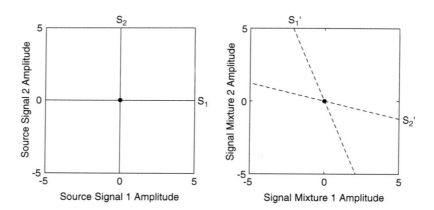

Figure 4.2

Left: The horizontal and vertical axes S_1 and S_2 are orthogonal.

Right: The same transformation that maps source signals **s** to signal mixtures **x** also maps the signal axes S_1 and S_2 in S to a pair of skewed axes S_1' and S_2' in X.

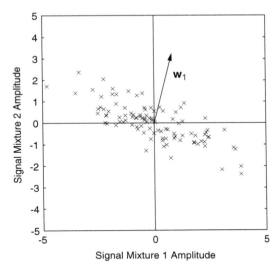

Figure 4.3
In a graph of mixture values x_1 vs. mixture values x_2, the pair of unmixing coefficients (α, β) defines a point with coordinates $\mathbf{w}_1 = (\alpha, \beta)^T$, where $\mathbf{w}_1$ is a weight vector drawn as a solid line. The weight vector defined by these unmixing coefficients extracts source signal $s_1 = \alpha x_1 + \beta x_2$ from the mixtures $\mathbf{x} = (x_1, x_2)^T$. A different weight vector $\mathbf{w}_2 = (\gamma, \delta)^T$ (not shown) extracts source signal s_2.

the mixtures does not contain any influence from s_2 then that signal can only be s_1.[1] This can be extended to multiple signals, by ignoring all orientations in X except that particular orientation associated with one signal. We now examine this analysis in more detail.

4.2   Unmixing Coefficients as Weight Vectors

A source signal s_1 can be extracted from a pair of mixtures $\mathbf{x} = (x_1, x_2)^T$ using a pair of unmixing coefficients (α, β) to recombine the mixtures $\mathbf{x}$,

$$s_1 = \alpha x_1 + \beta x_2. \tag{4.1}$$

Now, just as every pair $\mathbf{x}^t = (x_1^t, x_2^t)^T$ of signal mixture values at time t defines a point with coordinates (x_1^t, x_2^t) in X, so the pair of unmixing coefficients (α, β) defines a point with coordinates $\mathbf{w}_1 = (\alpha, \beta)^T$, as shown in figure 4.3. Note that $\mathbf{w}_1$ is a column vector,

---

1. The extracted signal is actually proportional to s_1, as described in subsection 4.5.1.

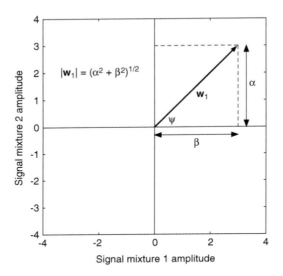

Figure 4.4
A weight vector $\mathbf{w}_1 = (\alpha, \beta)^T$ defines a point with coordinates (α, β). The length $|\mathbf{w}_1|$ of the vector $\mathbf{w}_1$ is simply the distance of the point at (α, β) from the origin. This distance is given by the length of the hypotenuse of a triangle with sides α and β. Thus the vector $\mathbf{w}_1$ has length $|\mathbf{w}_1| = (\alpha^2 + \beta^2)^{1/2}$.

and is referred to as a *weight vector* in this book. In geometric terms, what is special about the vector $\mathbf{w}_1$ that permits it to extract s_1^t from any pair of mixture data points $\mathbf{x}^t$?

Well, any vector can change in only two types of ways. It can change its *length*, and it can change its *orientation*. The length $|\mathbf{w}_1|$ of $\mathbf{w}_1$ is simply the distance of the coordinates (α, β) from the origin, and the orientation of $\mathbf{w}_1$ is the angle ψ between the horizontal axis X_1 and $\mathbf{w}_1$, as shown in figure 4.4.

4.2.1   Extracted Signals Depend on the Orientation of Weight Vectors

We can confirm that changing the length of $\mathbf{w}_1$ by a factor[2] λ only makes the extracted signal larger or smaller (e.g., more loud or more quiet), as follows. If we consider each element of a vector $\mathbf{w}_1 = (\alpha, \beta)^T$ as one side of a triangle, as depicted in figure 4.4 then the length $|\mathbf{w}_1|$ of that vector is the length of the hypotenuse of that triangle

$$|\mathbf{w}_1| = \sqrt{\alpha^2 + \beta^2}. \tag{4.2}$$

---

2. This is the Greek letter lambda.

Changing the length of $\mathbf{w}_1$ by a factor λ can therefore be achieved simply by changing each element of $\mathbf{w}_1$ by the factor λ

$$\lambda|\mathbf{w}_1| \;=\; \lambda\sqrt{\alpha^2 + \beta^2}, \tag{4.3}$$

$$=\; \sqrt{(\lambda\alpha)^2 + (\lambda\beta)^2}. \tag{4.4}$$

Given that $\mathbf{w}_1 = (\alpha, \beta)^T$, it follows that $\lambda\mathbf{w}_1 = ((\lambda\alpha), (\lambda\beta))^T$. The signal extracted by the scaled vector $\lambda\mathbf{w}_1$ at time t is simply a scaled version of the source signal s_1^t,

$$(\lambda\mathbf{w}_1^T)\mathbf{x}^t \;=\; (\lambda\alpha)x_1^t + (\lambda\beta)x_2^t, \tag{4.5}$$

$$=\; \lambda(\alpha x_1^t + \beta x_2^t), \tag{4.6}$$

$$=\; \lambda s_1^t. \tag{4.7}$$

The length of $\mathbf{w}_1$ therefore affects the amplitude of the extracted signal, but does not otherwise affect the nature of that signal. Thus, the extracted signal is a louder or attenuated version of s_1, depending on of the length of $\mathbf{w}_1$.

As noted by Sherlock Holmes, *When you have excluded the impossible, whatever remains, however improbable, must be the truth.*[3] Accordingly, if the length of $\mathbf{w}_1$ does not determine what sort of signal is extracted by $\mathbf{w}_1$ from the mixtures $\mathbf{x}$ then it must be the orientation of $\mathbf{w}_1$.

We can now ask the more specific question: in geometric terms, what is special about the *orientation* of the weight vector $\mathbf{w}_1$ that permits it to extract the source signal value s_1^t from any pair of signal mixture values $\mathbf{x}^t = (x_1^t, x_2^t)^T$?

We will explore this question fully over the next few pages, but the short answer is that the axes S_1 and S_2 in S get transformed to a pair of skewed axes S_1' and S_2' in X (see figure 4.2), such that $\mathbf{w}_1$ extracts s_1 only if $\mathbf{w}_1$ is at 90 degrees to S_2', as shown in figure 4.9. At every other angle, a different mixture y of s_1 and s_2 is extracted, where the relative proportions of s_1 and s_2 in y depends on the orientation of $\mathbf{w}_1$.

In order to investigate why this true, we need to define some additional vector-matrix operations.

4.3 The Inner Product

For the present, consider how the mixtures $\mathbf{x}^t = (x_1^t, x_2^t)^T$ at a given time t are recombined to yield a source signal value s_1^t at that time

$$s_1^t = \alpha x_1^t + \beta x_2^t. \tag{4.8}$$

---

3. From "The Beryl Coronet" by A.C. Doyle.

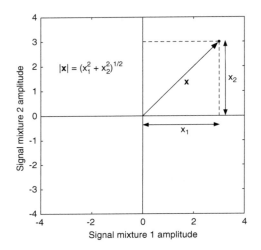

Figure 4.5
A single data point $\mathbf{x} = (x_1^t, x_2^t)^T$ defines a vector with coordinates (x_1^t, x_2^t) (the time index is omitted in the graph above, so that $\mathbf{x}$ refers to a single data point). The length of the vector $\mathbf{x}^t$ is simply the distance of the point at (x_1^t, x_2^t) from the origin. This distance is given by the length of the hypotenuse of a triangle with sides x_1^t and x_2^t. Thus the vector $\mathbf{x}^t$ has length $|\mathbf{x}^t| = (x_1^2 + x_2^2)^{1/2}$ (where the t superscripts have been omitted on the right hand side of this equation).

The particular mixture values $\mathbf{x}^t = (x_1^t, x_2^t)^T$ at time t define a vector which can be plotted on a graph of x_1 vs. x_2, as depicted in figure 4.5. Similarly, the pair of unmixing coefficients (α, β) defines a vector, which can also be plotted as a point on a graph of x_1 vs. x_2 (see figures 4.6 and 4.7). In fact, equation (4.8) is a longhand way of writing the *inner product* of these two vectors.

The pair of unmixing coefficients α and β define a weight vector, which is by convention a *column vector*

$$\mathbf{w}_1 = \begin{pmatrix} \alpha \\ \beta \end{pmatrix}. \tag{4.9}$$

As (α, β) will later form one row of a *matrix* of weight vectors, we need to be able to rewrite $\mathbf{w}_1$ as a *row vector*. This is achieved using the *transpose operator* T introduced in the previous chapter (also see appendix A).

$$\mathbf{w}_1^T = \begin{pmatrix} \alpha \\ \beta \end{pmatrix}^T \tag{4.10}$$

$$= (\alpha, \beta). \tag{4.11}$$

We can now rewrite equation (4.8) as

$$s_1^t = \mathbf{w}_1^T \mathbf{x}^t. \tag{4.12}$$

The the transpose operator T should not be confused with the superscript t, which denotes a time index.

The multiplication or product of two vectors is known as the *scalar*, *dot*, or *inner product*. The inner product requires that there are as many columns in the first term $(\mathbf{w}_1^T)$ as there are rows in the second term $(\mathbf{x}^t)$. This is because the inner product is obtained by multiplying each element in the row vector $\mathbf{w}_1$ by a corresponding element in the column vector $\mathbf{x}^t$, and then adding these products together,

$$s_1^t = \mathbf{w}_1^T \mathbf{x}^t \tag{4.13}$$

$$= (\alpha, \beta) \begin{pmatrix} x_1^t \\ x_2^t \end{pmatrix} \tag{4.14}$$

$$= \alpha x_1^t + \beta x_2^t. \tag{4.15}$$

The result of an inner product is a scalar, which in this case is s^t. If we consider s^t over all N time steps then we have

$$(s_1^1, s_1^2, \ldots, s_1^N) = (\alpha, \beta) \begin{pmatrix} x_1^1, x_2^2 \ldots, x_1^N \\ x_2^1, x_2^2, \ldots, x_2^N \end{pmatrix} \tag{4.16}$$

$$= \alpha x_1 + \beta x_2. \tag{4.17}$$

$$= \mathbf{w}_1^T \mathbf{x}, \tag{4.18}$$

where each single-element column s_1^t is given by the inner product of the row vector $\mathbf{w}_1^T$ and the corresponding column in $\mathbf{x}$. The left hand side of equation (4.18) is simply the source signal s_1, so that

$$s_1 = \mathbf{w}_1^T \mathbf{x}. \tag{4.19}$$

For completeness, the inner product can also be defined in terms of the lengths of $\mathbf{x}^t$ and $\mathbf{w}_1$ and the angle θ between them,

$$s_1^t = |\mathbf{x}^t||\mathbf{w}_1| \cos \theta. \tag{4.20}$$

From this, a key fact regarding inner products can be deduced algebraically. If $\theta = 90$ degrees then $\cos \theta = 0$. Thus, if $\mathbf{x}$ and $\mathbf{w}_1^T$ are orthogonal then their inner product is zero. This can also be deduced geometrically from figure 4.6, as discussed in the next section.

While this describes the syntax of the inner product, it does not yield insight into the underlying geometry, which can be shown to provide the length of the orthogonal projection of $\mathbf{x}^t$ onto $\mathbf{w}_1$.

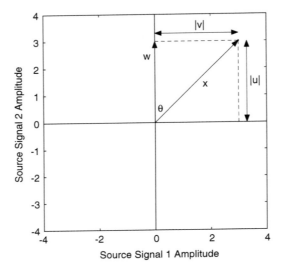

Figure 4.6
The inner product of a vector $\mathbf{w}_1$ with a vector defined by a data point $\mathbf{x}^t$ effectively decomposes $\mathbf{x}^t$ into two orthogonal vectors (superscripts and the subscripts are omitted in the figure). If $\mathbf{w}_1$ has unit length then the value of the inner product $\mathbf{w}_1^T \mathbf{x}^t$ is equal to the length $|\mathbf{u}|$ of the vector parallel to $\mathbf{w}_1$. Note that if $\mathbf{x}^t$ is a pair of mixture values at time t then the inner product $\mathbf{w}^T \mathbf{x}^t$ decomposes $\mathbf{x}^t$ into the vectors $\mathbf{u}$ and $\mathbf{v}$, such that $|\mathbf{u}|$ is proportional to the value of source signal s_1 at time t.

4.3.1 The Geometry of the Inner Product

Consider the inner product of a unit length vector[4] $\mathbf{w}_1$ (that is, a vector with length one) with a vector defined by a data point $\mathbf{x}^t$. One interpretation of the inner product $\mathbf{w}^T \mathbf{x}^t$ is that it splits, or decomposes, $\mathbf{x}^t$ into two orthogonal vectors $\mathbf{u}$ and $\mathbf{v}$ (t superscripts are omitted from $\mathbf{u}$ and $\mathbf{v}$ for clarity). These two orthogonal component vectors are related to $\mathbf{w}_1$ such that $\mathbf{w}_1$ is parallel to $\mathbf{u}$, and is orthogonal to $\mathbf{v}$ as shown in figure 4.6. If $\mathbf{w}_1$ has unit length then the inner product is the length of the component $\mathbf{u}$ parallel to $\mathbf{w}_1$. In figure 4.6, the vector $\mathbf{w}_1$ happens to be colinear with the vertical axis, so that $\mathbf{u}$ and $\mathbf{v}$ are colinear with the vertical and horizontal axes, respectively. However, this orthogonal decomposition of $\mathbf{x}^t$ occurs regardless of the orientation of $\mathbf{w}_1$, as depicted in figure 4.7. There, $\mathbf{w}_1$ is orthogonal to the projected axis S_2', a fact that will prove critical for extracting source signal s_1.

There are two crucial points to note in the case of a unit length vector $\mathbf{w}_1$. First, the value of the inner product is equal to the length of the vector $\mathbf{u}$, denoted $|\mathbf{u}|$. The vector

---

4. The vector $\mathbf{w}_1$ can always be made to have unit length by dividing $\mathbf{w}_1$ by its length, so that $\mathbf{w}_1 = \mathbf{w}_1/|\mathbf{w}_1|$.

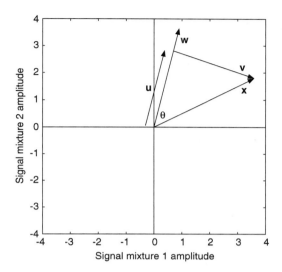

Figure 4.7

The inner product of a vector $\mathbf{w}_1$ with a vector defined by a data point $\mathbf{x}^t$ decomposes $\mathbf{x}^t$ into two orthogonal vectors, $\mathbf{u}$ and $\mathbf{v}$, where $\mathbf{u}$ is colinear with $\mathbf{w}_1$ and $\mathbf{v}$ is orthogonal to $\mathbf{w}_1$ and therefore to $\mathbf{u}$ (superscripts and the subscripts are omitted in the figure). If $\mathbf{w}_1$ has unit length then the value of the inner product $\mathbf{w}_1^T \mathbf{x}^t$ is equal to the length $|\mathbf{u}|$ of the component $\mathbf{u}$ parallel to $\mathbf{w}_1$. Thus the inner product effectively provides the length $|\mathbf{u}|$ of the orthogonal projection $\mathbf{u}$ of $\mathbf{x}^t$ onto $\mathbf{w}_1$. Note that the vector $\mathbf{v}$, which is orthogonal to $\mathbf{w}_1$, has no impact on the inner product $\mathbf{w}_1^T \mathbf{x}^t$.

$\mathbf{u}$ is also the orthogonal projection of $\mathbf{x}^t$ onto $\mathbf{w}_1$. Thus, *the inner product implements orthogonal projection* and provides the length $|\mathbf{u}|$ of the orthogonal projection $\mathbf{u}$ of $\mathbf{x}^t$ onto $\mathbf{w}_1$. Second, *if any two vectors are orthogonal then their inner product is zero* (basically because the length $|\mathbf{u}|$ of the orthogonal projection ($\mathbf{u}$) of $\mathbf{x}^t$ onto $\mathbf{w}_1$ is zero). Thus if $\mathbf{w}_1$ and $\mathbf{x}^t$ are orthogonal then their inner product is zero, as implied by equation (4.20).

4.4   Matrices as Geometric Transformations

4.4.1   Geometric Transformation of Signals

Thus far, we know two apparently unrelated facts about source signals and their mixtures: (1) each signal mixture is obtained by combining source signals, where the precise nature of this combination is determined by a set of *mixing coefficients* (a, b, c, d),

$$
\begin{aligned}
x_1 &= as_1 + bs_2 \\
x_2 &= cs_1 + ds_2,
\end{aligned}
\tag{4.21}
$$

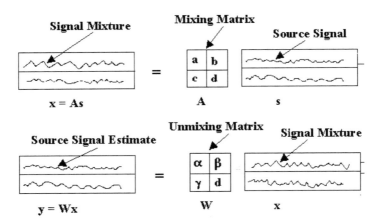

Figure 4.8
Schematic diagram of vector-matrix representation of mixing (top) and unmixing (bottom).
Top: Two source signals $\mathbf{s} = (s_1, s_2)^T$ are transformed by an unknown 2×2 mixing matrix $\mathbf{A}$ to form two signal mixtures $\mathbf{x} = (x_1, x_2)^T$.
Bottom: Two signal mixtures $\mathbf{x} = (x_1, x_2)^T$ are transformed by a 2×2 unmixing matrix $\mathbf{W}$ to form two estimated source signals $\mathbf{y} = (y_1, y_2)^T$.

and, (2) each source signal s_j can be obtained by recombining signal mixtures, where the precise nature of this recombination is determined by a set of *unmixing coefficients* $(\alpha, \beta, \gamma, \delta)$,

$$
\begin{aligned}
s_1 &= \alpha x_1 + \beta x_2 \\
s_2 &= \gamma x_1 + \delta x_2.
\end{aligned}
\tag{4.22}
$$

As might be suspected, these facts are not actually unrelated, as illustrated in figure 4.8. In order to explore precisely how they are related we need to establish a vector-matrix notation for combining signals.

4.4.2 The Unmixing Matrix

Given a single data point $\mathbf{x}_1^t$, we have $s_1^t = \mathbf{w}_1^T \mathbf{x}^t$. As shown in equation (4.18), if we consider all N data points $\mathbf{x} = (x_1, x_2)$ then we have

$$
\begin{aligned}
(s_1^1, s_1^2, \ldots, s_1^N) &= (\alpha, \beta) \begin{pmatrix} x_1^1, & x_1^2, & \ldots, & x_1^N \\ x_2^1, & x_2^2, & \ldots, & x_2^N \end{pmatrix} \tag{4.23} \\
&= (\alpha, \beta)(x_1, x_2)^T \tag{4.24} \\
&= \mathbf{w}_1^T \mathbf{x}. \tag{4.25}
\end{aligned}
$$

Here, each single-element column s_1^t is given by the inner product of the row vector $\mathbf{w}_1^T$ and the corresponding column in $\mathbf{x}$. This can now be rewritten succinctly as

$$s_1 = \mathbf{w}_1^T \mathbf{x}. \tag{4.26}$$

Notice that the vector $\mathbf{w}_1$ essentially extracts s_1 from the signal mixtures $\mathbf{x}$. Similarly, a vector $\mathbf{w}_2 = (\gamma, \delta)^T$ extracts s_2 from the signal mixtures $\mathbf{x}$,

$$(s_2^1, s_2^2, \ldots, s_2^N) = (\gamma, \delta) \begin{pmatrix} x_1^1, & x_1^2, & \cdots, & x_1^N \\ x_2^1, & x_2^2, & \cdots, & x_2^N \end{pmatrix} \tag{4.27}$$

$$= (\gamma, \delta)(x_1, x_2)^T \tag{4.28}$$

$$= \mathbf{w}_2^T \mathbf{x}. \tag{4.29}$$

which can be rewritten succinctly as

$$s_2 = \mathbf{w}_2^T \mathbf{x}. \tag{4.30}$$

Finally, we can define the mapping from $\mathbf{x}$ to $\mathbf{s}$ in terms of an *unmixing matrix* $\mathbf{W} = (\mathbf{w}_1, \mathbf{w}_2)^T$ with rows $\mathbf{w}_1^T$ and $\mathbf{w}_2^T$

$$\begin{pmatrix} s_1^1, & s_1^2, & \cdots, & s_1^N \\ s_2^1, & s_2^2, & \cdots, & s_2^N \end{pmatrix} = \begin{pmatrix} \alpha & \beta \\ \gamma & \delta \end{pmatrix} \begin{pmatrix} x_1^1, & x_1^2, & \cdots, & x_1^N \\ x_2^1, & x_2^2, & \cdots, & x_2^N \end{pmatrix}$$

$$= (\mathbf{w}_1, \mathbf{w}_2)^T (x_1, x_2) \tag{4.31}$$

$$= \mathbf{W}\mathbf{x}. \tag{4.32}$$

The first term on the left is the pair of source signals $\mathbf{s} = (s_1, s_2)^T$, so that this can be rewritten as

$$\mathbf{s} = \mathbf{W}\mathbf{x}. \tag{4.33}$$

Given that $s_1^t = \alpha x_1^t + \beta x_2^t$ the correct way to read equation (4.32) is as follows.

Each column in s_1 is a scalar value which is obtained by taking the inner product of the corresponding column in $\mathbf{x}$ with the first row vector $\mathbf{w}_1^T$ in $\mathbf{W}$. Similarly, each column in s_2 is obtained by taking the inner product of the corresponding column in $\mathbf{x}$ with the second row vector $\mathbf{w}_2^T$ in $\mathbf{W}$. More generally, the jth row s_j in $\mathbf{s}$ is obtained by taking the inner product of each column in $\mathbf{x}$ with the jth row in $\mathbf{W}$.

The reason that a source signal can be extracted by taking the inner product of a weight vector and a signal mixture is described after the next section, in which we examine how signals are mapped to mixtures using vector-matrix notation.

Finally, for completeness, the transpose of $\mathbf{s}$, in which each *column* is a source signal, is given by swapping the order in which $\mathbf{x}$ and $\mathbf{W}$ are written, and transposing them

$$\mathbf{s}^T = \mathbf{x}^T \mathbf{W}^T. \tag{4.34}$$

In this book, and in most other texts, each signal is defined as a row vector. This is an arbitrary decision, and we could equally well have defined each signal as a column vector.

Notation: The size of a data array such as $\mathbf{x}$ or a matrix $\mathbf{W}$ is by convention described as being $M \times N$, where the first figure M is the number of *rows* and N is the number of *columns*.

4.4.3   The Mixing Matrix

Just as the transformation from $\mathbf{x}$ to $\mathbf{s}$ can be written succinctly using vector-matrix notation, so the transformation from $\mathbf{s}$ to $\mathbf{x}$ can be written in vector-matrix form by considering how each mixture is obtained. The mixture x_1 is a combination of source signals, and the mixing coefficients define a vector $\mathbf{v}_1 = (a, b)^T$:

$$
\begin{align}
x_1 &= as_1 + bs_2 & (4.35) \\
&= (a, b)(s_1, s_2)^T & (4.36) \\
&= \mathbf{v}_1^T \mathbf{s}. & (4.37)
\end{align}
$$

Similarly, the mixture x_2 is defined in terms of the mixing coefficients (c, d), which define a vector $\mathbf{v}_2 = (c, d)^T$:

$$
\begin{align}
x_2 &= cs_1 + ds_2 & (4.38) \\
&= (c, d)(s_1, s_2)^T & (4.39) \\
&= \mathbf{v}_2^T \mathbf{s}. & (4.40)
\end{align}
$$

The two row vectors $\mathbf{v}_1^T = (a, b)$ and $\mathbf{v}_2^T = (c, d)$ can be combined into a single *mixing matrix* $\mathbf{A} = (\mathbf{v}_1, \mathbf{v}_2)^T$ such that

$$
\begin{align}
\begin{pmatrix} x_1^1, & x_1^2, & \ldots, & x_1^N \\ x_2^1, & x_2^2, & \ldots, & x_2^N \end{pmatrix} &= \begin{pmatrix} a & b \\ c & d \end{pmatrix} \begin{pmatrix} s_1^1, & s_1^2, & \ldots, & s_1^N \\ s_2^1, & s_2^2, & \ldots, & s_2^N \end{pmatrix} \\
&= (\mathbf{v}_1, \mathbf{v}_2)^T (s_1, s_2) & (4.41) \\
&= \mathbf{A}\mathbf{s}. & (4.42)
\end{align}
$$

Finally the above can be rewritten

$$
\mathbf{x} = \mathbf{A}\mathbf{s}. \tag{4.43}
$$

In summary, a mixing matrix $\mathbf{A}$ maps points $\mathbf{s}$ to the points $\mathbf{x}$, and an unmixing matrix $\mathbf{W}$ maps $\mathbf{x}$ back to $\mathbf{s}$, as depicted in figures 4.1 and 4.8. These mappings are defined by the matrices $\mathbf{A}$ and $\mathbf{W}$:

$$\mathbf{x} = \mathbf{As} \tag{4.44}$$

$$\mathbf{s} = \mathbf{Wx}. \tag{4.45}$$

It can be seen that $\mathbf{W}$ reverses, or inverts, the effects of $\mathbf{A}$, and indeed $\mathbf{W}$ could be estimated from the *matrix inverse* $\mathbf{A}^{-1}$, if $\mathbf{A}$ were known (the matrix inverse is analogous to the more familiar inverse for scalar variables, such as $x^{-1} = 1/x$). However, as we are ultimately concerned with finding $\mathbf{W}$ when $\mathbf{A}$ is not known, we cannot estimate $\mathbf{W}$ from the inverse of $\mathbf{A}$, and will not therefore describe how matrix inverses are estimated. The point is that $\mathbf{A}$ and $\mathbf{W}$ are complementary, inasmuch as each reverses the effects of the other.

For now we will examine how unmixing occurs if we know $\mathbf{W}$, by considering how a single axis S_2 is mapped to a line S_2' in a graph of x_1 vs. x_2.

4.5   The Mixing Matrix Transforms Source Signal Axes

Recall that the space defined by the axes S_1 and S_2 is S, and the space defined by axes X_1 and X_2 is X. The vector with coordinates $(0, 1)$ lies in the axis S_2 in S. We will use the symbol S_2 to refer to the vector $(0, 1)$ and to the axis S_2. The mixing matrix $\mathbf{A}$ can be used to transform the vector S_2 just as if it were a data point:

$$S_2' = \mathbf{A}S_2 \tag{4.46}$$

$$= \begin{pmatrix} a & b \\ c & d \end{pmatrix} \begin{pmatrix} 0 \\ 1 \end{pmatrix} \tag{4.47}$$

$$= \begin{pmatrix} 0a + 1b \\ 0c + 1d \end{pmatrix} \tag{4.48}$$

$$= \begin{pmatrix} b \\ d \end{pmatrix}. \tag{4.49}$$

Thus the axis S_2 in S maps to a line colinear with the vector $S_2' = (b, d)^T$ in X. We shall use the symbol S_2' to refer to both the line and vector here. Similarly, the axis S_1 in S maps to a vector $S_1' = (a, c)^T$ in X, as shown in figure 4.2. We can thus rewrite the matrix $\mathbf{A}$ in terms of the transformed axes S_1' and S_2',

$$\mathbf{A} = \begin{pmatrix} a & b \\ c & d \end{pmatrix} \tag{4.50}$$

$$= (S_1', S_2'). \tag{4.51}$$

Critically, changes in the value of source signal s_1 induce movement of data points along lines parallel to S_1 in S, and these same changes also induce movement of data points along lines parallel to the transformed axis S_1' in X.

4.5.1   Extracting One Source Signal from Two Mixtures

We have seen how a mixing matrix $\mathbf{A}$ maps points $\mathbf{s}$ to the points $\mathbf{x}$, and that an unmixing matrix $\mathbf{W}$ maps $\mathbf{x}$ back to $\mathbf{s}$. In order to examine how this unmixing occurs, we consider how a single source signal s_1 is extracted by the unmixing vector $\mathbf{w}_1$,

$$s_1 = \mathbf{w}_1^T \mathbf{x}. \tag{4.52}$$

If we substitute $\mathbf{x} = \mathbf{As}$ into equation (4.52) then we have

$$s_1 = \mathbf{w}_1^T (\mathbf{As}). \tag{4.53}$$

This can be considered in terms of the inner product of each column in $\mathbf{A}$ with the row vector $\mathbf{w}_1^T$,

$$s_1 = \mathbf{w}_1^T \mathbf{As} \tag{4.54}$$
$$= \mathbf{w}_1^T (S_1', S_2')(s_1, s_2). \tag{4.55}$$

Recall that the inner product of two orthogonal vectors is zero. Now, *if $\mathbf{w}_1^T = (\alpha, \beta)$ is orthogonal to the transformed axis $S_2' = (b, d)^T$ then, by definition,*

$$\mathbf{w}_1^T S_2' = 0. \tag{4.56}$$

In contrast, as shown in figure 4.9, the vectors S_1' and $\mathbf{w}_1$ are not orthogonal so that the inner product $\mathbf{w}_1^T S_1' = (\alpha, \beta)(a, c)^T$ yields a non-zero constant k,

$$\mathbf{w}_1^T S_1' = k, \tag{4.57}$$
$$= |S_1'||\mathbf{w}_1|\cos\theta, \tag{4.58}$$

where θ is the angle between S_1' and $\mathbf{w}_1$ (see equation (4.20)). Note that the value of k does not depend on which data point $\mathbf{x}^t$ is considered because $\mathbf{x}^t$ does not appear in equation (4.57). Substituting equations (4.56) and (4.57) into equation (4.55) yields

$$s_1 = (k, 0)(s_1, s_2)^T \tag{4.59}$$
$$= ks_1 + 0s_2 \tag{4.60}$$
$$= ks_1. \tag{4.61}$$

Thus, a scaled version ks_1 of the source signal s_1 is extracted from the mixture $\mathbf{x}$ by taking the inner product of each mixture data point $\mathbf{x}^t$ with a vector $\mathbf{w}_1^T$ *that is orthogonal to the transformed axis S_2' in X.*

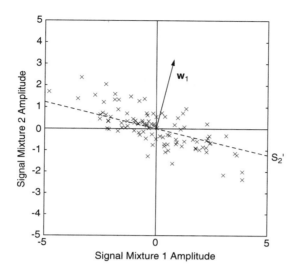

Figure 4.9

The vertical axis S_2 (which is colinear with the vector $(0, 1)^T$) in S gets mapped to a line $S_2' = (b, d)^T$ in X by the mixing matrix $\mathbf{A}$. The weight vector $\mathbf{w}_1^T = (\alpha, \beta)$ extracts source signal $s_1 = \mathbf{w}_1^T \mathbf{x}$ from the mixture $\mathbf{x} = (x_1, x_2)^T$ only if $\mathbf{w}_1$ is orthogonal to the transformed axis S_2'. At any other orientation, $\mathbf{w}_1$ simply extracts a different mixture of the source signals s_1 and s_2.

The fact that s_1 is scaled by an unknown constant factor k does not matter for our purposes. This implies that we can extract source signals from signal mixtures, but we cannot recover the *amplitude* of each source signal. Indeed, given source signal s_1, the signal extracted by ICA is actually ks_1, where $k = |S_1'||\mathbf{w}_1| \cos \theta$. For simplicity we assume $k = 1$ here so that

$$s_1 = \mathbf{w}_1^T \mathbf{x}. \tag{4.62}$$

Recall that the length of $\mathbf{w}_1$ does not affect the form of s_1, only its amplitude. Similarly, the source signal s_2 is extracted from the mixture $\mathbf{x}$ by taking the inner product of each mixture data point $\mathbf{x}^t$ with a vector $\mathbf{w}_2$ that is orthogonal to the transformed axis S_1' in X:

$$s_2 = \mathbf{w}_2^T \mathbf{x}. \tag{4.63}$$

Given that $\mathbf{W} = (\mathbf{w}_1, \mathbf{w}_2)^T$ and $\mathbf{s} = (s_1, s_2)^T$, these equations can be combined to yield

$$\mathbf{s} = \mathbf{W}\mathbf{x}. \tag{4.64}$$

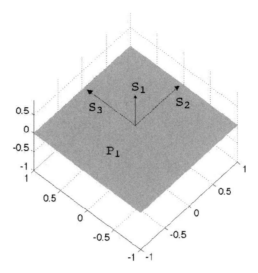

Figure 4.10
Three-dimensional source signal space.
Three-dimensional space S defined by three orthogonal axes, drawn here as three orthogonal vectors S_1, S_2, and S_3. Any pair of vectors define a plane, and the plane P_1 defined by vectors S_2 and S_3 is shown as a shaded region. Different values of the source signal s_1 are associated with different locations along the vector S_1, and different values of the source signals s_2 and s_3 are associated with different locations along the vectors S_2 and S_3, respectively. Note that the value of three source signals s_1, s_2, and s_3 at one time t defines a point with coordinates $\mathbf{s}^t = (S_1 = s_1^t, S_2 = s_2^t, S_3 = s_3^t)$ (not shown).

Thus, the matrix $\mathbf{W}$ extracts multiple sources signals from the mixtures $\mathbf{x}$ because *each row in $\mathbf{W}$ is a vector which is orthogonal to one transformed signal axis, S_1' or S_2'.*

Unfortunately, we do not know the matrices $\mathbf{W}$ nor $\mathbf{A}$. However, provided we know that each row vector in $\mathbf{W}$ extracts one source signal, and we know what a source signal should look like (see chapter 2), then we could rotate each row vector in $\mathbf{W}$ until the signal extracted by that vector looks like a source signal. This is the key to implementing ICA.

4.5.2   Extracting Source Signals from Three Mixtures

Just as a source signal s_1 can be extracted from a pair of mixtures $\mathbf{x} = (x_1, x_2)^T$ by finding that weight vector $\mathbf{w}_1^T$ which is orthogonal to the transformed axis S_2', is it also possible to extract s_1 from three mixtures $\mathbf{x} = (x_1, x_2, x_3)^T$ (see figures 4.10 and 4.11).

Consider three source signals $\mathbf{s} = (s_1, s_2, s_3)^T$. The signal values at a given time

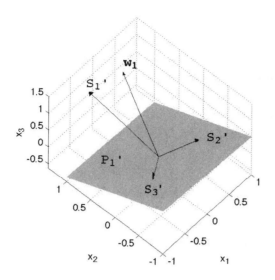

Figure 4.11

Three-dimensional signal mixture space.

Any pair of orthogonal vectors (e.g., S_1 and S_2) in S of figure 4.10 are mapped by a 3×3 mixing matrix $\mathbf{A}$ to a pair of (usually) non-orthogonal vectors (e.g. S_2' and S_3') in the 3D mixture space X, where they define a plane P_1' (shaded area). Different values of the source signal s_1 are associated with different locations along the transformed vector S_1', and different values of the source signals s_2 and s_3 are associated with different locations along the transformed vectors S_2' and S_3', respectively. If an unmixing vector $\mathbf{w}_1$ is orthogonal to P_1' then any signal extracted by $\mathbf{w}_1$ is unaffected by the changes in the signals s_2 and s_3 associated with the mapped axes S_2' and S_3'. The signal extracted by $\mathbf{w}_1$ is therefore proportional to s_1, where the constant of proportionality is determined by the cosine of the angle θ between $\mathbf{w}_1$ and the transformed vector S_1'.

$\mathbf{s}^t = (s_1^t, s_2^t, s_3^t)^t$ define a point in a three dimensional space, so that the set of values in $\mathbf{s} = (s_1, s_2, s_3)^T$ defines a cluster of points in this space. For brevity, the term three-dimensional space is often abbreviated to 3D space, or simply 3-space.

These three source signals are transformed to three signal mixtures $\mathbf{x} = (x_1, x_2, x_3)^T$ by a 3×3 mixing matrix $\mathbf{A}$

$$\mathbf{x} = \mathbf{As}. \tag{4.65}$$

In common with the two-dimensional (2D) case (i.e., two signals and two mixtures), each column of $\mathbf{A}$ is a vector which specifies the orientation of a mapped axis in the 3D space X of mixtures. Thus, changes in the amplitude of source signal s_1 are associated with the mapped axis S_1', changes in the amplitude of source signal s_2 are associated with the mapped axis S_2', and changes in the amplitude of source signal s_3 are associated with the mapped axis S_3'.

In the 2D case, it sufficed to find that weight vector $\mathbf{w}_1$ which was orthogonal to one mapped axis S_2' in order to extract s_1. In the 3D case, it is necessary to find that weight vector $\mathbf{w}_1$ which is orthogonal to *two* mapped axes S_2' and S_3' in order to extract s_1. This is because *any signal extracted by such a vector is unaffected by the changes in s_2 and s_3 associated with the mapped axes S_2' and S_3'.*

In fact, finding such a vector is not as difficult as it sounds, because the mapped axes S_2' and S_3' are just two lines in X, and any two lines define a plane (provided they are not colinear). Therefore, in order to extract s_1 it is necessary to find that weight vector $\mathbf{w}_1$ which is orthogonal to the plane P_1' defined by the two mapped axes S_2' and S_3' in X. Note that the plane P_1' is simply a transformed version of the plane P_1 defined by the orthogonal axes S_2 and S_3 in S.

Thus, the source signals s_1, s_2 and s_3 can be extracted if the weight vectors $\mathbf{w}_1, \mathbf{w}_2,$ and $\mathbf{w}_3$ are each orthogonal to a different transformed plane P_1', P_2' and P_3', respectively. As before, each weight vector forms one row of a 3×3 unmixing matrix $\mathbf{W}$:

$$\mathbf{W} = (\mathbf{w}_1, \mathbf{w}_2, \mathbf{w}_3)^T. \tag{4.66}$$

The key observation is made explicit in the 3D case, as follows. In a 3D space, any vector *defines* a 2D plane to which it is orthogonal. If two transformed axes, say S_2' and S_3', lie in this plane then the signal extracted by the vector $\mathbf{w}_1$ is unaffected by changes in every source signal except for changes s_1. In other words, $\mathbf{w}_1$ extracts source signal s_1.

Extracting Source Signals from More Than Three Mixtures   The extension beyond two mixtures can be carried on indefinitely. In an M-dimensional (MD) space any vector defines an $(M-1)$-dimensional plane to which it is is orthogonal (a 'plane' with more than two dimensions is called a *hyperplane*).

A set of M source signals define a cloud of points in an MD space S. These M source signals are transformed from S to M mixtures in X by an $M \times M$ mixing matrix $\mathbf{A}$. In X, a weight vector $\mathbf{w}_i$ defines an $(M-1)$D hyperplane P_i' such that $\mathbf{w}_i$ is orthogonal to P_i'. The orientation of $\mathbf{w}_i$ is chosen such that $(M-1)$ transformed axes lie in the hyperplane P_i'. Such a choice ensures that the signal extracted by the vector $\mathbf{w}_i$ is unaffected by changes in every source signal except for changes in s_i. In other words, $\mathbf{w}_i$ extracts source signal s_i from a set of M signal mixtures.

4.6 Summary

Changes in the value of each source signal in signal space are associated with a single unknown "source signal orientation". This orientation is determined by the mapping ($\mathbf{A}$) from signal space to mixture space.

Unmixing coefficients define weight vectors in mixture space, and each weight vector can be used to extract a single source signal. In order for a weight vector to extract one source signal that weight vector must be orthogonal to the orientations associated with all but one source signal.

Just as unmixing coefficients define a weight vector, so each set of signal mixtures values at a given time define a vector. A signal is extracted by taking the inner product of a weight vector with the set of vectors defined by signal mixtures. This essentially implements orthogonal projection of the signal mixture vectors onto the weight vector. As this weight vector is orthogonal to all but one "source signal orientation," the inner product of the weight vector is zero with all but one source signal orientation. Consequently, only one source signal amplitude is reflected in the signal extracted by each weight vector.

A complete set of weight vectors defines an unmixing matrix, where each weight vector extracts a different source signal. The unmixing matrix implements a geometric transformation from signal mixture space to source signal space. The mixing matrix implements the reverse transformation from mixture space to source signal space.

ICA and related methods find a set of weight vectors such that each vector is orthogonal to all source signal orientations except one. This chapter showed only how each source signal could be extracted if the weight vector associated with each source signal had been obtained by such a method.

5 Independence and Probability Density Functions

5.1 Introduction

Thus far we have established that the correct weight vector can extract exactly one source signal from a set of signal mixtures, but we do not yet have a strategy for finding such a weight vector. Fortunately, if we know of some property possessed by source signals, which is not also possessed by signal mixtures, then it is possible to extract source signals from signal mixtures (see chapter 2). In practice, this translates to assuming that source signals have *more* of some property (e.g., statistical independence) than signal mixtures, and, then finding a set of unmixing coefficients that maximizes the amount of this property in extracted signals, on the understanding that such signals are the required source signals.

In principle, it is possible to find the correct weight vector (and therefore the unmixing coefficients) for one source signal by rotating a weight vector $\mathbf{w}_1$ around the origin, and evaluating the extracted signal $y = \mathbf{w}_1^T \mathbf{x}$ at each orientation, until the chosen property is maximized. In practice, there are more efficient gradient based methods for doing this, but the "brute force" exhaustive search method just described gives a flavor of the basic problem. This exhaustive search method is illustrated for each of the properties considered below, and the gradient based search method is described in chapter 9.

In order to be able to estimate how much of a given property is possessed by a putative source signal which has been extracted by a weight vector $\mathbf{w}_1$, we need to define a formal measure of that property. The properties of interest to us (normality, independence, and complexity) are defined in terms of *moments* of *probability density functions*, which are essentially a form of normalized *histograms*.

5.2 Histograms

If you measure the height of a thousand people, and count the number of people with each height, then the resultant set of counts can be used to construct a *histogram*. A histogram is a graphical representation of a set of such counts (see figure 5.1).

Specifically, the heights $x = \{x^1, x^2, \ldots, x^N\}$ of $N = 1000$ people could be used to construct a histogram as follows. As we want to count the number of people with different heights, we need to divide the range of measured heights into a number of intervals, say, $\Delta x = 1$ inch, between 60 and 84 inches. This yields a total of 24 *bins*, where each bin is defined by a lower and upper bound (e.g., the first bin's bounds are between 60 and 61 inches, the second between 61 and 62 inches, and so on). For each bin, we count the number of measured heights that fall between the lower and upper bound of that bin. We would expect relatively few measurements to fall in the first bin (with bounds 60 and 61 inches) and last bins (with bounds 83 and 84 inches), because they lie at the extreme ranges of human height. Conversely, we would expect a large proportion of measurements

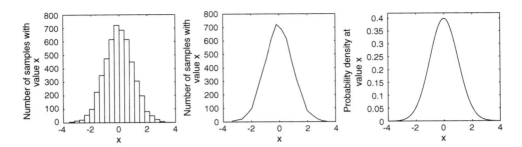

Figure 5.1

A histogram is a graphical representation of the number of times each signal amplitude, or value, occurs in that signal.

Left: A histogram of N amplitude values in a normal or gaussian signal mixture x sampled at each of N points $\{x^1, x^2, \ldots, x^N\}$. A histogram is constructed by dividing possible values of x into a number of intervals or bins $[x, x + \Delta x]$ where each bin has width Δx, and then counting how many sampled values of x lie within the interval associated with each bin. The value of x corresponding to the centre of each bin is plotted on the horizontal axis, and the number of samples $n(i)$ in the ith bin is plotted on the vertical axis.

Middle: Outline of the histogram (obtained by drawing a curve through adjacent bin heights) it can be seen that this is an approximation to the *probability density function* (pdf) $p_x(x)$ (right) of x.

Right: The probability density function $p_x(x)$ of x. A probability density function is essentially a normalized version of a histogram in which the number of signal samples is assumed to be infinite, and the bin width $\Delta x = dx$ is infinitesimally small. The area under the probability density function curve is unity.

to fall in bins with bounds around 72 inches, because this is a common human height. The resultant histogram has a typical bell shape.

In a histogram, the ith bin with bounds $[x_i, x_i + \Delta x]$ provides an estimate of the number m_i of measured values that fall between x_i and $(x_i + \Delta x)$ (e.g., between 65 and 66 inches). If the histogram is based on N measurements partitioned into M bins then the estimated probability that x falls within the interval defined by the ith bin is equal to the area occupied by the ith bin expressed as a proportion of the sum of areas occupied by all M bins. The area of the ith bin is its height m_i times its width Δx, $m_i \Delta x$, and the sum of all M bin areas is therefore

$$m_1 \Delta x + m_2 \Delta x +, \ldots, + m_M \Delta x \qquad (5.1)$$

$$= (m_1 + m_2 +, \ldots, + m_M) \times \Delta x \qquad (5.2)$$

$$= \left(\sum_{i=1}^{M} m_i \right) \times \Delta x, \qquad (5.3)$$

where the symbol $\sum$ denotes summation over M terms (bins). The limits of this summation ($i = 1$ to $i = M$) are specified as subscripts and superscripts, but these are often omitted if the values of limits are obvious. Thus the probability that x falls in the ith bin is

$$p(x_i < x \le (x_i + \Delta x)) \quad = \quad \frac{m_i \Delta x}{\sum_j m_j \Delta x} \tag{5.4}$$

$$= \quad \frac{m_i \Delta x}{\Delta x \sum_j m_j} \tag{5.5}$$

$$= \quad \frac{m_i}{N} \tag{5.6}$$

where $(x_i < x \le (x_i + \Delta x))$ is interpreted as, "x_i is less than x, and x is less than or equal to $(x_i + \Delta x)$," that is, x lies between x_i and $(x_i + \Delta x)$; and $p(x_i < x \le (x_i + \Delta x))$ is the probability that x lies between x_i and $(x_i + \Delta x)$.

Probability Density

For convenience, we can express each bin area as a probability by dividing it by the sum total of all bin areas, so that the sum total of all bin areas becomes unity. Note that the probability associated with a given bin is not the height of that bin expressed as a proportion of the height of all bins. It is the *area* of that bin expressed as a proportion of the total area of all bins. If the probability associated with a bin is its area, and this is given by its height times its width, then it follows that the height of a bin can be interpreted as a *probability density*. By analogy, the mass (probability) of a small section of wire can be obtained as its mass per unit length (density) multiplied by the length of the section (bin width) under consideration.

The fact that we have used a finite sample N to construct the histogram of x values means that it has a lumpy appearance. As the sample size is increased, the bin widths can be made smaller. In the limiting case as the bin width approaches zero (denoted $\Delta x \to 0$), the height of each bin approaches a probability density, and the shape of the histogram of x values approaches that of the *probability density function* (pdf) of the variable x, denoted $p_x(x)$. Thus, a pdf can be considered as an idealized histogram of some variable or signal.

Notation Before embarking on a description of probability density functions it should be emphasized that the letter p without superscripts or subscripts always denotes a probability. For example, $p(x < x_i)$ is the probability that x is less than x_i. In contrast, the subscripted letter x in p_x denotes a function, in this case a probability density function. When written within parentheses this denotes the probability density $p_x(x)$ of its argument x.

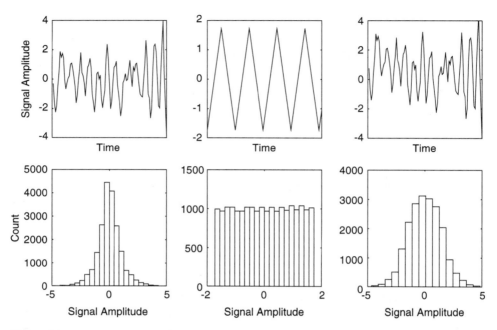

Figure 5.2

Left: A speech source signal (top) and its histogram (bottom). Speech signals tend to contain a large proportion of silence, so that the amplitude value with the largest count in the histogram is at zero. Note that the histogram disregards any information about the temporal ordering of values in the speech signal.

Middle: A sawtooth source signal (top) and its histogram (bottom).

Right: A signal mixture (top) which is the sum of the source signals on the left and middle, and its histogram (bottom).

Any mixture of source signals has a histogram that tends to be more bell-shaped (normal or gaussian) than that of any of its constituent source signals, even if the source signals have very different histograms. For clarity, the top panels display only a small time interval of the signals used to construct the histograms in the bottom panels. The speech and sawtooth signals were each normalized have unit variance.

5.3 Histograms and Probability Density Functions

A histogram is a graphical representation of a set of counts, and a histogram of people's heights typically yields a bell shape (see figure 5.1). This ubiquitous histogram is a good approximation to the *normal* or *gaussian* pdf. The normal pdf is not only ubiquitous in the sense that it is the pdf of choice when confronted with hard statistical problems (see any

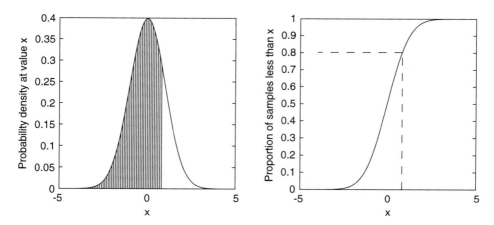

Figure 5.3

Left: A gaussian pdf $p_x(x)$ defined by equation (5.7). The probability that x is less than or equal to some value $x0 = 0.9$ is given by the total area of the shaded region.

Right: A cdf is a function g which is the integral $X = g(x)$ of its pdf $p_x(x)$, and therefore returns the area under the pdf for any specified value $x0$ of x. As can be seem from the pdf on the left, the area under $p_x(x)$ between $x = -\infty$ and $x0 = 0.9$ is the probability that x is less than or equal to $x0 = 0.9$, and is given by $g(x0) = 0.8$, indicated by the dashed line.

statistics book), it is ubiquitous for the following remarkable fact. Almost any measured quantity which depends on several underlying factors has a gaussian pdf (see figure 5.2). Naturally, there are multiple caveats to this claim, but it is essentially true, and captures the essence of the *central limit theorem* (CLT) (stated more formally at the end of this chapter).

In the case of human height it is not implausible that this depends on many underlying factors. The CLT ensures that if we could make a histogram of the amount of each factor across all individuals in a population then the shape of the histogram for each factor would not substantially alter the gaussian distribution of heights in the population. In other words, *the gaussian distribution is nature's default distribution* if many factors contribute to a given physical attribute, such as height, or arm length. This will prove crucial because we will seek out those factors with distributions that are as *non-gaussian* as possible, on the understanding that such factors cannot be mixtures, and must therefore be source signals.

For completeness, the shape of a normal pdf is shown in figure 5.3, and is defined by the following equation

$$p_x(x) = \frac{1}{\sqrt{2\pi\sigma^2}} \exp\left(-\frac{(x - \overline{x})^2}{2\sigma^2}\right), \tag{5.7}$$

where σ is the *standard deviation*, which is a measure of the variability of x (see section 5.6), and $\bar{x}$ is the mean of x. The first term $(1/\sqrt{2\pi\sigma^2})$ is a normalization constant which ensures that the area under the normal pdf sums to unity.

5.4   The Central Limit Theorem

We can now state the central limit theorem more formally from a proof provided by A. Liapunov in 1901 (see (DeGroot, 1986), p276),

> If a set of signals $\mathbf{s} = (s_1, s_2, \ldots, s_M)$ are independent with means $(\mu_1, \mu_2, \ldots, \mu_M)$ and variances $(\sigma_1^2, \sigma_2^2, \ldots, \sigma_M^2)$ then, for a large number M of signals $\mathbf{s}$, the signal
>
> $$x = \sum_{j=1}^{M} s_j, \tag{5.8}$$
>
> has a pdf which is approximately gaussian with mean $\sum_j \mu_j$ and variance $\sum_j \sigma_j^2$.

Note that the CLT, as stated above, does not exactly match the mixing process we are considering because the mixture x is formed using a set of mixing coefficients, all of which are implicitly equal to unity. Fortunately, the CLT does not place restrictions on how much of each source signal contributes to a signal mixture, so that the above result holds true even if the mixing coefficients are not equal to unity

$$x = \sum_{j=1}^{M} a_j s_j, \tag{5.9}$$

where the a_j's are non-zero mixing coefficients. This implies that for a mixture formed using mixing coefficients $a = a_1$ and $b = a_2$

$$x = a s_1 + b s_2, \tag{5.10}$$

the pdf of x is approximately gaussian.

Here $M = 2$, which cannot be considered to be a large number of mixtures, so that the approximation of x's pdf to a gaussian pdf is not usually very impressive. However, this does not matter for our purposes, because the CLT ensures that the pdf of the mixture x is almost always *more* gaussian than the pdf of its constituent source signals.

As for the means and variances of the signals mixtures, we assume throughout that source signals have zero mean, and the variance of a mixture is simply related to its amplitude, which (as we shall see in the later chapters) is disregarded during extraction of source signals.

5.5 Cumulative Density Functions

Note that a pdf is not just an idealized histogram, it is a *function* which returns a *probability density* $p_x(x)$. From a purely practical point of view, a graph of a pdf is a useful means to observe the probability associated with different values of x. More importantly, it allows us to answer questions of the form: what is the probability that x is less than or equal to $x0$? Clearly, the probability that $x \leq x0$ is the probability $p_x(x)dx$ summed over all values up to and including $x0$,

$$p(x \leq x0) = \int_{x=-\infty}^{x0} p_x(x)\,dx. \tag{5.11}$$

This integral yields the area under the curve defined by $p_x(x)$ between $x = -\infty$ and $x = x0$ as shown in figure 5.3, and yields an important class of function, the *cumulative density function*, or cdf, usually denoted as g in this book,

$$g(x) = p(x \leq x0) \tag{5.12}$$

$$= \int_{x=-\infty}^{x0} p_x(x)\,dx. \tag{5.13}$$

Conversely, the probability $p(x \geq x0)$ that $x \geq x0$ is given by the area between $p_x(x0)$ and $p_x(\infty)$. This can be evaluated with a corresponding change in the *limits of integration*

$$p(x \geq x0) = \int_{x=x0}^{\infty} p_x(x)\,dx. \tag{5.14}$$

Finally, the definition of the cdf as the integral of a pdf implies that the pdf $p_x(x)$ is given by the *derivative* $dg(x)/dx$ of $g(x)$ with respect to x:

$$p_x(x) = \frac{dg(x)}{dx}. \tag{5.15}$$

This result will prove crucial later.

Maximum Entropy Pdfs   For our purposes, the cdf will prove to be important for the following reason, explored more fully in chapter 7. If any signal x has a pdf $p_x(x)$ and cdf g then the signal $X = g(x)$ obtained by transforming x with g has a uniform (i.e., flat) or *maximum entropy* pdf.

5.6 Moments: Mean, Variance, Skewness and Kurtosis

The pdf of a signal x can be characterized in terms of its *moments*.

First Moment

The first moment of a pdf p_x corresponds to the mean value $\bar{x}$ of the signal x. This mean value $\bar{x}$ is also known as the *expected value* or *expectation* $E[x]$ of the variable x. For a variable x with pdf p_x the first moment is

$$E[x] = \int_{x=-\infty}^{+\infty} p_x(x) \, x \, dx, \tag{5.16}$$

where the summation is between $-\infty$ and $+\infty$. This integration corresponds to a weighted sum, where each value of x is weighted by its probability density $p_x(x)$.

This can be viewed in terms of a physical analogy to probability density. Specifically, we know that the height of a pdf p_x at x is a probability density, analogous to the density of physical objects. In this case let us suppose that the object is a metal rod and consists of different proportions of various metals, so that its density $p_x(x)$ varies with position x along the rod, like a pdf. How could we find that point x_B which would support the rod in a balanced position? The position x_B corresponds to the *center of mass* of the rod, and this is obtained as

$$x_B = \int_{x=0}^{R} p_x(x) \, x \, dx, \tag{5.17}$$

where R is the length of the rod.[1] This center of mass is also known as the mean value $\bar{x}$, or expected value $E[x]$ of the pdf p_x. For example, if the rod has uniform density then x_B would be at its mid-point $x_B = R/2$. Note that, like a pdf, the rod has been normalized so that it has unit mass.

Central Moments

Note that subtracting $\bar{x}$ from x yields a variable $x_0 = (x - \bar{x})$ which has zero mean, and the first moment of x_0 is known as the first *central moment* of x. In general, the nth central moment of a variable is given by

$$E[(x - \bar{x})^n]. \tag{5.18}$$

It is often convenient to assume that variables have a mean of zero (i.e., a zero first moment)

---

1. If the limits of integration were $-\infty$ and ∞ as in the general definition defined in equation (5.16) then this would not alter the result because $p_x(x) = 0$ for $x < 0$ and for $x > R$.

Second Moment

The *second moment* $E[x^2]$ of the pdf of x is

$$E[x^2] = \int_{x=-\infty}^{+\infty} p_x(x)\, x^2 \, dx, \tag{5.19}$$

which can be shown to be

$$E[x^2] = E[x]^2 + E[(x - E[x])^2] \tag{5.20}$$
$$= \bar{x}^2 + E[(x - \bar{x})^2], \tag{5.21}$$

where $E[(x - \bar{x})^2]$ is known as the *variance* of x. The second central moment of x^2 is the variance of $(x - \bar{x})$.

In terms of physical analogy, the second moment is related to the moment of inertia. Given a metal rod with density p_x, the second moment defines that point at which the moment of inertia is smallest, such that the force required to rotate the rod around this point is minimal. For a rod with uniform density this point is at the middle of the rod.

The square root of the variance is the *standard deviation*, denoted σ, and is an important measure of variability

$$\sigma = \sqrt{E[(x - \bar{x})^2]}. \tag{5.22}$$

This permits equation (5.21) to be re-written as

$$E[x^2] = \bar{x}^2 + \sigma^2. \tag{5.23}$$

Third Moment

The *third moment* $E[x^3]$ of the pdf of x is

$$E[x^3] = \int_{x=-\infty}^{+\infty} p_x(x)\, x^3 \, dx. \tag{5.24}$$

The central moment of x^3 is known as *skewness* of x. More generally, skewness is defined as

$$E[(x - \bar{x})^3] = \int_x p_x(x)\, (x - \bar{x})^3 \, dx. \tag{5.25}$$

Skewness takes account of the sign of signal values (e.g., $-3^3 = -27$), which is why it provides a measure of the asymmetry of a pdf. The third moment will not be used in this book, and is not considered further here.

Fourth Moment

The *fourth moment* $E[x^4]$ of the pdf of x is

$$E[x^4] = \int_{x=-\infty}^{+\infty} p_x(x)\, x^4\, dx. \tag{5.26}$$

If x has zero-mean then a normalized version of $E[x^4]$ is known as *kurtosis*, where kurtosis is defined in terms of a ratio that includes the fourth and second central moments,

$$K = \frac{E[x^4]}{E[x^2]^2} - 3. \tag{5.27}$$

Essentially, kurtosis provides a measure of the fourth central moment which takes account of a signal's variance $E[x^2]$. Kurtosis provides a measure of how super-gaussian or "peaky" a pdf is (see figure 5.2). The constant 3 ensures that a gaussian pdf has zero kurtosis, super-gaussian pdfs have positive kurtosis, and sub-gaussian pdfs have negative kurtosis.

Evaluating Moments

The different moments defined above require an infinite number of signal values. For a finite number N of sampled points, these can be estimated as follows.

The first moment $E[x]$ of a signal x is estimated as the mean $\overline{x}$,

$$E[x] \quad = \quad \overline{x} \tag{5.28}$$

$$\approx \quad \frac{1}{N}\sum_{t=1}^{N} x^t, \tag{5.29}$$

where x^t denotes the tth value of x, and not x raised to the power t here.

From equation 5.23, the second moment $E[x^2]$ of x is estimated as

$$E[x^2] \quad = \quad \overline{x}^2 + \sigma^2 \tag{5.30}$$

$$\approx \quad \left(\frac{1}{N}\sum_{t=1}^{N} x^t\right)^2 + \frac{1}{N}\sum_{t=1}^{N}(x^t - \overline{x})^2. \tag{5.31}$$

$$\tag{5.32}$$

Note that if x has zero-mean (i.e., $\overline{x} = 0$) then the second moment is equal to the variance σ^2,

$$E[x^2] \quad = \quad \sigma^2, \tag{5.33}$$

$$\approx \frac{1}{N} \sum_{t=1}^{N} (x^t)^2. \tag{5.34}$$

We will not make use of the third moment, and its evaluation is therefore omitted here. Finally, the fourth moment is evaluated in terms of kurtosis:

$$K \approx \frac{\sum_t (x^t)^4}{\sum_t (x^t)^2} - 3. \tag{5.35}$$

5.7 Independence and Correlation

The term "correlated" tends to be used in colloquial terms to suggest that two variables are related in a very general sense. For example, it might be stated in a heated argument that "there is absolutely no correlation between poverty and longevity." In this case, the intention is to imply that a person's income and their longevity are completely unrelated, or independent. However, this is not implied by the above statement, if we used the term "correlation" according to its formal definition. All that is implied is that income and longevity are uncorrelated, but this does not imply that they are unrelated. The essence of this more general notion of relatedness is captured by *statistical independence*, which is defined in terms of pdfs.

Just as a single variable x has a pdf p_x, so a pair of variables has a *joint pdf* p_{xy}, as shown in figure 5.4. In this case, the joint pdf specifies the probability density associated with a pair of values x and y. More generally, given a vector valued variable $\mathbf{z} = (z_1, z_2, \ldots, z_M)$ with M entries, a joint pdf specifies the probability density associated with any value of $\mathbf{z}$.

Two variables x and y are independent if and only if

$$p_{xy}(x, y) = p_x(x) \, p_y(y), \tag{5.36}$$

where (for any joint pdf) the pdfs $p_x(x)$ and $p_y(y)$ are known as the *marginal pdfs* of the joint pdf $p_{xy}(x, y)$. If two variables are independent then the joint pdf p_{xy} can be obtained exactly from the product of its marginal pdfs $p_x(x)$ and $p_y(y)$, as implied by equation (5.36).

Independence implies that knowing the marginal pdfs p_x and p_y is equivalent to knowing the joint pdf p_{xy}. In other words, the entire structure of the joint pdf is implicit in the structure of its marginal pdfs because the joint pdf can be reconstructed exactly from the product of its marginal pdfs. In contrast, if two variables are not independent then their joint pdf cannot be obtained from the marginal pdfs of the joint pdf.

If x and y are independent then equation (5.36) implies that

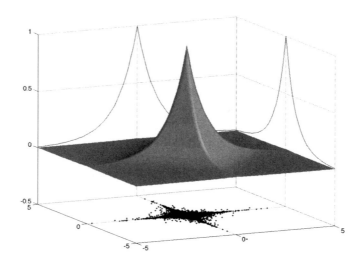

Figure 5.4

The joint probability density function (pdf) of two independent high kurtosis variables (e.g., speech signals) is indicated by the solid surface. The *marginal pdf* of each high kurtosis variable x and y is plotted along one horizontal axis as a solid curve. The joint probability of observing values (x^t, y^t) is indicated by the local density of plotted points on the horizontal plane. This local density is an approximation to the joint pdf $p_{xy}(x, y)$, which is indicated by the height of the solid surface.

$$E[x^p y^q] \quad = \quad E[x^p]E[y^q], \tag{5.37}$$

If $p = 1$ and $q = 1$ then $E[x^p y^q] = E[xy]$ is the first moment of the joint pdf p_{xy}. The expectation $E[xy]$ is also known as the *covariance* between x and y,

$$E[xy] \quad = \quad \int_x \int_y p_{xy}(x, y) \, x \, y \, dx \, dy, \tag{5.38}$$

where $E[xy]$ is evaluated for a finite sample of N samples of the zero-mean variables x and y as

$$E[xy] = \sum_{t=1}^{N} x^t y^t. \tag{5.39}$$

Covariance is closely related to *correlation* $\rho(x, y)$, which is a normalized version of covariance,

$$\rho(x, y) = \frac{E[xy]}{\sigma_x \sigma_y}, \tag{5.40}$$

where σ_x and σ_x are the standard deviations of x and y, respectively,

$$\sigma_x = E[xx]^{1/2}, \quad \sigma_y = E[yy]^{1/2}. \tag{5.41}$$

This normalization ensures that ρ varies between $\rho = -1$ and $\rho = 1$. A value of $\rho = 1$ implies that as x increases, so y increases in proportion to x, a value of $\rho = -1$ implies that as x increases, so y *decreases* in proportion to x, and a value of $\rho = 0$ implies that as x increases, *on average* y neither increases nor decreases in proportion to x.

Note that a correlation assumes $p = q = 1$, so that if x and y are uncorrelated then

$$E[xy] \quad = \quad E[y]E[x]. \tag{5.42}$$

This equates to assuming that the first moment of the joint pdf p_{xy} is equal to the product of the first moments of the marginal pdfs p_x and p_y of p_{xy}

$$E[x^1.y^1] = E[x^1]E[y^1]. \tag{5.43}$$

In contrast, independence involves *all* positive integer values of p and q. Thus independence places many more constraints on the joint pdf p_{xy} than correlation does.

The formal similarity between measures of independence and correlation can be interpreted as follows. Correlation is a measure of the amount of covariation between x and y, and depends on the first moment of the pdf p_{xy} only. In contrast, independence is a measure of the covariation between [x raised to powers p] and [y raised to powers q], and depends on *all* moments of the pdf p_{xy}. Thus, independence can be considered as a generalized measure of correlation, such that $\rho(x^p, y^q) = 0$ for all positive integer values of p and q.

5.8   Uncorrelated Pendulums

Consider the simple physical example of two pendulums swinging exactly in phase (i.e., the pendulums reach their peak and zero velocity at exactly the same time). In this case, there is clearly a positive correlation ρ between the velocities of the pendulums. However, what if the pendulums are started at different times, with a phase difference of 90 degrees (as depicted in figure 5.5)? In this case, if one pendulum reaches the upper extreme of its swing (i.e., zero velocity) at the same time as the other pendulum reaches the lower extreme of its swing (i.e., maximum velocity) then $\rho = 0$. This seems counterintuitive because the velocities of the two pendulums are obviously related to each other. Clearly, the formal definition of correlation does not fit well with our intuitive notion of relatedness. This notion is captured more accurately by statistical independence than it is by correlation.

In order to examine this example in more detail, we need to formalize the quantities involved. Pendulum velocity varies with time, so that we can define a time variable t with a range between zero and π, $t = \{0, ..., (4 \times 360)\}$, which allows us to examine

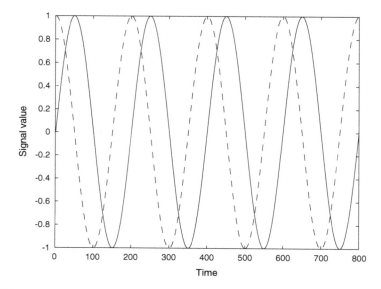

Figure 5.5
Graph of $x = \sin(t)$ (solid line) and $y = \cos(t)$ (dashed line). The variables x and y represent the velocities of two pendulums swinging with the same frequency but with a phase difference of 90 degrees, so that when one pendulum is at the bottom of its swing (maximum velocity), the other is at the top of its swing (zero velocity). Even though x and y are clearly related to each other, the correlation between them is $\rho(x, y) = 0$.

pendulum behavior over 4 full cycles. If the two pendulums are started with a time difference of 90 (degrees) then the velocity of the pendulums are given by $x = \sin(t)$ and $y = \sin(t + 90) = \cos(t)$. Intuitively, it can be seen that both x and y depend on t. As can be seen from figure 5.6, the variables x and y are highly interdependent. However, the the correlation of x and y is zero because $E[xy] = 0$,

$$\rho(x, y) = \frac{E[xy]}{\sigma_x \sigma_y} \tag{5.44}$$

$$= \frac{E[\cos(t)\sin(t)]}{\sigma_x \sigma_y} \tag{5.45}$$

$$= 0. \tag{5.46}$$

In contrast, the correlation between the variables x^p and y^q as depicted in figures 5.7 and 5.8 for $p = q = 2$ is given by the central moment (i.e., $x = (\overline{x} - x), y = (\overline{y} - y)$)

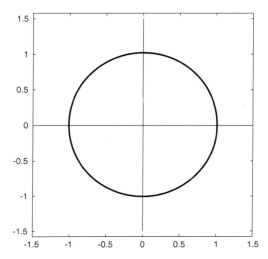

Figure 5.6
Graph of $x = \sin(t)$ versus $y = \cos(t)$ for $t = 0, \ldots, 4 \times 360$ defines a circle. Even though x and y are clearly related to each other, the correlation between them is $\rho(x, y) = 0$. Thus correlation does not reflect all forms of dependence between two variables.

$$\rho(x^2, y^2) = \frac{E[x^2 y^2]}{\sigma_{x^2} \sigma_{y^2}} \quad < \quad 0, \tag{5.47}$$

where σ_{x^2} and σ_{y^2} are the standard deviations of x^2 and y^2, respectively. Thus, whereas the correlation between $x = \sin(t)$ and $y = \cos(t)$ is zero, the fact that the value of x provides information about the value of y is implicit in the non-zero high order correlations between x^p and y^q (e.g., between x^2 and y^2).

5.9   Summary

In this chapter, we have learned several important facts.

- A *histogram* is a graphical representation of the values in a given signal x, and a *probability density function* (pdf) $p_x(x)$ is essentially an idealized histogram.

- Changing the ordering of values in a given signal has no effect on the pdf of that signal.

- The *central limit theorem* ensures that almost any mixture of signals has a pdf which is approximately gaussian.

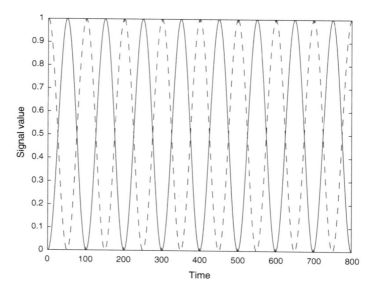

Figure 5.7
Graph of $x^2 = \sin^2(t)$ (solid line) and $y^2 = \cos^2(t)$ (dashed line). The variables x^2 and y^2 are anti-correlated because for any value of x^2, the value of $y^2 = 1 - x^2$. The correlation between x^2 and y^2 $\rho(x^2, y^2)$ is therefore negative.

- A *cumulative density function* $g(x)$ of a signal x is the *integral* of its pdf $p_x(x)$, and returns the proportion of values below a specified value of x. By implication, the pdf of a signal is the *derivative* of that signal's cdf.

- Two signals x and y are *statistically independent* only if their *joint pdf* $p_{xy}(x, y)$ is given by the product $p_x(x)p_y(y)$ of its *marginal* pdfs $p_x(x)$ and $p_y(y)$. This implies that if two signals are independent then the *central moment* $E[x^p y^q]$ of their joint pdf is equal to the product $E[x^p]E[y^q]$ for *all* positive integer values of p and q.

- If two signals are *uncorrelated* then the *first central moment* of their joint pdf $E[xy] = E[x]E[y]$. However, two such signals are independent if $E[x^p y^q] = E[x^p]E[y^q]$ for *all* positive integer values of p and q.

With these facts, we can now examine the details of how to implement several source separation methods.

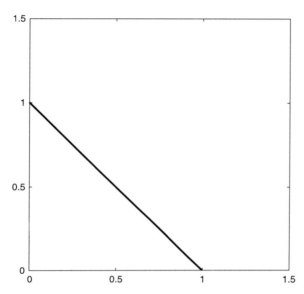

Figure 5.8
Graph of $x^2 = \sin(t)^2$ versus $y^2 = \cos(t)^2$ for $t = 0, \ldots, 4 \times 360$. The dependence between x and y variables is not apparent in their correlation (see figure 5.6). However, this dependence is apparent in high order correlations between x and y, such as the correlation $\rho(x^2, y^2)$ between x^2 and y^2, which is non-zero (and negative). If the variables x and y are statistically independent then all high order correlations are zero; that is, $\rho(x^p, y^q) = 0$ for all positive integer values of p and q.

III METHODS FOR BLIND SOURCE SEPARATION

6 Projection Pursuit

6.1 Introduction

We know that signal mixtures tend to have gaussian (normal) probability density functions, and that source signals have non-gaussian pdfs. We also know that each source signal can be extracted from a set of signal mixtures by taking the inner product of a weight vector and those signal mixtures where this inner product provides an orthogonal projection of the signal mixtures. But we do not yet know precisely how to find such a weight vector. One type of method for doing so is exploratory projection pursuit, often referred to simply as *projection pursuit* (Kruskal, 1969, Friedman et al., 1974, Fyfe & Baddeley, 1995).

Projection pursuit methods seek one projection at a time such that the extracted signal is as non-gaussian as possible. This contrasts with ICA, which typically extracts M signals simultaneously from M signal mixtures, which requires estimating a (possibly very large) $M \times M$ unmixing matrix. One practical advantage of projection pursuit over ICA is that less than M signals can be extracted if required, where each source signal is extracted from M signal mixtures using an M-element weight vector.

The name projection pursuit derives from the fact that this method seeks a weight vector which provides an orthogonal projection of a set of signal mixtures such that each extracted signal has a pdf which is as non-gaussian as possible.

6.2 Mixtures Are Gaussian

Let us reconsider the example of human height. Suppose that the height of an individual h^i is the outcome of many underlying factors which include a genetic component s_G^i, and dietary component s_D^i (i.e., nature versus nurture). Let us further suppose that the contribution of each factor to height is the same for all individuals (i.e., the nature/nurture ratio is fixed). Finally, we need to assume that the total effect of these different factors in each individual is the sum of their contributions. If we consider the contribution of each factor as a constant coefficient then we can write

$$h^i = as_G^i + bs_D^i, \tag{6.1}$$

where a and b are non-zero coefficients. Each coefficient determines how height increases with the factors s_G^i and s_D^i. Note that s_G^i and s_D^i vary across individuals, whereas the coefficients a and b are the same for all individuals. The central limit theorem (see section 5.4) ensures that the pdf of h^i values is approximately gaussian irrespective of the pdf of s_G^i or s_D^i values, and irrespective of the constants a and b.

Of course, we should recognize equation (6.1) for what it is: the formation of a signal mixture h by a linear combination of source signals s_G and s_D, using mixing coefficients a and b. Note that h could equally well be a mixture of two voice signals.

As a further example, in signal processing it is almost always assumed that, after the signals of interest have been extracted from a noisy stream of data, the residual noise is gaussian. As stated above, this assumption is mathematically very convenient, but it is also usually valid. If the residual noise is the result of many processes whose outputs are added together then the central limit theorem (CLT) guarantees that this noise is indeed approximately gaussian.

6.3   Gaussian Signals: Good News, Bad News

We now have to confront some good news and some bad news, when interpreting the above in terms of signals generated by physical systems. The bad news is that the converse of the CLT is not true in general; that is, it is not true that any gaussian signal is a mixture of non-gaussian signals. The good news is that, in practice, gaussian signals often do consist of a mixture of non-gaussian signals. This is good news because it means we can treat any gaussian signal as if it consists of a mixture of non-gaussian source signals. Given a set of such gaussian mixtures, we can then proceed to find each source signal by finding that unmixing vector which extracts the most non-gaussian signal from the set of mixtures.

We could now proceed using two different strategies. We could define a measure of the "distance" between the signal extracted by a given unmixing vector and a gaussian signal, and then find the unmixing vector that maximizes this distance. This distance is known as the *Kullback-Leibler divergence* (see Hyvärinen et al., 2001a). A simpler strategy consists of defining a measure of non-gaussianity and then finding the unmixing vector that maximizes this measure. This is the strategy that will be examined here.

The fact that there are actually two types of non-gaussian signals will not detain us long, because we shall assume (in common with most blind source separation methods) that our source signals are of one type only. The two types are known by various terms, such as *super-gaussian* and *sub-gaussian*, or equivalently as *platykurtotic* and *leptokurtotic*, respectively; and a signal with zero kurtosis is *mesokurtotic*. A signal with a super-gaussian pdf has most of its values clustered around zero, whereas a signal with a sub-gaussian pdf does not, as illustrated in figure 5.2. As examples, a speech signal has a super-gaussian pdf, and a sawtooth function and white noise have sub-gaussian pdfs (see figure 5.2). This implies that super-gaussian signals have pdfs that are more peaky than that of a gaussian signal, whereas a sub-gaussian signal has a pdf that is less peaky than that of a gaussian signal. We will assume that our source signals are super-gaussian (i.e., like speech), although projection pursuit methods based on Kullback-Leibler divergence can extract source signals from mixtures of super- and sub-gaussian source signals, e.g., FastICA Hyvärinen et al., 2001a).

The informal descriptor "peaky" has a formal concomitant, which is usually defined as the *kurtosis* of a signal's pdf. If we can find an unmixing vector $\mathbf{w}$ that maximizes the kurtosis of an extracted signal $y = \mathbf{w}^T \mathbf{x}$ then we can assume that y is a source signal. But first, we need to explore what is meant by kurtosis.

6.4   Kurtosis as a Measure of Non-Normality

The kurtosis of the pdf of a signal (often simply referred to as the kurtosis of the signal) was defined in equation 5.26. For a finite sample, kurtosis is computed as

$$K = \frac{\frac{1}{N}\sum_{t=1}^{N}(\bar{y} - y^t)^4}{\left(\frac{1}{N}\sum_{t=1}^{N}(\bar{y} - y^t)^2\right)^2} - 3, \tag{6.2}$$

where $\bar{y}$ is the mean value of y^t. This rather complex expression has only one important term, and that is the numerator. The other terms ensure that the measured value of kurtosis is well behaved. The constant (3) ensures that gaussian signals have zero kurtosis, super-gaussian signals have positive kurtosis, and sub-gaussian signals have negative kurtosis. The denominator is the *variance* of y, and ensures that the measured kurtosis takes account of signal variance.

Equation (6.2) can be written more succinctly in terms of means or *expected values*, denoted $E[.]$. Note that the numerator consists of the sum of N terms divided by N, and is therefore an expectation (i.e., the mean of $(\bar{y} - y^t)^4$ over all t). As the denominator contains a mean we can rewrite equation (6.2)

$$K = \frac{E[(\bar{y} - y)^4]}{(E[(\bar{y} - y)^2])^2} - 3. \tag{6.3}$$

6.5   Weight Vector Angle and Kurtosis

Using kurtosis as a measure of non-normality, we can now examine how the kurtosis of a signal $y = \mathbf{w}^T \mathbf{x}$ extracted from a set of M mixtures $\mathbf{x} = (x_1, x_2, \ldots, x_M)^T$ varies as the weight vector $\mathbf{w}$ is rotated around the origin. Given our assumption that each source signal s is super-gaussian we would expect

1. the kurtosis of the extracted signal y to be maximal precisely when $y = s$

2. the kurtosis of the extracted signal y to be maximal when $\mathbf{w}$ is orthogonal to the projected axes S_1' or S_2', because we know the optimal weight vector should be orthogonal to a transformed axis S_1' or S_2'.

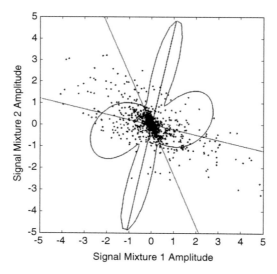

Figure 6.1

Graph showing how the kurtosis of an extracted signal varies with weight vector orientation for two speech signal mixtures. The plotted points represent signal mixture 1 (x_1) versus signal mixture 2 (x_2). For any given orientation of a weight vector $\mathbf{w}$ the recovered signal y is given by the inner product of $\mathbf{w}$ with the two signal mixtures $\mathbf{x} = (x_1, x_2)$, $y = \mathbf{w}^T \mathbf{x}$. The kurtosis of y varies as $\mathbf{w}$ is rotated around the origin. For each value of $\mathbf{w}$ the associated kurtosis is plotted as a distance from the origin in the direction of $\mathbf{w}$, giving a continuous curve. Critically, kurtosis is maximal when $\mathbf{w}$ is orthogonal to a transformed axis S_1' or S_2' (plotted as dashed lines), and $\mathbf{w}$ recovers exactly one source signal at these orientations. The orientation of $\mathbf{w}$ corresponding to one maximum in kurtosis is plotted as a solid line.

Figure 6.1 demonstrates such a case. Note that 2 above does not provide a means of finding source signals; because the projected axes S_1' or S_2' are not usually known, it simply provides confirmation of the geometry of the optimal weight vector in relation to the projected axes.

In principle, the correct value of $\mathbf{w}$ can be found using the brute force exhaustive search method illustrated in figure 6.1. This involves finding that weight vector orientation at which the kurtosis of the extracted signal is maximal. Alternatively, we could use a more efficient gradient based method, as described in Chapter 9.

Note that the length $|\mathbf{w}|$ of $\mathbf{w}$ is irrelevant (see section 4.2.1), provided it is greater than zero (i.e., $|\mathbf{w}| > 0$), because kurtosis defined in such a way that it is unaffected by the length of $\mathbf{w}$.

The issue of how to extract more than one source signal is addressed in next section.

6.6   Using Kurtosis to Recover Multiple Source Signals

The strategy for recovering multiple source signals is very simple. It involves removing each recovered source signal from the set of signal mixtures and then using the above procedure to recover the next source signal from the "reduced" set of signal mixtures. This sequential procedure is often referred to as *deflation*.

The only tricky part of this strategy is removing each recovered source signal from the set of remaining signal mixtures. This is achieved using a method known as *Gram-Schmidt orthogonalisation* (GSO) (see appendix C).

In geometric terms, given M signal mixtures represented as points in an M-dimensional (MD) space, GSO projects these data points onto an $(M - 1)$D space. Critically, if projection pursuit extracts the Mth source signal using a vector $\mathbf{w}_M$ then this $(M - 1)$D space contains the $(M - 1)$ transformed axes $(S_1', S_2', \ldots, S_{M-1}')$.

To take an example, consider the case for which initially there are $M = 3$ mixtures of three sources. We can recover one source using a vector $\mathbf{w} = \mathbf{w}_3$, as described in the previous section. Note that in order for $\mathbf{w}_3$ to recover exactly one source signal $y_3 = s_3$, it must be orthogonal to the plane $P_{1,2}'$ defined by the transformed axes S_1' and S_2'. Additionally, after the signal y_3 is recovered we are really only interested in this plane. This is where GSO is useful, because it projects data points in a three-dimensional (3D) space onto a two-dimensional (2D) space (i.e., a plane). Moreover, because we know $\mathbf{w}_3$, we can ensure that GSO does not project data onto any old 2D plane, but onto that 2D plane $P_{1,2}'$ which contains the transformed axes S_1' and S_2'.

6.7   Projection Pursuit and ICA Extract the Same Signals

The sequential procedure described above is guaranteed to find the same independent source signals as are found by ICA, provided certain formal conditions apply (e.g., the source signals are independent and non-gaussian) (Hyvärinen & Oja, 1997, Hyvärinen et al., 2001a) (p202). This appears counterintuitive because ICA explicitly maximizes a measure of independence of an entire set of extracted signals, whereas projection pursuit maximizes a measure of non-gaussianity for each sequentially extracted signal. Despite this sequential extraction, projection pursuit extracts a set of mutually independent extracted signals.

In fact, this result makes perfect sense, provided the source signals are independent and non-gaussian. The proof can be summarized as follows.

Consider a set of M non-gaussian source signals each of which contributes to each of M signal mixtures. If projection pursuit is used to find a signal that is maximally non-gaussian then this signal will be one of the source signals. This is because, of all the possible signals that could be extracted by an unmixing vector $\mathbf{w}_1$, the particular unmixing vector $\mathbf{w}_1$ which extracts a source signal will yield the most non-gaussian signal.

Having obtained one source signal, and then removed it from the set of mixtures (e.g., using GSO), projection pursuit is then used to find another maximally non-gaussian signal. As far as projection pursuit is concerned, this is just another set of mixtures. Just as projection pursuit extracted a source signal from the original set of M mixtures, so it will extract a source signal from the new set of $M - 1$ signal mixtures, because (as before), in so doing, projection pursuit extracts that signal which is maximally non-gaussian. Thus, if the source signals are independent and non-gaussian then the sequential application of projection pursuit to a decreasing number of signal mixtures results in exactly the same set of source signals as would be obtained by ICA.

However, if the source signals are not independent then differences between the signals extracted by ICA and projection pursuit emerge. In this case, the different functions maximized as part of ICA and projection pursuit (i.e., independence and non-gaussianity, respectively) will have different consequences for the estimated signals extracted by ICA and projection pursuit.

6.8   When to Stop Extracting Signals

How can we tell when all of the source signals have been extracted? This is a fundamental issue for all BSS methods, but it has no simple answer. In order to provide a flavour of the type of problem we are up against, consider the following example.

There are two people speaking at the same time whilst being recorded by three microphones. A scatterplot of the two voice source signals would be a 2D graph. A scatter plot of the three voice mixtures recorded by the microphones would show points in a 3D graph. However, because the mixing process is linear, all of the points in this 3D space would be in a plane. In other words, the source signals occupy a 2D subspace of the 3D mixture space. Recall that, in general, we do not know how many sources are present.

If projection pursuit were applied to these data then the first two extracted signals would be voices, but there would be literally nothing left to extract after this. In this case it is easy to know when to stop: when we run out of signals to extract. However, such noise-free cases are rarely encountered in practice. Each microphone adds noise, so that the recorded data would not lie exactly in a plane. In this more realistic case, the "signal" is actually microphone or *sensor noise*. If the sensor noise has a small amplitude relative to the signal mixtures then the data can be preprocessed to remove such noise.

Principal Component Analysis

One standard method for reducing the amount of noise in data is principal component analysis (PCA). Briefly, for our speech example, PCA would identify the 2D subspace containing the source signals, and would identify the remaining one-dimensional (1D) subspace as containing low-energy data, which we would classify as noise. Using PCA, we could discard this 1D subspace, and use the 2D subspace as input to a source separation method. More generally, PCA can be used to discard low-energy subspaces from high dimensional data (see chapter 10 and appendix F).

More sophisticated methods for estimating how many sources to extract usually involve Bayesian estimation (e.g., see Penny et al., 2001). Such methods seek a compromise between model complexity (e.g., the number of weight vectors in the unmixing matrix) and the extent to which the model accounts for the observed data.

Projection Pursuit Ignores Signal Structure

It is worth noting that projection pursuit (and ICA) disregards any spatial or temporal structure in signals. This is because projection pursuit depends on the assumption that source signals are non-gaussian, an assumption defined in terms of the pdfs of extracted signals. However, the pdf of any signal does not contain any information regarding the ordering of amplitude values in that signal. The pdf of a speech signal would be the same if the temporal order of amplitude values were re-arranged (permuted) in any order. For example, if the temporal order of signal values were reversed, so that the speech was heard backwards then this would have no effect on the pdf, and would therefore not affect projection pursuit results.

This is counter-intuitive because we, as efficient processors of temporal signals (e.g., speech), depend on assumptions different from those of projection pursuit, and would therefore find it hard to separate the sound of one voice in a mixture of voices if the mixtures were played backwards, for example (see chapter 5).

6.9   Summary

Different mixtures of a set of non-gaussian source signals tend to be gaussian. Projection pursuit seeks a weight vector such that the signal extracted from a set of signal mixtures is as non-gaussian as possible. It is common practice to assume that source signals are super-gaussian, which is consistent with being highly kurtotic. Using this assumption, it was demonstrated that if the signal extracted by a weight vector is as kurtotic as possible then the extracted signal is a source signal.

MatLab Code   Simple demonstration code is provided in appendix B.

7 Independent Component Analysis

"I shouldn't be surprised if it hailed a good deal tomorrow," Eeyore was saying. "Blizzards and what-not. Being fine to-day doesn't Mean Anything. It has no sig—what's that word? Well, it has none of that."
— The House at Pooh Corner, AA Milne, 1928.

7.1 Introduction

ICA is essentially a multivariate, parallel version of projection pursuit. Thus, whereas projection pursuit extracts a series of signals one at a time from a set of M signal mixtures, ICA extracts M signals in parallel. This tends to make ICA more robust than projection pursuit.

Statistical independence lies at the core of the ICA methods. Therefore, in order to understand ICA, it is essential to understand independence. At an intuitive level, if two variables y_1 and y_2 are independent then the value of one variable provides absolutely no information about the value of the other variable. For example, the phase of the moon (y_1) provides no information regarding what the President had for breakfast today (y_2). The moon phase and the President's breakfast are said to be *statistically independent* variables.

7.2 Independence of Joint and Marginal Distributions

7.2.1 Independent Events: Coin Tossing

Consider the pedestrian example of tossing a coin. If every toss has an outcome that is independent of all other tosses and the probability of obtaining a head is $p_h = 0.5$ then the probability of obtaining two heads is

$$p_h \times p_h = \prod_{i=1}^{2} p_h \qquad (7.1)$$

$$= 0.5^2 \qquad (7.2)$$

$$= 0.25, \qquad (7.3)$$

where the symbol Π is standard notation for representing products. Similarly, the probability of obtaining exactly N heads from N coin tosses is

$$\prod_{i=1}^{N} p_h = p_h^N. \qquad (7.4)$$

If the coin is biased such that $p_h = 0.2$ then the the probability of obtaining exactly N heads is simply p_h raised to the power N,

$$p_h^N = 0.2^N. \qquad (7.5)$$

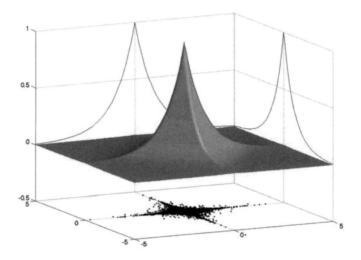

Figure 7.1
The joint probability density function (pdf) of two high-kurtosis variables (e.g., speech signals) is indicated by the solid surface. The marginal pdf of each high-kurtosis variable s_1 and s_2 is plotted along one horizontal axis as a solid curve. The joint probability of observing values $\mathbf{s}^t = (s_1^t, s_2^t)$ at time t is indicated by the local probability density of plotted points on the horizontal plane. This probability density is an approximation to the joint pdf p_s, which is indicated by the height of the solid surface.

For example, the probability of obtaining 5 heads with such a coin is $0.2^5 = 0.00032$. Note that the probability of obtaining a number of heads can be obtained as the product of the probability of obtaining each head only because the outcomes of coin tosses are *independent* events.

7.2.2   Independent Signals: Speech

We can extend this discussion to more interesting examples, such as speech. By definition, the probability that the amplitude of a voice signal s lies within an extremely small range around the value s^t is given by the value of the *probability density function* (pdf) $p_s(s^t)$ of that signal at s^t. For brevity, we will often abuse this technically correct, but lengthy, definition by stating that $p_s(s^t)$ is simply the probability that the variable s adopts the value s^t. Given that speech signals spend most of their time with near-zero amplitude, the pdf of speech signals has a peak at $s = 0$, as shown in figures 2.3 and 7.1. The typical gaussian pdf associated with signal mixtures is depicted in figure 7.2.

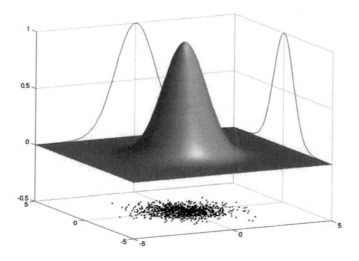

Figure 7.2
The joint probability density function (pdf) of two gaussian variables (e.g., signal mixtures) is indicated by the solid surface. The *marginal* pdf of each gaussian variable x_1 and x_2 is plotted along one horizontal axis as a solid curve. The joint probability of observing values $\mathbf{x}^t = (x_1^t, x_2^t)^T$ is indicated by the local *probability density* of plotted points on the horizontal plane. This probability density is an approximation to the joint pdf p_x, which is indicated by the height of the solid surface.

Now, we assume that two speech signals s_1 and s_2 from two different people are independent. This implies that the *joint probability* $p_s(s_1^t, s_2^t)$ that $s_1 = s_1^t$ when $s_2 = s_2^t$ is given by the probability $p_{s1}(s_1^t)$ that $s_1 = s_1^t$ times the probability $p_{s2}(s_2^t)$ that $s_2 = s_2^t$

$$p_s(s_1^t, s_2^t) = p_{s1}(s_1^t) \times p_{s2}(s_2^t). \tag{7.6}$$

The joint probability for all values of $\mathbf{s}$ is the joint pdf p_s, and can be visualized for two variables as shown in figure 7.1, such that the probability that $\mathbf{s} = (s_1^t, s_2^t)$ is given by the height $p_s(\mathbf{s})$ above two horizontal axes representing values of s_1 and s_2. The pdfs p_{s1} and p_{s2} are known as the *marginal* pdfs of the joint pdf p_s. A key feature of this joint pdf is that it can be obtained as the product of its two marginal pdfs p_{s1} and p_{s2}. It bears repeating that this is true only because the variables s_1 and s_2 of the marginal pdfs p_{s1} and p_{s2} are independent.

From equation (7.6), the vector valued variable $\mathbf{s}^t = (s_1^t, s_2^t)$ has a pdf which can be written as

$$p_s(\mathbf{s}^t) = p_{s1}(s_1^t) \times p_{s2}(s_2^t). \tag{7.7}$$

If we assume that all speech signals can be approximated by the same super-gaussian pdf p_s, so that $p_s = p_{s1} = p_{s2}$, then we can write

$$p_s(\mathbf{s}^t) \quad = \quad p_s(s_1^t) \times p_s(s_2^t) \tag{7.8}$$

$$= \quad \prod_{i=1}^{2} p_s(s_i^t). \tag{7.9}$$

If we also assume that all values of each signal are independent then the probability of obtaining the observed N values in each signal is

$$p_s(s_1) \quad = \quad \prod_{t=1}^{N} p_s(s_1^t) \tag{7.10}$$

$$p_s(s_2) \quad = \quad \prod_{t=1}^{N} p_s(s_2^t), \tag{7.11}$$

so that the probability of obtaining the N pairs of signal values is

$$p_s(\mathbf{s}) \quad = \quad \prod_{t=1}^{N} p_s(\mathbf{s}^t). \tag{7.12}$$

The price paid for the assumption that all values of each speech signal are independent is that we ignore the ordering of signal values. Whilst this assumption is patently invalid, it does permit the probability of any signal to be estimated (albeit, incorrectly if consecutive values are similar to each other). Moreover, it permits the probability of any set of M independent signals to be estimated over N time steps. If we substitute equation 7.9 in equation (7.12) then

$$p_s(\mathbf{s}) = \prod_{t=1}^{N} \prod_{i=1}^{M=2} p_s(s_i^t). \tag{7.13}$$

This is the probability of obtaining the observed values if the signals s_1 and s_2 are independent, and if *all* values of $\mathbf{s}^t$ are independent.

Finally, it is common practice to express the product of terms as a sum of logarithms. If we take the logarithm of equation (7.13) then we have

$$\ln p_s(\mathbf{s}) \quad = \quad \ln \prod_{t=1}^{N} \prod_{i=1}^{M=2} p_s(s_i^t) \tag{7.14}$$

$$= \quad \sum_{t=1}^{N} \sum_{i=1}^{M=2} \ln p_s(s_i^t). \tag{7.15}$$

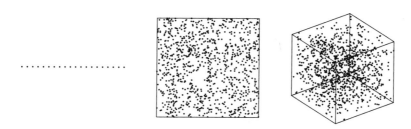

Figure 7.3
Uniform densities of points for 1, 2 and 3 variables define maximum entropy distributions. In each case, the distribution of points has no structure and fills the bounded space defined by the variable(s). Variables with maximum entropy distributions are statistically independent of each other.

7.3   Infomax: Independence and Entropy

Given a set of signal mixtures and an unmixing matrix which extracts a set of signals, how do we know that the extracted signals are source signals? One way is to ascertain whether or not the extracted signals are mutually independent. This suggests that a method for finding source signals is to seek out those signals that are independent. In order to find such a set, we need a measure that will let us know how close the extracted signals are to being independent. This permits us to iteratively change the unmixing matrix so as to increase the degree of independence of the extracted signals.

We cannot measure independence, but we can measure another quantity, *entropy*, which is related in a useful way to independence.[1]

Entropy is a measure of the uniformity of the distribution of a bounded set of values, such that complete uniformity corresponds to *maximum entropy* (see figure 7.5). Specifically, if we have a discrete set of N signal values then the entropy of this set depends on the uniformity of the values in the set. The entropy of a set of variables is known as *joint entropy*. For example, for three variables with a fixed range between zero and unity, their entropy can be visualized as the degree of uniformity in the unit cube (see figure 7.3). Note that if a variable is actually defined to be a probability density then its range is unity.

One way to obtain mutually independent signals is to find an unmixing matrix that maximizes the entropy (of a fixed nonlinear function g) of the signals extracted by that matrix. The unmixing matrix that maximizes the entropy of these signals also maximizes

---

1. For an informal introduction to entropy, mutual information and information theory, see (Jessop, 1995). Otherwise, see (Cover & Thomas, 1991, Reza, 1961)

Figure 7.4

Infomax ICA overview for two sound source signals. *Left*: Pairs of signals with time along the vertical axes, and signal amplitude along the horizontal axis. *Right*: Scatter plots of two signals shown on left. Each scatter plot approximates the joint probability density function of two signals. An unknown pair of source signals $\mathbf{s} = (s_1, s_2)^T$ is transformed to a pair of observed signal mixtures $\mathbf{x} = (x_1, x_2)^T$ by an unknown mixing matrix $\mathbf{A}$, such that $\mathbf{x} = \mathbf{As}$. This pair of source signal mixtures $\mathbf{x} = (x_1, x_2)^T$ is transformed to a pair of extracted signals $\mathbf{y} = (y_1, y_2)^T$ by an unmixing matrix $\mathbf{W}$, such that $\mathbf{y} = \mathbf{Wx}$. If this matrix is the optimal unmixing matrix then the signals $\mathbf{y}$ extracted by $\mathbf{W}$ from $\mathbf{x}$ are the required source signals $\mathbf{s}$, and the signals $\mathbf{Y} = (Y_1, Y_2)$ obtained by transforming $\mathbf{y}$ by a model cumulative density function (cdf) g (defined by $\mathbf{Y} = g(\mathbf{y})$) have a uniform (i.e., *maximum entropy*) joint distribution.

ICA works by adjusting the unmixing coefficients of $\mathbf{W}$ in order to maximize the uniformity (entropy) of the distribution of $\mathbf{Y} = g(\mathbf{y})$ (top right), where g is assumed to be the cdf of the source signals. If g is the cdf of the source signals then the extracted signals $\mathbf{y} = \mathbf{Wx}$ approximate the source signals. Note that the joint pdf of $\mathbf{Y}$ (top right) is usually not exactly uniform because the match between the model cdf g and the cdf of the source signals is usually not exact, nor does this match need to be exact for ICA to work (Cardoso, 2000, Amari, 1998).

the amount of shared entropy or *mutual information*[2] between them and the set of signal mixtures. Accordingly, finding independent signals by maximizing entropy is known as *infomax* (Bell & Sejnowski, 1995).

7.3.1   Infomax Overview

First, it is important to bear in mind that maximizing entropy is simply a means to an end, and depends on three crucial facts about bounded signals[3] (Cover & Thomas, 1991):

- a set of signals with a uniform joint pdf has maximum joint entropy;

- a set of signals that have maximum joint entropy are mutually independent;

- any *invertible function*[4] of maximum entropy signals (which are therefore mutually independent) yields signals that are also mutually independent.

---

2. The mutual information between two signals is a measure of the amount of information each signal contains about the other, and is given by the difference between the sum of their individual entropies and the joint entropy of the two signals.

3. For the sake of brevity we assume that all signals are bounded.

4. If a function $Y = g(y)$ is invertible then every value of Y is associated with only one value of y. As a counterexample, $Y = \sin(y)$ is a noninvertible function because every value of Y is associated with an infinite number of values of y.

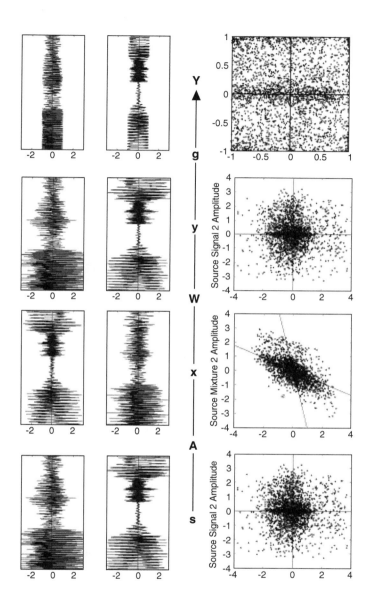

The facts listed above allow us to pursue the following strategy, summarized in figure 7.4. Given an invertible multivariate function g of signals $\mathbf{y} = \mathbf{Wx}$ extracted by the unmixing matrix $\mathbf{W}$, find a $\mathbf{W}$ such that the signals $\mathbf{Y} = g(\mathbf{y})$ have maximum entropy.

Notation We use functions such as g to indicate both univariate and multivariate functions, where the argument of g indicates the form is intended. For example, for a univariate variable we have $g(y)$, whereas for a vector valued variable $\mathbf{y} = (y_1, y_2, \ldots, y_M)^T$ we have $g(\mathbf{y}) = (g(y_1), g(y_2), \ldots, g(y_M))^T$.

It turns out that the entropy of the signals $\mathbf{Y}$ is maximized if the extracted signals have a cumulative density function (cdf) which matches the cdf g. This *"cdf-matching"* property is a key aspect of ICA, and is usually somewhat understated. As the derivative of a cdf defines a corresponding pdf (see chapter 5), ICA can also be interpreted as a method for extracting signals that match a specific pdf. For example, if is assumed that source signals consist of images containing small bright regions then a skew-pdf model can be used to perform spatial ICA of a sequence of observed images, e.g., see (Stone et al., 2002). Alternatively, if it is assumed that source signals have super-gaussian pdfs (e.g., speech) or sub-gaussian pdfs then corresponding pdf models can be used. It is thus possible to "tune" the model pdf to the nature of the source signals to be extracted.

Note that the required signals $\mathbf{y}$ are found by maximizing the entropy of a related, but different, set of signals $\mathbf{Y} = g(\mathbf{y})$. This is why maximizing entropy is a means to an end.

In order to complete the strategy, we need one more fact

- if any function g is invertible then its inverse g^{-1} is also invertible.

It follows that if the signals $\mathbf{Y} = g(\mathbf{y})$ are independent then the extracted signals $\mathbf{y} = g^{-1}(\mathbf{Y})$ are also independent.

In geometric terms, as the entropy of the signal mixtures $\mathbf{x}$ is fixed, maximizing the *change* in entropy involved in the mapping $\mathbf{x} \rightarrow \mathbf{Y}$ has the effect of spreading out the points $\mathbf{Y}$ as much as possible, and therefore maximizes the entropy of the points $\mathbf{Y}$.

In summary, given a set of signal mixtures $\mathbf{x}$ and a set of identical independent model cdfs g, we seek that unmixing matrix $\mathbf{W}$ which maximizes the joint entropy of the signals $\mathbf{Y} = g(\mathbf{y})$, where $\mathbf{y} = \mathbf{Wx}$ are the signals extracted by $\mathbf{W}$. Given the optimal $\mathbf{W}$, the signals $\mathbf{Y}$ have maximum entropy and are therefore independent, which ensures that the extracted signals $\mathbf{y} = g^{-1}(\mathbf{Y})$ are also independent because g is an invertible function. After a brief introduction to entropy, we will examine this strategy in more detail.

7.3.2 Entropy

As stated above, entropy is essentially a measure of the uniformity of the distribution of a variable Z with values $Z^1, Z^2, \ldots, Z^N$, such that complete uniformity corresponds to a *maximum entropy* distribution.

Entropy can also be interpreted in terms of the average amount of *surprise* associated with a given event. For example, getting hit by lightning, denoted $Z^i = 1$ (Z could stand for "zapped" here), on a given day i would be a surprise (to say the least) because it is an event deemed to be of very low probability:

$$p(Z^i = 1) \approx 0. \tag{7.16}$$

The precise amount of surprise associated with the outcome $Z^i = 1$ can be defined as

$$-\ln p(Z^i = 1) \tag{7.17}$$

which is large for small values of p and small for large values of p.

In contrast, not getting hit by lightning, denoted $Z^i = 0$ on a given day i would be unsurprising because this has a very high probability

$$p(Z^i = 0) \approx 1. \tag{7.18}$$

If the probability of getting hit by lightning on a given day is $p(Z^i = 1)$ then the probability of not getting hit by lightning is $(1 - p(Z^i = 1))$. In this case, the amount of surprise is:

$$-\ln(1 - p(Z^i = 1)). \tag{7.19}$$

For notational simplicity we define $p = p(Z^i = 1)$.

The standard symbol for *entropy* is H, which is defined as the average amount of surprise associated with the variable Z, and is given by

$$H(Z) = -p\ln(p) - (1 - p)\ln(1 - p). \tag{7.20}$$

We now return to the more familiar example of coin tossing. In this case the average amount of surprise is related to the bias of a given coin. If bias is defined as probability p that a tossed coin will land heads up $Z^i = 1$ on the ith toss then the ability to predict the outcome of a coin toss is maximal if the coin is very biased, for example $p = 1$ or $p = 0$ (see figure 7.5). In these two cases of bias, the average amount of surprise associated with a series of coin tosses is zero because we know the outcome for every coin toss. Both cases correspond to a *minimal entropy* distribution of Z^i values.

In order to take account of the fact that $\ln p \to -\infty$ as $p \to 0$ or $\ln 0$ is undefined, we need to consider how $p \ln p$ changes in the limit as $p \to 0$. In fact, the rate at which p approaches zero is faster than the rate at which $\ln p$ approaches $-\infty$ and in the limit as $p \to 0$ the term $p \ln p$ approaches zero. The logic of this argument also applies to the term $(1 - p)\ln(1 - p)$ in the limit as $(1 - p) \to 0$. Thus, equation (7.20) evaluates to zero in the limit as $p \to 0$ and in the limit as $p \to 1$. A proof of this can be found in standard calculus texts.

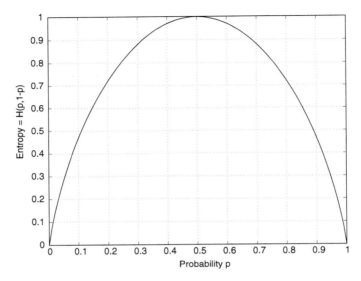

Figure 7.5
Entropy of coin tosses for different values of coin bias p_h between zero and one. If we denote heads as 1 and tails as 0 then the outcome of each toss is least predictable at $p_h = 0.5$, and the corresponding set of N outcomes has maximum entropy. This is true for entropy with log to any base, and we have used log to the base 2 in this graph.

If the coin is unbiased so that $p = 0.5$ then the ability to predict the outcome of a coin toss is minimal. In this case, the average amount of surprise associated with a series of coin toss outcomes is maximal, and the distribution of outcomes has *maximum entropy*. Specifically, if $p = 0.5$ then the entropy is

$$H(Z) = -\ln 0.5. \tag{7.21}$$

If we then construct a two-bin histogram of a series of coin toss outcomes for $p = 0.5$ then the number items in the first (zero) bin is approximately equal to the number of items in the second (one) bin. In this case, the distribution of values is uniform, and corresponds to a maximum entropy distribution. As the bias of the coin is varied between $p = 0$ and $p = 1$ the entropy of the distribution of zero/one values varies, as depicted in figure 7.5.

Here we have used logarithms to the base e, but the entropy is maximized by $p = 0.5$ irrespective of the base. If the entropy is calculated using logarithms to the base 2 then the units of measurement are called *bits*, and equation (7.21) would evaluate to unity, as in figure 7.5.

More generally, if the number of possible outcomes is n (e.g., for n-sided dice) where each outcome has probability p_i then the expected surprise or entropy is

$$H(Z) = -\sum_{i}^{n} p_i \ln p_i. \tag{7.22}$$

This has a maximum value of $\ln p_i$ if all p_i values are the same, that is, if the distribution of p_i's is uniform. Note that p_i's define a continuous pdf p_Z in the limit as $n \to \infty$. The important point to note is that, in general, a uniform distribution corresponds to a maximum entropy distribution.

The general definition of entropy[5] for a single (univariate) variable or signal Z with pdf p_Z is given by equation (7.22) in the limit as $n \to \infty$

$$H(Z) = -\int_{z=-\infty}^{+\infty} p_Z(z) \ln p_Z(z)\, dz. \tag{7.23}$$

Notice that this is a weighted mean of the term $\ln p_Z(z)$, analogous to the weighted means that defined each moment of a pdf in chapter 5. Just as a moment of a pdf can be expressed as an expected value, so entropy can be written as

$$H(Z) = -E[\ln p_Z(z)], \tag{7.24}$$

which, as we have already noted, is the average surprise of the variable Z.

Evaluating Entropy

There is one important but subtle distinction to be made when evaluating the entropy of a variable Z. We can evaluate entropy either from n values p_i of the pdf as in equation (7.22), or from a finite number N of event outcomes $Z^1, Z^2, \ldots, Z^N$, where each Z^t could be the outcome of a dice roll, for example. If the probability of obtaining outcome Z^t is $p_Z(Z^t)$ then the amount of surprise of each outcome is $-\ln p_Z(Z^t)$. If entropy is given by the average surprise then it follows that

$$H(Z) = -\frac{1}{N} \sum_{t}^{N} \ln p_Z(Z^t), \tag{7.25}$$

which looks alarmingly different from equation (7.22). It turns out that the entropy of a variable Z with pdf p_Z can be computed from two different sets of measurements, either from p_Z itself using equation 7.22, or from a set of N observed values $Z^1, Z^2, \ldots, Z^N$

---

5. If, as above, Z is a continuous variable (i.e., in the limit as $n \to \infty$) entropy is known as as *differential entropy*. However, we will use the term entropy to refer to the entropy of both discrete and continuous variables.

sampled from the pdf p_Z (e.g., from a set of dice rolls) using equation (7.25) (in this case, the number of values Z^t sampled from the ith bin will be proportional to the height of that bin). It is this latter form that is used in ICA.

7.3.3 Entropy of Univariate pdfs

If we now consider the signal $Y = g(y)$, where $y = \mathbf{w}^T \mathbf{x}$ is a signal extracted by a single row $\mathbf{w}^T$ of an unmixing matrix $\mathbf{W}$ then the entropy of Y is estimated as

$$H(Y) = -\frac{1}{N} \sum_{t=1}^{N} \ln p_Y(Y^t). \tag{7.26}$$

We now show that

- if y is a signal with cdf g then the signal $Y = g(y)$ has maximum entropy. This is equivalent to saying that the pdf of $Y = g(y)$ is uniform.

We begin by showing that the pdf p_Y of a signal $Y = g(y)$ is related to the pdf of the extracted signal $y = \mathbf{w}^T \mathbf{x}$ by

$$p_Y(Y) = \frac{p_y(y)}{\left| \frac{dY}{dy} \right|}, \tag{7.27}$$

where $|.|$ denotes absolute value.[6] (see figure 7.6).

If we define a small interval Δy around a value $y = y^1$ then the probability that y is between $y^1 - \Delta y/2$ and $y^1 + \Delta y/2$ is

$$p(y^1 - \Delta y/2 < y \le y^1 + \Delta y/2) \approx p_y(y^1)\Delta y, \tag{7.28}$$

where the equality becomes exact in the limit as $\Delta y \to 0$.

Similarly, the probability that Y is between $Y^1 - \Delta Y/2$ and $Y^1 + \Delta Y/2$ is

$$p(Y^1 - \Delta Y/2 < Y \le Y^1 + \Delta Y/2) \approx p_Y(Y^1)\Delta Y. \tag{7.29}$$

The increasing monotonic (and therefore invertible) function g maps the value y^1 (uniquely) to the value $Y^1 = g(y^1)$, and the interval Δy to the corresponding interval

$$\Delta Y = g(y^1 + \Delta y/2) - g(y^1 - \Delta y/2). \tag{7.30}$$

Given that $Y^1 = g(y^1)$, the probability of observing y in the range $y^1 \pm \Delta y/2$ is equivalent to the probability of observing Y in the range $Y^1 \pm \Delta Y/2$,

---

6. This account is based on that given in (Sivia, 1996, p70).

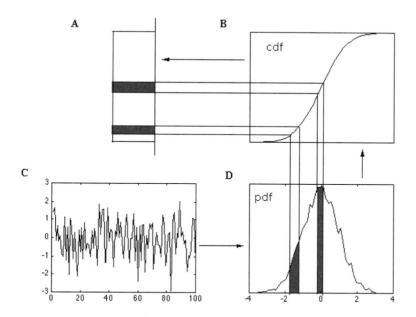

Figure 7.6
Schematic diagram of how a uniform distribution (**A**) is obtained if a signal is transformed by its own cdf. A signal $y = (y^1, \ldots, y^{5000})$ is used to construct a normalized (i.e., unit area) histogram (**D**), which is an approximation to the signal's pdf p_y. Only 100 of the 5000 signal values of y are shown in **C**. Note that the range of signal values in y is reflected in the x-axis of the histogram in **D**. The integral of p_y yields an approximation to the cdf g of y, with a range between zero and unity (**B**). The signal $Y = g(y)$ (not shown) has a pdf p_Y with a uniform distribution, shown rotated through 90 degrees in **A**. The signal Y has a uniform distribution because each of the (equivalent) shaded areas $p_Y(Y)\Delta Y$ in **A** must equal the corresponding shaded areas $p_y(y)\Delta y$ in **D**. Thus, certain intervals Δy on the x-axis of **D** get compressed when they are mapped by the cdf g to a corresponding interval ΔY in **A**, while others get expanded. Note that the amount of compression/expansion of an interval centered on a value y^t depends on the slope (derivative) of the cdf g at y^t.

$$p_Y(Y^1)\Delta Y = p_y(y^1)\Delta y. \tag{7.31}$$

Omitting superscripts and rearranging yields

$$p_Y(Y) = p_y(y)\frac{\Delta y}{\Delta Y} \tag{7.32}$$

$$= \frac{p_y(y)}{\frac{\Delta Y}{\Delta y}}, \tag{7.33}$$

and in the limit as $\Delta y \to 0$ this implies

$$p_Y(Y) = \frac{p_y(y)}{\frac{dY}{dy}}. \tag{7.34}$$

If g were monotonically decreasing then the derivative dY/dy would be negative. In order to take account of monotonically increasing and decreasing functions we take the absolute value of the derivative

$$p_Y(Y) = \frac{p_y(y)}{|\frac{dY}{dy}|}. \tag{7.35}$$

In fact, we do not need to use absolute values because all cdfs are monotonically increasing, but we include it here because it is required for the general multivariate case considered in the next section.

Note that the quantity $|dY/dy|$ represents the limit ($dy \to 0$) of a *ratio of lengths* (i.e., positive quantities), such that increments in y map to increments in Y. The quantity $|d(Y)/dy|$ is known as the *Jacobian* (denoted J), although this term is usually used to refer to the determinant of a matrix $\mathbf{J}$ of derivatives, as in the next section. We have now justified the result given in equation (7.27).

Given that $Y = g(y)$, we use a prime character to denote the derivative $|dY/dy| = g'(y)$

$$P_Y(Y) = \frac{p_y(y)}{g'(y)}. \tag{7.36}$$

We can omit the $|.|$ operator here because $g'(y)$ is a pdf, so that $g'(y') > 0$. We can replace g' by the pdf p_s assumed for the source signals $g' = p_s$

$$P_Y(Y) = \frac{p_y(y)}{p_s(y)}. \tag{7.37}$$

This can be substituted into equation (7.26)

$$H(Y) = -\frac{1}{N} \sum_{t=1}^{N} \ln \frac{p_y(y^t)}{p_s(y^t)}. \tag{7.38}$$

Recall that $y = \mathbf{w}^T \mathbf{x}$ is extracted by the weight vector $\mathbf{w}$. It follows that if a $\mathbf{w}$ exists such that the pdf p_y of the extracted signal y can be made to match the pdf p_s assumed for the source signals then the ratio $p_y(y)/p_s(y) = 1$, and is therefore constant. This implies that the pdf $p_Y(Y) = p_y(y)/p_s(y)$ is uniform, which, in turn, implies that $p_Y(Y)$ is a maximum entropy pdf.

It follows that if an unmixing vector $\mathbf{w}$ exists that maximizes the entropy of the signal $Y = g(y)$ then the pdf $p_y(y)$ of the extracted signal $y = \mathbf{w}^T \mathbf{x}$ will match the pdf $p_s(y)$.

Thus, the function p_s acts as an implicit model of the pdfs of signals to be extracted from the mixtures $\mathbf{x}$. In other words, the function p_s can be used to *specify* the pdf of extracted signals because the $\mathbf{w}$ that maximizes entropy is the $\mathbf{w}$ that extracts a signal y with pdf $p_y(y) = p_s(y)$.

Notice that equation (7.38) provides a measure of the similarity between the pdfs p_y and p_s. In fact, the *negative* of equation 7.38 is the discrete version of a standard measure of the *difference* between two pdfs, known as the *Kullback-Leibler divergence* or *relative entropy*. Therefore maximizing equation 7.38 corresponds to minimizing the Kullback-Leibler divergence or relative entropy between p_y and p_s. Some authors prefer to interpret ICA in terms of minimizing the Kullback-Leibler divergence between p_y and p_s. The Kullback-Leibler divergence can be applied to both univariate pdfs (as here) or to joint pdfs.

The pdf assumed for a source signal s is $p_s = g'$ which implies that the function g is the cdf of s

$$g = \int g'(y)\,dy \qquad (7.39)$$

and if the pdf of an extracted signal y is $p_s = g' = p_y$ then

$$g = \int p_y(y)\,dy. \qquad (7.40)$$

If a weight vector exists that maximizes the entropy of $Y = g(y)$ then the extracted signal y has cdf g. For example, if we define g' to be a super-gaussian pdf (i.e., a pdf with high kurtosis) then the weight vector that maximizes the entropy of $Y = g(y)$ will also maximize the kurtosis of the extracted signal $y = \mathbf{w}^T\mathbf{x}$. This is the cdf-matching (and, equivalently, pdf-matching) property of ICA mentioned earlier.

In order to evaluate equation (7.38) for a given extracted signal y, we need an expression for $p_y(y)$. Whilst it is possible to evaluate this in the univariate case considered here, the resultant expression is both complicated to derive and unnecessary. This is because ICA simultaneously extracts multiple source signals, for which the expression corresponding to $p_y(y)$ is relatively simple, as shown in the next section.

7.3.4 Entropy of Multivariate pdfs

Here we follow the general line of reasoning in the previous section to show that the above result generalizes to multivariate pdfs.

Given two bounded variables, their *joint entropy* can be visualized in terms of the amount of scatter when the values of one signal are plotted against corresponding values of the other signal (see figure 7.3, center panel).

More formally, the joint entropy of two variables $\mathbf{Z} = (Z_1, Z_2)$ is defined as

$$H(\mathbf{Z}) = -\int_{z_1=-\infty}^{+\infty}\int_{z_2=-\infty}^{+\infty} p_Z(z_1, z_2) \ln p_Z(z_1, z_2) \, dz_1 \, dz_2, \qquad (7.41)$$

where the joint pdf $p_Z(\mathbf{z}) = p_Z(z_1, z_2)$ is the density at $\mathbf{z} = (z_1, z_2)$. This can be written more succinctly using the vector variable $\mathbf{z} = (z_1, z_2)$

$$H(\mathbf{Z}) = -\int_{\mathbf{Z}} p_Z(\mathbf{z}) \ln p_Z(\mathbf{z}) \, d\mathbf{z}, \qquad (7.42)$$

where the joint pdf $p_Z(\mathbf{z}) = p_Z(z_1, z_2)$ is the density at (z_1, z_2).

Just as the one-dimensional integral in equation (7.24) provides a weighted mean of the univariate function $\ln p_Z(z)$, so equation (7.42) is a weighted mean of the multivariate function

$$\ln p_Z(\mathbf{z}) = (\ln p_Z(z_1), \ln p_Z(z_2), \ldots, \ln p_Z(z_M)), \qquad (7.43)$$

so that the joint entropy defined in equation (7.42) can be written succinctly as

$$H(\mathbf{Z}) = -E[\ln p_Z(\mathbf{z})]. \qquad (7.44)$$

If the M marginal pdfs $(p_Z(z_1), p_Z(z_2), \ldots, p_Z(z_M))$ of the multivariate pdf $p_Z(\mathbf{z})$ are independent then

$$\ln p_Z(\mathbf{z}) = \ln \prod_{i}^{M} p_Z(z_i) \qquad (7.45)$$

$$= \sum_{i}^{M} \ln p_Z(z_i). \qquad (7.46)$$

This is a critical equation for the infomax method, because it will be used to embody the assumption that the multivariate pdf used as a model for the source signals consists of independent marginal pdfs, which implies that the source signals are also assumed to be independent.

For a finite set of N values sampled from a distribution with pdf p_Z, equation (7.44) can be estimated as

$$H(\mathbf{Z}) = -\frac{1}{N}\sum_{t=1}^{N} \ln p_Z(\mathbf{Z}^t). \qquad (7.47)$$

We can now consider the entropy of the vector variable $\mathbf{Y} = g(\mathbf{y})$, where $\mathbf{y} = \mathbf{W}\mathbf{x}$ is the set of signals extracted by the unmixing matrix $\mathbf{W}$. For a finite set of values sampled from a distribution with pdf p_Y, the entropy of $\mathbf{Y}$ can be estimated as

$$H(\mathbf{Y}) \;=\; -\frac{1}{N}\sum_{t=1}^{N}\ln p_Y(\mathbf{Y}^t). \tag{7.48}$$

Following the same line of reasoning as was applied for a single variable Y above, it can be shown that the entropy $H(\mathbf{Y})$ of a multivariate pdf $p_Y(\mathbf{Y})$ is maximized if it is a uniform joint pdf.

Given that $\mathbf{Y} = g(\mathbf{y})$, the joint pdf p_Y can be shown to be related to the joint pdf p_y of the extracted signals by the multivariate form of equation (7.35)

$$P_Y(\mathbf{Y}) = \frac{p_y(\mathbf{y})}{\left|\dfrac{\partial \mathbf{Y}}{\partial \mathbf{y}}\right|}, \tag{7.49}$$

where $\partial \mathbf{Y}/\partial \mathbf{y}$ is a Jacobian matrix, and the vertical bars $|.|$ denote absolute value of the *determinant* of this matrix. This will not be proven here. Instead, a geometric account follows, which is summarized in figure 7.7.

In general, the Jacobian J is a scalar value, and is the determinant of a *Jacobian matrix* $\mathbf{J}$, which is an $M \times M$ matrix of *partial derivatives*.[7] If $M = 2$ then the Jacobian matrix is

$$\mathbf{J} = \frac{\partial \mathbf{Y}}{\partial \mathbf{y}} = \begin{pmatrix} \partial Y_1/\partial y_1 & \partial Y_2/\partial y_1 \\ \partial Y_1/\partial y_1 & \partial Y_2/\partial y_2 \end{pmatrix}. \tag{7.50}$$

It will prove useful to note that equation (7.49) holds for any invertible function: given any vector variable $\mathbf{Z} = (Z_1, Z_2, \ldots, Z_M)$ which is any invertible function g of the variable $\mathbf{z} = (z_1, z_2, \ldots, z_M)$, such that $\mathbf{Z} = g(\mathbf{z})$, the pdfs of $\mathbf{z}$ and $\mathbf{Z}$ are related by

$$p_Z(\mathbf{Z}) = \frac{p_z(\mathbf{z})}{\left|\dfrac{\partial \mathbf{Z}}{\partial \mathbf{z}}\right|}. \tag{7.51}$$

In the univariate case, the Jacobian was shown to be the limit of the ratio of lengths associated with corresponding values of z^t and Z^t. Here, the value $\mathbf{z}^t$ defines a point in an M dimensional space and the Jacobian is the ratio of volumes $(\mathrm{volume}(p_Z(\mathbf{Z}^t))/\mathrm{volume}(p_z(\mathbf{z}^t)))$ in the limit as $\mathrm{volume}(p_z(\mathbf{z}^t)) \to 0$ associated with the mapping from the point $\mathbf{z}^t$ to the point $\mathbf{Z}^t = g(\mathbf{z}^t)$.

Following the line of reasoning given in the univariate case, we can write

$$|\mathbf{J}| = |\partial \mathbf{Y}/\partial \mathbf{y}| = g'(\mathbf{y}). \tag{7.52}$$

---

7. See chapter 9 for a brief account of partial derivatives.

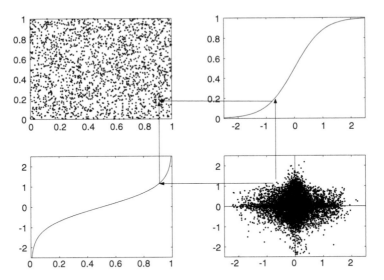

Figure 7.7
Maximum entropy distribution obtained from a scatter plot of two (unmixed) speech signals. If the matrix $\mathbf{W}$ used to extract two signals $\mathbf{y} = \mathbf{Wx}$ from two mixtures $\mathbf{x}$ is optimal then $\mathbf{y} = \mathbf{s}$, where $\mathbf{s}$ are the required speech signals. The resultant joint distribution of points from $\mathbf{y}$ appears as shown in the *lower right* scatter plot. The cdf g of the extracted signals $\mathbf{y} = (y_1, y_2)^T$ is the same for y_1 and y_2, and is depicted in the *top right* graph, and in the *lower left* graph (reflected through the diagonal). If each extracted signal is transformed by the function g then the joint distribution the signals $\mathbf{Y} = g(\mathbf{y})$ is uniform (i.e., has maximum entropy), as shown in the *top left* scatter plot. As an example, the arrows show how a single data point $\mathbf{y}^t = (y_1^t, y_2^t)^T$ is transformed to a corresponding data point $\mathbf{Y}^t = (g(y_1^t), g(y_2^t))^T = g(\mathbf{y}^t)$ of the maximum entropy joint distribution. Here, the cdf g is the tanh function, which implies a super-gaussian pdf for the signals plotted in the lower right graph.

We can define g' to be the pdf assumed for the source signals $g' = p_s$. Substituting this into equation (7.49) yields

$$P_Y(\mathbf{Y}) = \frac{p_y(\mathbf{y})}{p_s(\mathbf{y})}. \tag{7.53}$$

This can then be substituted into equation (7.48):

$$H(\mathbf{Y}) = -\frac{1}{N} \sum_{t=1}^{N} \ln \frac{p_y(\mathbf{y}^t)}{p_s(\mathbf{y}^t)}. \tag{7.54}$$

If an optimal unmixing matrix $\mathbf{W}$ exists such that the extracted signals $\mathbf{y} = \mathbf{Wx}$ have a joint pdf

$$p_y(\mathbf{y}^t) = p_s(\mathbf{y}^t) \tag{7.55}$$

then the ratio defined in equation (7.53) is constant. This implies that *the joint pdf $P_Y(\mathbf{Y})$ is uniform and that the entropy $H(\mathbf{Y})$ defined in equation 7.54 is maximized by the optimal matrix $\mathbf{W}$. This, in turn, implies that the variables $\mathbf{Y}$ are independent, so that the extracted signals $\mathbf{y} = g^{-1}(\mathbf{Y})$ are also independent (see subsection 7.3.1).*

As in the univariate case, if an unmixing matrix $\mathbf{W}$ exists that maximizes the entropy of the signal $\mathbf{Y} = g(\mathbf{y})$ then the pdf p_y of each extracted signal in $\mathbf{y} = \mathbf{Wx}$ will match the pdf p_s. Thus, the function p_s acts as a *model pdf* for signals to be extracted from the mixtures $\mathbf{x}$. The function p_s can therefore be used to *specify* the pdf of extracted signals because the $\mathbf{W}$ that maximizes entropy is the $\mathbf{W}$ that extracts a set of signals $\mathbf{y}$ with pdf $p_y = p_s$.

However, in order to evaluate equation (7.54) for a given set of extracted signals $\mathbf{y}$, we need an expression for $p_y(\mathbf{y})$. Given the result expressed in equation 7.51, and the mapping $\mathbf{y} = \mathbf{Wx}$ we can deduce that

$$p_y(\mathbf{y}) = \frac{p_x(\mathbf{x})}{\left|\frac{\partial \mathbf{y}}{\partial \mathbf{x}}\right|}. \tag{7.56}$$

We state without proof that the Jacobian $|\partial \mathbf{y}/\partial \mathbf{x}|$ evaluates to

$$\left|\frac{\partial \mathbf{y}}{\partial \mathbf{x}}\right| = |\mathbf{W}|, \tag{7.57}$$

where $|\mathbf{W}|$ is the absolute value of the determinant of the unmixing matrix $\mathbf{W}$, so that

$$p_y(\mathbf{y}) = \frac{p_x(\mathbf{x})}{|\mathbf{W}|}. \tag{7.58}$$

Note that the Jacobian $|\mathbf{W}|$ is a constant and, in contrast to the Jacobian $|\partial \mathbf{Y}/\partial \mathbf{y}|$, does not depend on the value of $\mathbf{y}$. This reflects the fact that $\mathbf{y}$ is a linear function of $\mathbf{x}$.

We cannot evaluate the pdf $p_x(\mathbf{x})$, but this does not matter for our purposes, as we will see shortly. Substituting equation (7.58) into equation (7.54) yields

$$H(\mathbf{Y}) = -\frac{1}{N} \sum_{t=1}^{N} \ln \frac{p_x(\mathbf{x}^t)}{|\mathbf{W}| p_s(\mathbf{y}^t)}. \tag{7.59}$$

This can be rearranged

$$H(\mathbf{Y}) = \frac{1}{N} \sum_{t=1}^{N} \ln p_s(\mathbf{y}^t) + \ln |\mathbf{W}| - \frac{1}{N} \sum_{t=1}^{N} \ln p_x(\mathbf{x}^t), \tag{7.60}$$

where, from the general definition in equation 7.47, we can deduce that the final term in equation 7.60 is the entropy $H(\mathbf{x})$ of the set of mixtures $\mathbf{x}$

$$H(\mathbf{x}) = -\frac{1}{N}\sum_{t=1}^{N}\ln p_x(\mathbf{x}^t). \qquad (7.61)$$

Substituting this into equation (7.60) yields

$$H(\mathbf{Y}) = \frac{1}{N}\sum_{t=1}^{N}\ln p_s(\mathbf{y}^t) + \ln|\mathbf{W}| + H(\mathbf{x}). \qquad (7.62)$$

The unmixing matrix $\mathbf{W}$ that maximizes the entropy $H(\mathbf{Y})$ does so irrespective of the pdf $p_x(\mathbf{x})$ because $p_x(\mathbf{x})$ defines the entropy $H(\mathbf{x})$ of the mixtures $\mathbf{x}$ which cannot therefore be affected by $\mathbf{W}$. We can therefore ignore $H(\mathbf{x})$ when seeking a $\mathbf{W}$ that maximizes equation (7.62), and can instead define a simpler function which does not include $H(\mathbf{x})$

$$h(\mathbf{Y}) = \frac{1}{N}\sum_{t=1}^{N}\ln p_s(\mathbf{y}^t) + \ln|\mathbf{W}|. \qquad (7.63)$$

Finally, if the M marginal pdfs of the model joint pdf p_s are independent then we can rewrite equation (7.63) as

$$h(\mathbf{Y}) = \frac{1}{N}\sum_{i=1}^{M}\sum_{t=1}^{N}\ln p_s(y_i^t) + \ln|\mathbf{W}|. \qquad (7.64)$$

If we substitute a commonly used super-gaussian (high-kurtosis) model pdf for the source signals $p_s = (1 - \tanh(\mathbf{s})^2)$ then we have

$$h(\mathbf{Y}) = \frac{1}{N}\sum_{i}^{M}\sum_{t}^{N}\ln(1 - \tanh(\mathbf{w}_i^T\mathbf{x}^t)^2) + \ln|\mathbf{W}|. \qquad (7.65)$$

In summary, given a set of observed mixtures $\mathbf{x}$, and a corresponding set of extracted signals $\mathbf{y} = \mathbf{W}\mathbf{x}$ we can now evaluate the quality of any putative unmixing matrix $\mathbf{W}$ using equation (7.64). If the specified pdf $p_s = g'$ corresponds to a high-kurtosis signal then equation (7.64) will be maximized by a $\mathbf{W}$ that extracts high-kurtosis signals from $\mathbf{x}$. As equations 7.64 and 7.62 differ by a constant $(H(\mathbf{x}))$ the unmixing matrix that maximizes the simpler equation (7.64) also maximizes the entropy of $\mathbf{Y}$ defined in equation (7.62). Thus we can deduce that, for the optimal unmixing matrix, the signals $\mathbf{Y} = g(\mathbf{y})$ have maximum entropy and are therefore independent. As our model joint cdf has independent marginal cdfs, this implies that the extracted signals $\mathbf{y} = g^{-1}(\mathbf{Y})$ are also independent.

7.3.5   Using Entropy to Extract Independent Signals

In order to make use of entropy to recover source signals it is clearly necessary to consider more than one recovered signal at a time so that the joint entropy of the set of recovered signals can be estimated.

Having obtained a formal definition of entropy in terms of the recovered signals and the unmixing matrix $\mathbf{W}$ we need a method for finding that $\mathbf{W}$ which maximizes entropy of $\mathbf{Y}$, and which therefore maximizes the independence of $\mathbf{y}$. Once again, the brute force exhaustive search method will do for now. In the case of two signals, this involves trying all possible orientations for the row vectors $\mathbf{w}_1^T$ and $\mathbf{w}_2^T$ in $\mathbf{W} = (\mathbf{w}_1, \mathbf{w}_2)^T$. In figure 7.8, $\mathbf{w}_2$ is kept constant at the optimal orientation (i.e., orthogonal to S_1') for illustrative purposes, and the value of h is plotted as $\mathbf{w}_1$ is rotated through 360 degrees. As $\mathbf{w}_2$ is constant, the changing value of h reflects the changing entropy associated with the signal y_1 extracted by $\mathbf{w}_1$. As can be seen, entropy is maximal only when $\mathbf{w}_1$ is at the correct orientation (i.e., orthogonal to S_2').

Finally, note that if the model pdf p_s matches the pdf p_y of the extracted signals then maximizing the joint entropy of $\mathbf{Y}$ also maximizes the amount of *mutual information* between $\mathbf{x}$ and $\mathbf{Y}$ see (Bell & Sejnowski, 1995). For this reason, the above exposition of ICA is known as *infomax*. Next, we consider a different interpretation, which also leads to equation (7.64).

7.4   Maximum Likelihood ICA

One common interpretation of ICA is as a *maximum likelihood* (ML) method for estimating the optimal unmixing matrix. Maximum likelihood estimation (MLE) is a standard statistical tool for finding parameter values (e.g., the unmixing matrix $\mathbf{W}$) that provide the best fit of some data (e.g., the extracted signals $\mathbf{y}$) to a given a model (e.g., the assumed joint pdf p_s of source signals).

The ML "model" includes a specification of a pdf, which in this case is the pdf p_s of the unknown source signals $\mathbf{s}$. Using ML ICA, the objective is to find an unmixing matrix that yields extracted signals $\mathbf{y} = \mathbf{Wx}$ with a joint pdf as similar as possible to the joint pdf p_s of the unknown source signals $\mathbf{s}$. As noted before, just because we do not know the source signals does not mean that we cannot know their pdfs.

Somewhat perversely, we can consider the probability of obtaining the observed data $\mathbf{x}$ in the context of such a model. We can then pose the question: given that the source signals have a pdf p_s, which particular mixing matrix $\mathbf{A}$ is most likely to have generated the observed signal mixtures $\mathbf{x}$? In other words, if the probability of obtaining the observed mixtures (from some unknown source signals with pdf p_s) were to vary with $\mathbf{A}$ then which particular $\mathbf{A}$ would maximize this probability?

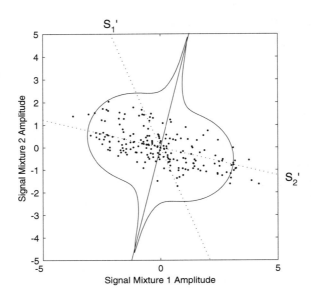

Figure 7.8

Graph showing how joint entropy varies with weight vector orientation for two speech signal mixtures. The plotted points represent signal mixture 1 (x_1) versus signal mixture 2 (x_2). For the purposes of this demonstration we have cheated by fixing one weight vector $\mathbf{w}_2$ (not shown) in the 2×2 weight matrix $\mathbf{W} = (\mathbf{w}_1, \mathbf{w}_2)^T$ to be optimal (i.e., orthogonal to S_1'). This allows us to examine the effects of rotating the weight vector $\mathbf{w}_1$ on entropy as it is rotated around the origin.

For any given orientation of the weight vector $\mathbf{w}_1$ the extracted signal y_1 is given by the inner product of $\mathbf{w}_1^T$ with the two signal mixtures $\mathbf{x} = (x_1, x_2)$, $y_1 = \mathbf{w}_1^T \mathbf{x}$. The joint entropy of the pdf of the pair of signals $\mathbf{Y} = (g(y_1), g(y_2))$ varies as $\mathbf{w}_1$ is rotated around the origin, where $g = \tanh$ is the high-kurtosis model cdf assumed for source signals. At each orientation sampled by $\mathbf{w}_1$, the associated entropy is plotted as a distance from the origin in the direction of $\mathbf{w}_1$, giving a continuous curve. Critically, entropy is maximal when $\mathbf{w}_1$ is orthogonal to the transformed axis S_2', at which point $\mathbf{w}_1$ extracts exactly one source signal $s_1 = y_1$. Here entropy is defined as in equation (7.65).

The orientation of $\mathbf{w}_1$ corresponding to one maximum in entropy is plotted as a solid line. Note that this line has the same *orientation* as the *direction* of $\mathbf{w}_1$. This line actually connects two *identical* maxima in entropy, because the vectors $\mathbf{w}_1$ and $-\mathbf{w}_1$ both have the same orientation and both therefore extract the same signal with a simple sign reversal (e.g., $\mathbf{w}_1$ extracts y_1 and $-\mathbf{w}_1$ extracts $-y_1$). Note that this line is orthogonal to the transformed axis S_1'.

Note that, as $\mathbf{A}$ and $\mathbf{W}$ are inverses of each other, it does not matter whether the model parameters are expressed in terms of $\mathbf{A}$ or $\mathbf{W}$.

MLE is thus based on the assumption that if the model pdf p_s and the model parameters $\mathbf{A}$ are correct then a high probability should be obtained for the data $\mathbf{x}$ that were actually observed. Conversely, if $\mathbf{A}$ is far from the correct parameter values then a low probability of the observed data would be expected.

Using MLE, we call the probability of the observed data for a given set of model parameter values (e.g., a pdf p_s and a matrix $\mathbf{A}$) the *likelihood* of the model parameter values given the observed data.

We will assume that all source signals have the same pdf p_s, and that source signals have high-kurtosis pdfs. This may not seem much to go on, but as we have seen before, it turns out to be a perfectly adequate criterion for extracting source signals from signal mixtures.

Consider a (mixture) vector variable $\mathbf{x}$ with joint pdf p_x, and a (source) vector variable $\mathbf{s}$ with joint pdf p_s, such that $\mathbf{y}$ is related to $\mathbf{x}$ by

$$\mathbf{x} = \mathbf{As}. \qquad (7.66)$$

In general the relation between the pdfs of $\mathbf{x}$ and $\mathbf{s}$ is

$$p_x(\mathbf{x}) = p_s(\mathbf{s}) \left| \frac{\partial \mathbf{s}}{\partial \mathbf{x}} \right|, \qquad (7.67)$$

where $|\partial \mathbf{s}/\partial \mathbf{x}|$ is the Jacobian of $\mathbf{s}$ with respect to $\mathbf{x}$. Given equation (7.66), it follows that

$$\mathbf{s} = \mathbf{A}^{-1}\mathbf{x} \qquad (7.68)$$
$$= \mathbf{W}^*\mathbf{x}, \qquad (7.69)$$

where the optimal unmixing matrix $\mathbf{W}^*$ is the inverse of the mixing matrix $\mathbf{A}$. As before, the Jacobian is

$$\left| \frac{\partial \mathbf{s}}{\partial \mathbf{x}} \right| = |\mathbf{W}^*|. \qquad (7.70)$$

Substituting equation (7.70) into equation (7.67)

$$p_x(\mathbf{x}) = p_s(\mathbf{s}) \left| \mathbf{W}^* \right|. \qquad (7.71)$$

This is the probability of the observed data given the optimal unmixing matrix and the source signals $\mathbf{s} = \mathbf{W}^*\mathbf{x}$. For any non-optimal unmixing matrix $\mathbf{W}$ the extracted signals are $\mathbf{y} = \mathbf{Wx}$, and the signal mixtures $\mathbf{x}$ have probability

$$p_x(\mathbf{x}) \quad = \quad p_s(\mathbf{y})\,|\mathbf{W}|\,, \tag{7.72}$$

$$= \quad p_s(\mathbf{Wx})\,|\mathbf{W}|\,. \tag{7.73}$$

We would naturally expect $p_x(\mathbf{x})$ to be maximal if $\mathbf{W}$ is the optimal unmixing matrix. Thus equation (7.73) can be used to evaluate the quality of any putative unmixing matrix $\mathbf{W}$ in order to find that particular $\mathbf{W}$ which maximizes $p_x(\mathbf{x})$.

We let equation (7.73) define a *likelihood function* $L(\mathbf{W})$ of $\mathbf{W}$:

$$L(\mathbf{W}) = p_s(\mathbf{Wx})|\mathbf{W}|. \tag{7.74}$$

Thus, if we wish to find a $\mathbf{W}$ that is most likely to have generated the observed mixtures $\mathbf{x}$ from the unknown source signals $\mathbf{s}$ with pdf p_s then we need only(!) find that $\mathbf{W}$ which maximizes the likelihood $L(\mathbf{W})$. The unmixing matrix that maximizes equation 7.74 is known as the MLE of the optimal unmixing matrix.

We can examine this in more detail if we assume that the source signals are independent, which implies that the joint pdf p_s is the product of its M marginal pdfs, each of which is the pdf p_s of one signal y_i

$$L(\mathbf{W}) \quad = \quad p_s(\mathbf{y})|\mathbf{W}| \tag{7.75}$$

$$= \quad \prod_{i=1}^{M} p_s(y_i)|\mathbf{W}| \tag{7.76}$$

$$= \quad \prod_{i=1}^{M} p_s(\mathbf{w}_i^T \mathbf{x})|\mathbf{W}|, \tag{7.77}$$

where $\mathbf{w}_i^T$ is a single weight vector and is a row of $\mathbf{W}$. If we assume that all values of each source signal are independent then we can write

$$L(\mathbf{W}) \quad = \quad \prod_{i=1}^{M}\prod_{t=1}^{N} p_s(y_i^t)|\mathbf{W}| \tag{7.78}$$

$$= \quad \prod_{i}\prod_{t} p_s(\mathbf{w}_i^T \mathbf{x}^t)|\mathbf{W}|. \tag{7.79}$$

Finally, it is common practice to use the *log likelihood*, because this is easier to evaluate. As the logarithm is a monotonic function, the $\mathbf{W}$ that maximizes the function $L(\mathbf{W})$ also maximizes its logarithm $\ln L(\mathbf{W})$. This allows us to take the logarithm of equation (7.79), which yields the *log likelihood function*

$$\ln L(\mathbf{W}) = \sum_{i}\sum_{t} \ln p_s(\mathbf{w}_i^T \mathbf{x}^t) + N\,\ln|\mathbf{W}|. \tag{7.80}$$

We can divide this by N without affecting the optimal $\mathbf{W}$:

$$\frac{1}{N} \ln L(\mathbf{W}) = \frac{1}{N} \sum_{i=1}^{M} \sum_{t=1}^{N} \ln p_s(y_i^t) + \ln |\mathbf{W}|. \tag{7.81}$$

Note that this is the same as equation (7.64).

If we substitute a commonly used high-kurtosis model pdf for the source signals $p_s = (1 - \tanh(\mathbf{s})^2)$ then we have

$$\ln L(\mathbf{W}) = \frac{1}{N} \sum_{i}^{M} \sum_{t}^{N} \ln(1 - \tanh(\mathbf{w}_i^T \mathbf{x}^t)^2) + \ln |\mathbf{W}|. \tag{7.82}$$

The matrix $\mathbf{W}$ that maximizes this function is the *maximum likelihood estimate* of the optimal unmixing matrix $\mathbf{W}^*$.

7.5 Maximum Likelihood and Infomax Equivalence

It is noteworthy that both the infomax and ML approaches to ICA lead to exactly the same equation. The infomax approach yields equation (7.64) and the MLE approach yields equation (7.81), a convergence which has been noted by many authors, e.g., (Cardoso, 1997).

Both methods depend on the frankly unrealistic assumption that the model pdf is an exact match for the pdf of the required source signals. However, the pdf of the source signals is not known in general. Despite this, ICA works because if the model pdf is an approximation to the source signal pdf then the extracted signals are the source signals (Cardoso, 2000, Amari, 1998).

7.6 Extracting Source Signals Using Gradient Ascent

Given a set of signal mixtures $\mathbf{x}$, we seek an unmixing matrix $\mathbf{W}$ which maximizes the entropy $H(\mathbf{Y})$ of the signals $\mathbf{Y} = g(\mathbf{Wx})$, or equivalently, an unmixing matrix which maximizes the likelihood $L(\mathbf{W})$.

We can find an estimate $\mathbf{W}$ of the optimal matrix $\mathbf{W}^*$ using the gradient ascent method described in chapter 9 to iteratively adjust $\mathbf{W}$ in order to maximize the entropy of $\mathbf{Y}$. In order to perform gradient ascent efficiently, we require an expression for the gradient of entropy with respect to the matrix $\mathbf{W}$. This expression is derived in appendix D.

7.7 Temporal and Spatial ICA

In "standard" ICA, each of M temporal signal mixtures is measured over N time steps, and M temporal source signals are recovered as $\mathbf{y} = \mathbf{Wx}$, where each source signal is independent *over time* of every other source signal. However, when considering temporal

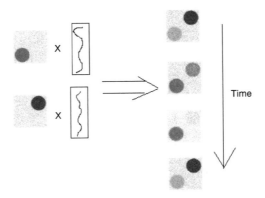

Figure 7.9
The general mixing process assumed for ICA for an observed temporal sequence of images (right). Here, each of two images (left) is multiplied by a different time-varying signal (shown in two vertical panels) to yield a temporal sequence of images, such that each image in the sequence is a different mixture of the two images on the left.

Spatial ICA: For sICA, it is assumed that each observed image (right) is a mixture of independent source images (left), where the contribution of each source image to the observed image sequence varies over time, as determined by a temporal signal (drawn in vertical panels).

Temporal ICA: For tICA, it is assumed that the observed temporal sequence of gray-levels of each pixel is a mixture of independent temporal source signals (drawn in vertical panels), where the contribution of each source signal to an observed temporal sequence varies over (image) space.

Note that ICA usually requires that there are as many source signals as mixtures, and this constraint not reflected in the figure.

sequences of images each image consists of a set of pixels, and each row of the data array $\mathbf{x}$ is the temporal sequence of one pixel over time. Thus each column of $\mathbf{x}$ is an image recorded at one point in time. So far, we have been treating the rows of $\mathbf{x}$ as mixtures, and using ICA to find a set of *independent temporal signals*. If we treat the columns of $\mathbf{x}$ as mixtures then the set of signals found by ICA are *spatially independent images*. ICA can therefore be used to maximize independence over *time* or to maximize independence over *space* (see figures 7.9 and 7.10).

Thus, ICA can be used in one of two complementary ways to extract either temporal source signals from the rows of $\mathbf{x}$ using *temporal ICA* (tICA), or spatial source signals from the rows of $\mathbf{x}^T$ using *spatial ICA* (sICA). Extracting speech source signals from speech mixtures is an example of tICA. In contrast, extracting features from sets of functional magnetic resonance (fMRI) images or from a spatial array of electroencephalographic (EEG) electrodes are examples of sICA.

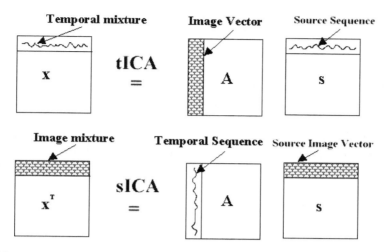

Figure 7.10
Vector-matrix representation of mixing process for tICA and sICA. Given a temporal sequence of images, ICA can be used to decompose signal mixtures into temporally independent signals or spatially independent images. Note that each image is represented as an image vector by concatenating its rows, so that an $M \times M$ image yields a single image vector with $M \times M$ elements.

tICA: Each row of the array $\mathbf{x}$ is a temporal mixture of the different independent temporal source signals in the rows of $\mathbf{s}$. Using tICA, the set of observed signal mixtures $\mathbf{x}$ is decomposed into a set of independent temporal source signals and a corresponding set of unconstrained image vectors. Each independent temporal source signal determines how the contribution of one image vector (column of $\mathbf{A}$) to the observed image sequence varies over time.

sICA: Each row of the array $\mathbf{x}^T$ is an image mixture of the different independent spatial source signals (images) in the rows of $\mathbf{s}$. Using sICA, the set of observed image mixtures $\mathbf{x}^T$ is decomposed into a set of independent source images and a corresponding set of unconstrained temporal signals. Each independent source image vector determines how the contribution of one temporal signal (column of $\mathbf{A}$) to the observed temporal sequence varies over space. An alternative perspective is that each temporal sequence determines how one independent source image vector contributes to the observed image sequence over time.

In essence, both sICA and tICA produce a set of images and a corresponding set of temporal sequences. However, tICA produces a set of mutually independent temporal sequences and a corresponding *dual* set of unconstrained images, whereas sICA produces mutually independent images and a corresponding dual set of unconstrained temporal sequences.

The problems solved by tICA and sICA are essentially the same, and the algorithm used is the same for both tICA and sICA. The difference depends on whether the data are assumed to be independent over time (as in speech), or independent over space (as in fMRI). In order to examine this difference in more detail we will consider a data set which can be analysed using either tICA or sICA.

sICA and fMRI Consider the temporal series of two-dimensional (2D) images of a brain collected under fMRI during the course of an experiment. A simple experiment might consist of flashing a black and white grating on and off in order to induce activation in visual areas of the brain, such as the primary visual cortex. Even though the entire brain is imaged as a set of 2D images about every 2 seconds, we will consider only one horizontal slice that passes through the visual cortex. This results in a temporal sequence of 150 2D images of the visual cortex during the course of a typical five minute scanning session. For convenience we will assume that the temporal image sequence actually consists of 144 images.

The 144-element time course of each pixel's gray level is assumed to consist of a mixture of underlying temporal source signals, and is analogous to the amplitude of a microphone output. Specifically, it is assumed that each pixel's temporal sequence is a mixture of the same set of underlying temporal source signals. For brevity, we refer to the time course of each pixel's gray level as a pixel temporal mixture. As an image is typically 256×256 pixels, this implies that there are effectively 65,536 temporal mixtures, which tICA would decompose into 65,536 temporal source signals. This unwieldy number of temporal source signals is physically implausible, so we will assume for now that each image is 12×12 pixels so that there are only 144 pixels in each image. This short "movie" of the activation of primary visual cortex can now be analysed using tICA or sICA. In practice, the number of pixels in each image can be reduced using principal components analysis (PCA) (see appendix F).

sICA and Microphone Arrays Alternatively, this could be considered in terms of an ordered spatial array of 144 microphones arranged in a 12×12 grid. If these microphones are on the ceiling of a room containing 144 members of a choir then the recorded data can be considered as a temporal sequence of images, in which each image consists of 12×12 'pixels' (microphones).

7.7.1 Temporal ICA

If the rows of the image acquired at time t are concatenated then the result is a 144-element (column) *image vector* $x^t = (x_1^t, x_2^t, \ldots, x_{144}^t)^T$, where x_i^t is the gray-level of the ith pixel. The temporal sequence of image vectors defines a vector-valued variable

$$\mathbf{x} = (x^1, x^2, \ldots, x^{144})^T. \tag{7.83}$$

Note that $\mathbf{x}$ is a 144×144 array of pixel values, in which each column is an image vector, and each row is the gray-level of one pixel over the 144 temporal sequence of image vectors. For example, x^2 is a column vector which is the image vector of the second image in the temporal sequence of images $\mathbf{x}$.

The method we have labeled as tICA would find a 144×144 unmixing matrix $\mathbf{W}_{tICA}$ such that the extracted temporal signals $\mathbf{y}_T$ are mutually independent (where the subscript T denotes temporal independence)

$$\mathbf{y}_T = \mathbf{W}_{tICA}\mathbf{x}, \tag{7.84}$$

where the rows of $\mathbf{y}_T$ are mutually independent temporal sequences

$$\mathbf{y}_T = (y_1, y_2, \ldots, y_{144})^T. \tag{7.85}$$

If y_i is the ith temporal sequence, we might reasonably ask, precisely what is it that varies over time in accordance with this sequence?

The short answer is that each temporal sequence y_i defines how a specific image contributes to the temporal sequence of image mixtures $\mathbf{x}$ over time. This can be seen if we assume for the present that matrices are subject to the laws of algebra which govern scalars. We could then multiply both sides of equation 7.84 by the inverse $\mathbf{W}_{tICA}^{-1}$ of the unmixing matrix $\mathbf{W}_{tICA}$

$$\mathbf{x} = \mathbf{W}_{tICA}^{-1}\mathbf{y}_T. \tag{7.86}$$

In fact, finding the inverse of a matrix is usually a nontrivial business, but we need to know only that it can be obtained for our purposes.

If we assume that the method has worked perfectly so that the extracted signals $\mathbf{y}_T$ are identical to the temporal source signals $\mathbf{s}_T$ then the similarity of equation (7.86) to the mixing process

$$\mathbf{x} = \mathbf{A}\mathbf{s}_T \tag{7.87}$$
$$= \mathbf{A}\mathbf{y}_T \tag{7.88}$$

implies that

$$\mathbf{A} = \mathbf{W}_{tICA}^{-1}. \tag{7.89}$$

More importantly, it implies that each column of $\mathbf{A}$ is an image vector, which contributes to every column (image mixture) in $\mathbf{x}$. The relative contribution of the tth image vector in $\mathbf{A}$ to every column in $\mathbf{x}$ is specified by the ith temporal sequence (row) of $\mathbf{y}_T$, as shown in figure 7.10. Thus, whereas each row y_i of $\mathbf{y}_T$ specifies a signal that is independent of all rows in $\mathbf{y}$, each column of $\mathbf{A}$ consists of an image that varies independently over time according to the amplitude of y_i. Note that, in general, the rows of $\mathbf{y}$ are constrained to be mutually independent, whereas the relationship between the columns (images) of $\mathbf{A}$ is completely unconstrained.

7.7.2 Spatial ICA

One way to interpret sICA is to consider an image as a mixture of underlying source images, and an image vector as a "spatial sequence" measured at a single point in time. This contrasts nicely with tICA in which a pixel's gray-level is considered as a temporal mixture of underlying temporal source signals, and each temporal mixture is measured at a single point in space (i.e., at one pixel's location in a temporal sequence of images).

Basically, ICA finds a set of independent source signals irrespective of whether these signals represent temporal or spatial (i.e., image vector) signals. Thus, in the case of tICA, each row of $\mathbf{x}$ contains a mixture of temporal source signals and ICA finds a set of independent temporal source signals. Similarly, if each row contained a mixture of spatial source signals (i.e., a mixture of images) then ICA finds a set of independent spatial source signals (i.e., source images).

Recall that $\mathbf{x}$ was defined in the previous section such that each column is an image vector formed from the concatenation of consecutive rows in an image. But, for sICA, we require that one image vector is in each *row*. This can be achieved as the transpose $\mathbf{x}^T$ of $\mathbf{x}$ (formed simply by rotating $\mathbf{x}$ through 90 degrees as indicated in figure 7.10).

The concatenation of rows might seem an odd thing to do to an image, but recall that ICA maximizes the independence between images (defined in terms of the pdf of images) which is the same irrespective of the spatial layout of pixel values in any single image. So it does not matter if ICA is presented with an image in the form of an image vector because ICA is concerned only with the set of pixel gray-levels, and not with their ordering. This argument also applies projection pursuit because kurtosis is also unaffected by the spatial layout of pixels. In other words, scrambling every image in the temporal sequence would have no effect on the results of ICA (provided the scrambling process was identical for all images in a given sequence, so that individual pixels remained aligned across a sequence of images).[8]

The method we have labeled as sICA would find an unmixing matrix $\mathbf{W}_{sICA}$ such that the extracted spatial signals (image vectors) $\mathbf{y}_S$ are mutually independent (where the subscript S denotes temporal independence)

$$\mathbf{y}_S = \mathbf{W}_{sICA}\mathbf{x}^T, \tag{7.90}$$

---

8. Note that we could equally well have concatenated the columns of each image instead of the rows, and it is only necessary to keep track of whether rows or columns were concatenated when it is required to reconstitute an image from an image vector.

where each row of $\mathbf{y}_S$ is an image vector

$$y_i = \mathbf{w}_i^T \mathbf{x}^T, \tag{7.91}$$

where $\mathbf{w}_i^T$ is the ith row of $\mathbf{W}_{sICA}$.

In summary, tICA is based on the assumption that the temporal sequence of the gray-levels of a pixel at every point in space is *independent over time* of temporal sequences of all other points in space. In contrast, sICA is based on the assumption that the spatial pattern ("spatial sequence") of gray-levels of all pixels at every point in time is *independent over space* of spatial patterns of all other points in time.

Clearly, if it reasonable to assume temporal independence for source signals underlying a particular data set then tICA should be applied. Conversely, if it reasonable to assume spatial independence for source signals underlying a particular data set then sICA should be applied.

7.7.3   Spatiotemporal ICA

If both spatial and temporal independence can be assumed then spatiotemporal ICA (stICA) can be applied. Whereas tICA assumes independence over time but not space, and sICA assumes independence over space but not time, stICA assumes independence over time *and* space (Stone *et al.*, 2002).

7.7.4   The Size of the Unmixing Matrix

In the above examples, we have cheated a little by assuming that there are as many images in a temporal sequence as there are pixels in each image. This yields a nice square (144×144) array for the entire sequence of images, and permits easy comparison of sICA and tICA. In general this assumption is invalid, but this does not affect the descriptions of sICA and tICA.

In the case of sICA, we treat the rows of the transposed matrix $\mathbf{x}^T$ as mixtures. The data array $\mathbf{x}^T$ has N rows and M columns, where each row contains one image vector. The unmixing matrix is then given by an $N \times N$ matrix $\mathbf{W}_{sICA}$, such that

$$\mathbf{y}_S = \mathbf{W}_{sICA}\mathbf{x}^T, \tag{7.92}$$

where $\mathbf{W}_{sICA}$ is often small enough to be estimated using ICA.

However, in the case of tICA, we treat the rows of $\mathbf{x}$ as mixtures, where each mixture is a temporal sequence. The number M of temporal sequences (pixels) can be much larger than the number N of images in a sequence ($M >> N$, as with EEG data). This yields a data array $\mathbf{x}$ with M rows and N columns, where each row contains one temporal sequence.

The unmixing matrix is then given by an $M \times M$ matrix $\mathbf{W}_{tICA}$, such that

$$\mathbf{y}_T = \mathbf{W}_{tICA}\mathbf{x}. \tag{7.93}$$

The $M \times M$ matrix $\mathbf{W}_{tICA}$ can be very large, because M is equal to the number of pixels in a single image.

If the square $M \times M$ unmixing matrix is too large then it is possible to reduce it to a smaller square $K \times K$ unmixing matrix using PCA (see appendix F). However, preprocessing with PCA depends on the assumption that signals of interest are distributed amongst the "largest" principal components (i.e., those associated with the largest eigenvalues), an assumption which is not necessarily valid (Green et al., 2002). Alternatively, it is possible to specify the exact number K (where K is no larger than the number M of signal mixtures) of signals to be extracted by ICA from the original data set using a non-square $K \times M$ unmixing matrix (Porrill & Stone, 1997, Amari, 1999, Penny et al., 2001).

ICA Ignores Signal Structure It is worth noting that ICA disregards any spatial or temporal structure in signals for the same types of reasons that projection pursuit does (see chapters 5 and 6).

7.8 Summary

Following an introduction to independence and entropy in terms of joint pdfs, the infomax account of ICA was described. Infomax ICA seeks that unmixing matrix which maximizes the entropy of extracted signals after they have been transformed by a specific model joint cdf. A key assumption is that the marginal cdfs of this joint cdf are independent (i.e., their product yields the joint cdf), which ensures that the extracted signals are also independent. It was noted that ICA is an essentially "cdf-matching" method which extracts signals with a joint cdf (or equivalently a joint pdf) that match that model cdf.

Maximum likelihood ICA was introduced for finding an estimate of the optimal unmixing matrix. It was shown that ML ICA and infomax ICA are actually equivalent.

In practice, ICA can be applied in either the spatial or in the temporal domain. The relation between temporal and spatial ICA was described.

MatLab Code Simple demonstration code is provided in appendix D, and code for spatial, temporal and spatiotemporal ICA of image sequences can be downloaded from http://www.shef.ac.uk/̃pc1jvs.

8 Complexity Pursuit

Entia non sunt multiplicanda praeter necessitatem.
(Entities are not to be multiplied beyond necessity.)
—William of Ockham (ca. 1285–1349)

Make everything as simple as possible, but not simpler.
—Albert Einstein

8.1 Introduction

Almost every signal measured within a physical system is actually a mixture of statistically independent source signals. However, because source signals are usually generated by the motion of mass (e.g., a membrane), the form of physically possible source signals is underwritten by the laws that govern how masses can move over time. This suggests that the most parsimonious explanation for the complexity of an observed signal is that it consists of a mixture of simpler source signals, each of which is from a different physical source. This observation can be used as a basis for extracting source signals from mixtures of those signals.

Given a set of source signals, a mixture of those signals is usually more complex than the simplest (i.e., least complex) of its constituent source signals (see chapter 2). For example, mixing two source signals yields a signal mixture which is more complex than the simplest (i.e., least complex) of the two source signals (see figure 2.4). This *complexity conjecture*[1] provides the basis of a method for separating signal mixtures into their underlying source signals, by seeking the *least complex* signal that can be obtained from a set of signal mixtures. In this respect, complexity pursuit implements a form of Ockham's razor in deciding which signals to extract from a set of signal mixtures. This strategy can also be used to model learning in the visual system (see section 11.7).

Complexity has received much less attention as a principle for blind source separation (BSS) than either normality or independence.[2] This may be due to the relative ease with which formal measures of normality and independence can be formulated, and to the difficulty in formalising the notion of complexity.

---

1. This conjecture is different from that expressed in (Stone, 2001) in a subtle but important manner. In (Stone, 2001), it was conjectured that each signal mixture is more complex than *each* of its constituent source signals, a conjecture which is refuted in (Xie et al., [in press]), where it is proved that any mixture has a complexity that lies between that of its least and most complex constituent source signals. The subtle difference between these conjectures has no implications for the algorithm described here, which is the same as in (Stone, 2001), and which is based on the simple assumption the least complex signal that can be extracted from a set of signal mixtures is a source signal.

2. However, several authors have augmented methods based on independence with constraints derived from complexity (e.g., Pearlmutter & Parra, 1996, Stone & Porrill, 1999, Penny et al., 2001).

The term *complexity pursuit* is used here to refer to a class of methods which seek minimally complex source signals, but the name is borrowed from a specific method described in (Hyvärinen, 2001). The name complexity pursuit derives from the fact that such methods seek a weight vector which provides an orthogonal projection of a set of signal mixtures such that each extracted signal is minimally complex.

While complexity pursuit methods can be derived directly from information-theoretic measures of complexity, such methods tend to be more general and more complicated than is required for many BSS problems. In contrast, the particular method described below (Stone, 2001) minimizes a very simple measure of *Kolmogorov complexity* (Cover & Thomas, 1991). The measure used here and in (Stone, 2001) is similar to measures of complexity defined in (Hyvärinen, 2001), where the connection to Kolmogorov complexity is made explicit.

Complexity Pursuit: A Physical Analogy Although the analogy is not exact, one useful way to gain an intuitive understanding of complexity pursuit is as follows. Consider a length of wire which has been bent into a complex three-dimensional (3D) shape. The shadow of this wire object is more or less complex depending on the direction of the light source and the orientation of the wire object. If the object is slowly rotated through all possible orientations then the projection of its 3D structure forms a shadow with varying degrees of complexity. Clearly, there exists one orientation for the object with a projection (shadow) that is less complex than at any other orientation. This would be the orientation found by complexity pursuit.

As you may have guessed, each point on the wire represents the amplitudes of three signal mixtures at one time, with contiguous points representing consecutive times. The light source represents the weight vector which extracts a single signal, and the shadow represents the signal extracted from the signal mixtures. However, instead of rotating the object, we should (equivalently) rotate the direction of the light source, and ensure that a planar surface is always opposite the light source in order to be able to observe the object's shadow. Here the analogy is inexact, because the shadow is two-dimensional, whereas complexity pursuit extracts a one-dimensional signal. Despite this, the analogy provides a rough idea of the strategy that underpins complexity pursuit.

8.2 Predictability and Complexity

One simple measure of complexity can be formulated in terms of predictability. Specifically, if each value of a signal is easy to predict on the basis of previous signal values then that signal has low complexity. Conversely, if successive values of a signal are random (i.e., independent of each other) then prediction is in principle impossible, and such a signal has high complexity.

As mentioned above, Kolmogorov complexity (Cover & Thomas, 1991) (which is related to entropy) provides a very robust measure of complexity. However, whereas temporal predictability is intuitive and relatively easy to measure, Kolmogorov complexity is less intuitive and is impractical to measure exactly.

We define a measure $F(\mathbf{w}_i, \mathbf{x})$ of temporal predictability, which is then used to estimate the complexity of a signal y_i extracted by a given weight vector $\mathbf{w}_i$, where $y_i = \mathbf{w}_i^T \mathbf{x}$. Given a set of source signals, if one source signal s_i is more predictable than any of the signal mixtures then the value of $\mathbf{w}_i$ which maximizes the predictability of the extracted signal y_i should yield a source signal (i.e., $y_i = s_i$). Note that maximal predictability corresponds to minimal complexity, and *vice versa*.

8.3   Measuring Complexity Using Signal Predictability

We proceed by first defining a measure F of predictability in terms of an extracted signal $y_i = \mathbf{w}_i^T \mathbf{x}$. In order to extract a source signal $y_i = s_i$ from a set of M signal mixtures $\mathbf{x} = (x_1, x_2, \ldots, x_M)^T$, we need to find that weight vector $\mathbf{w}_i$ which maximizes the predictability F of y_i, and which therefore minimizes its complexity.

Given a weight vector $\mathbf{w}_i$ which extracts a signal $y_i = (y_i^1, y_i^2, \ldots, y_i^N)$ from a set of M signal mixtures $\mathbf{x} = (\mathbf{x}^1, \mathbf{x}^2, \ldots, \mathbf{x}^N)$ observed over N time steps, the definition of predictability F used here is

$$F(\mathbf{w}_i, \mathbf{x}) \;=\; \ln \frac{\sum_{t=1}^N (\overline{y}_i - y_i^t)^2}{\sum_{t=1}^N (\tilde{y}_i^t - y_i^t)^2} \tag{8.1}$$

$$=\; \ln \frac{V_i}{U_i}, \tag{8.2}$$

where $y_i^t = \mathbf{w}_i^T \mathbf{x}^t$ is the value of the extracted signal y_i at time t, and $\mathbf{x}^t = (x_1^t, x_2^t, \ldots, x_M^t)^T$ is a vector variable of M signal mixture values at time t.

The numerator V_i is the overall variance of the extracted signal, and ensures that the signal is not so predictable that it is constant.

The denominator U_i is a measure of the temporal "roughness" of the extracted signal y_i, such that U_i is large for "rough" signals and small for "smooth" signals. Specifically, U_i reflects the extent to which y_i^t is predicted by a short-term 'moving average' $\tilde{y}_i^t$ of previous values in y_i. The predicted value $\tilde{y}_i^t$ of y_i^t is an exponentially weighted sum of signal values measured up to time $(t - 1)$, such that recent values have a larger weighting than those in the distant past:

$$\tilde{y}^t \;=\; \lambda \, \tilde{y}^{(t-1)} + (1 - \lambda) \, y^{(t-1)} \quad : 0 \le \lambda \le 1. \tag{8.3}$$

A typical value for λ is 0.9. Such a value implies that the predicted value for y^t is given by

$$
\begin{aligned}
\tilde{y}^t &= 0.9y^{t-1} + 0.9^2 y^{t-2} + 0.9^3 y^{t-3} \dots & (8.4) \\
&= 0.9y^{t-1} + 0.81y^{t-2} + 0.729y^{t-3} \dots & (8.5)
\end{aligned}
$$

Notice that, if $\lambda = 0$ then $\tilde{y}_i^t = y_i^{t-1}$ so that the predicted value of y_i^t is simply y_i^{t-1}.

$$
\begin{aligned}
\tilde{y}^t &= 0\,\tilde{y}^{(t-1)} + (1-0)\,y^{(t-1)} & (8.6) \\
&= y^{(t-1)}. & (8.7)
\end{aligned}
$$

This represents the simplest model of prediction because it is based on the assumption that y_i is constant (i.e., that $y_i^t = y_i^{t-1}$). The fact that this assumption is violated for most signals does not prevent the method from working because it attempts to extract signals that have high overall variance while varying smoothly over time (i.e., signals that are maximally consistent with the model implicit in F).

Note that maximizing F while holding U_i constant would result in a high variance signal with no constraints on its temporal structure. Conversely, maximizing F while holding V_i constant would result in a highly predictable and entirely useless (i.e., constant) signal. In both cases, trivial solutions would be obtained. In contrast, the ratio F can be maximized only if two constraints are satisfied: (1) y has a non-zero range (i.e., high variance), and (2) the values in y change 'slowly' over time (i.e., they can be predicted from previous values). Note also that the value of F is independent of the length $|\mathbf{w}_i|$ of $\mathbf{w}_i$, so that only changes in the *orientation* of $\mathbf{w}_i$ affect the value of F (see chapter 4).

Reinterpreting F in Terms of Complexity For a slightly different perspective on predictability it can be shown that the $\mathbf{w}_i$ which maximizes the predictability F of $y = \mathbf{w}^T \mathbf{x}$ also minimizes a simple measure of complexity

$$
\ln \sum_{t=1}^{N} (\tilde{y}_i^t - y_i^t)^2, \tag{8.8}
$$

subject to the constraint that $|\mathbf{w}_i| = 1$. As the logarithmic function is monotonic, it follows that any $\mathbf{w}_i$ which minimizes equation (8.8) also minimizes

$$
U_i = \sum_{t=1}^{N} (\tilde{y}_i^t - y_i^t)^2. \tag{8.9}
$$

In other words, the weight vector which extracts the most predictable signal from the set of mixtures can also be found by minimizing U_i, if the length of $\mathbf{w}_i$ is set to unity.

The condition that $|\mathbf{w}_i| = 1$ should be unsurprising given that we know (from section 4.2.1) that the length of the vector $\mathbf{w}_i$ does not affect the form of the extracted signal, and setting $|\mathbf{w}_i|$ to some non-zero constant simply ensures that it cannot shrink to zero.

If we set $\lambda = 0$ then U_i is just a measure of the differences between successive values in the extracted signal $y_i = \mathbf{w}_i^T \mathbf{x}$. (More generally, for $\lambda > 0$ U_i is a measure of the difference between a y_i^t and a weighted mean of values prior to time t.)

It follows that minimizing a measure of the complexity of an extracted signal yields a signal in which successive signal values are as similar as possible, without being the same. Note that the difference between successive signal values could be exactly equal to zero if $|\mathbf{w}_i| = 0$, but we have already specified the constraint that $|\mathbf{w}_i| = 1$.

8.4   Extracting Signals by Maximizing Predictability

The method can be demonstrated graphically for two source signals and two mixtures (x_1 and x_2) of these source signals by plotting x_1 against x_2 and then rotating a weight vector $\mathbf{w}_i$ around the origin until the value of F is maximal. The signal $y_i = \mathbf{w}_i^T \mathbf{x}$ extracted by the weight vector at the orientation that maximizes F has maximum predictability and therefore has minimal complexity (see figure 8.1).

Multiple signals can be extracted using two methods. First, signals can be extracted simultaneously using the fast eigenvalue method described in appendix E. Second, signals can be extracted sequentially, as in the case of projection pursuit. That is, each signal can be extracted using the general gradient based method described in chapter 9, followed by removal of that signal from the set of mixtures. After removing the first such signal, the conjecture given on the first page of this chapter should now hold true of the remaining set of signal mixtures. This implies that the next source signal can be obtained by seeking the least complex signal that can be obtained from the remaining set of signal mixtures. This process can then be repeated until all source signals have been extracted.

Separating Mixtures of Signals with Different Pdfs Unlike ICA which includes a model of the pdfs of extracted signals, complexity pursuit depends only on the complexity of signals. Therefore, complexity pursuit (in common with some forms of projection pursuit) can be used to extract signals with different pdfs (e.g., super-gaussian, sub-gaussian or gaussian).

Three source signals $\mathbf{s} = (s_1, s_2, s_3)$ are displayed in figure 8.2:

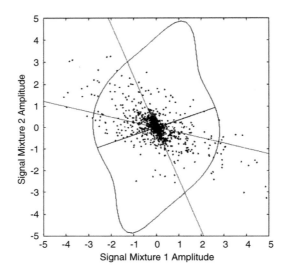

Figure 8.1

Plot of how complexity varies with weight vector orientation for two speech signal mixtures. The plotted points represent signal mixture 1 (x_1) versus signal mixture 2 (x_2). For any given orientation of a weight vector $\mathbf{w}$ the extracted signal y is given by the inner product of $\mathbf{w}^T$ with the two signal mixtures $\mathbf{x} = (x_1, x_2)^T$, $y = \mathbf{w}^T\mathbf{x}$. The complexity of y varies as $\mathbf{w}$ is rotated around the origin. For each orientation of $\mathbf{w}$ the associated complexity is plotted as a distance from the origin in the direction of $\mathbf{w}$, giving a continuous curve. Critically, complexity is minimal when $\mathbf{w}$ is orthogonal to a transformed axis S'_1 or S'_2 (plotted as dashed lines), and $\mathbf{w}$ extracts exactly one source signal at each of these orientations. Here complexity is defined as $1/F$, where F is the temporal predictability of the extracted signal (see text).

The orientation of $\mathbf{w}$ corresponding to one minimum in complexity is plotted as a solid line. Note that this line has the same *orientation* as the *direction* of $\mathbf{w}_2$. This line actually connects two *identical* minima in complexity, because the vectors $\mathbf{w}_2$ and $-\mathbf{w}_2$ both have the same orientation and both therefore extract the same signal with a simple sign reversal (i.e., $\mathbf{w}_2$ extracts y_2 and $-\mathbf{w}_2$ extracts $-y_2$). Note that $\mathbf{w}_2$ is orthogonal to the transformed axis S'_1

1. a super-gaussian signal (the sound of a train whistle)

2. a sub-gaussian signal (a sine wave)

3. a gaussian signal[3]

---

3. Signal 3 was generated using the *randn* procedure in MatLab, and temporal structure was imposed on the signal by sorting its values in ascending order.

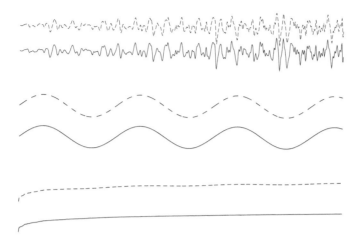

Figure 8.2
Three signals with different probability density functions. A super-gaussian train whistle sound, a sub-gaussian sine wave, and sorted gaussian noise are displayed from top to bottom. In each graph, the source signals used to synthesize the mixtures displayed in figure 8.3 are shown in bold, and corresponding signals recovered from those mixtures are shown as dashed lines. Each source signal and its corresponding recovered signal have been shifted vertically for display purposes. The correlations between source and recovered signals are greater than r=0.999. Only the first 1000 of the 9000 samples used are shown here. The ordinal axis displays signal amplitude.

These three signals were mixed using a random 3×3 matrix A to yield a set of three signal mixtures $\mathbf{x} = \mathbf{As}$. Each signal consisted of 3000 samples; the first 1000 samples of each mixture are shown in figure 8.3. The three recovered signals each had a correlation of $r > 0.99$ with only one of the source signals, and other correlations were close to zero. This method has also been demonstrated to work with speech signals (Stone, 2001), and for learning stereo disparity (see section 11.7).

Complexity Pursuit Does Not Ignore Signal Structure This class of methods includes all methods which depend on the assumption that source signals have informative temporal or spatial structure, e.g., (Stone, 2001, Hyvärinen, 2001) and (Molgedey & Schuster, 1994, Attias, 2000). As has already been discussed, this contrasts with ICA and projection pursuit which ignore all spatial and temporal structure.

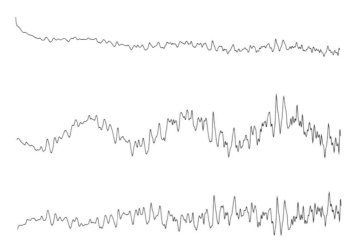

Figure 8.3
Three signal mixtures used as input to the method. See figure 8.2 for a description of the three source signals used to synthesize these mixtures. Only the first 1000 of the 9000 samples used in experiments are shown here. The vertical axis displays signal amplitude.

8.5   Summary

Source signals are usually generated by the motion of mass, so that the form of physically possible source signals is underwritten by the laws that govern how masses can move over time. This suggests that the most parsimonious explanation for the complexity of an observed signal is that it consists of a mixture of simpler source signals.

This simple observation was used as the basis of a method for separating signal mixtures into their underlying source signals, by seeking the least complex signals that can be obtained from a set of signal mixtures.

Complexity was discussed in terms of Kolmogorov complexity. A simple measure of complexity was defined, and the signal with the lowest complexity extracted by a weight vector was assumed to be a source signal. The method was demonstrated on mixtures of super-gaussian, sub-gaussian and gaussian signals.

MatLab Code   Simple demonstration code is provided in appendix E, and code for extraction of sound signals can be downloaded from
http://www.shef.ac.uk/~pc1jvs.

9 Gradient Ascent

9.1 Introduction

Thus far, we have considered different measures (e.g., independence) that can be used to ascertain when source signals have been recovered from signal mixtures. For example, the more independent the extracted signals are, the more likely they are to be the required source signals. However we have not considered how to set about maximizing such measures, other than by exhaustive search, which is a method that becomes increasingly exhausting as the number of source signals increases beyond two. Moreover, the time taken to perform the exhaustive search can grow rapidly to end-of-universe times for certain classes of computational problems.

For these reasons, a different search strategy is required. *Gradient ascent* is based on the observation that if it is desired to get to the top of a hill then one simple strategy is to keep moving uphill until there is no more uphill left, at which time the top of the hill should have been reached. There are several drawbacks to this strategy, but these can wait for later discussion.

For simplicity, we will examine this strategy using kurtosis. For our purposes the height on the "hill" corresponds to the amount of kurtosis, and the distance measured along a horizontal ground plane corresponds to different values of the two unmixing coefficients. Thus by incrementally changing the values of the unmixing coefficients so as to increase the kurtosis of an extracted signal a set of optimal unmixing coefficients are obtained that extract a maximally kurtotic signal, which we assume to be a source signal.

If you were standing on this hill of kurtosis, how would you know in which direction to move next? In other words, how would you know how much to change each unmixing coefficient in order to move in a direction which maximizes kurtosis? A natural and reasonably sensible tactic would be to choose that direction with the steepest uphill slope; that is, the direction with the steepest *gradient*. A small step uphill along the direction of steepest gradient is guaranteed to increase your height, which corresponds to increasing the kurtosis of extracted signals. This is why the method is called gradient ascent.

This is fine for people on hills because they can see which direction has the steepest slope. In contrast, any gradient ascent method must find an estimate of the direction of steepest ascent by other means.

The most efficient method for finding the direction of steepest ascent at a given point is to calculate the rate of change or *derivative* of the local kurtosis with respect to each unmixing coefficient. Specifically, we can obtain the direction of steepest ascent by calculating the derivative of kurtosis along the horizontal direction associated with each of the unmixing coefficients. At a given point, the gradient of kurtosis is different for each unmixing coefficient, so that, together, their combined gradients define a *direction* on the ground plane. This direction along the ground plane corresponds to the direction of steepest ascent on the hill of kurtosis. Accordingly, a small move in this direction on the ground plane is guaranteed to increase kurtosis more than any other direction. Specifically, moving in this direction defines new values for the coefficients (corresponding to the new position as measured on the ground plane), and these coefficients are guaranteed to extract a signal with increased kurtosis.

In order to examine how this translates to a mathematical method, we will begin with a simple gradient ascent problem.

9.2   Gradient Ascent on a Line

Suppose that the amount of kurtosis K of a signal extracted from a set of two signal mixtures depended on only one parameter, which we will call ψ. In order to maximize K we should move up the gradient of K.

In mathematical terms, the gradient of K can be obtained by taking the derivative of K with respect to ψ, where this derivative is denoted $dK/d\psi$. Note that we have not actually done anything yet, aside from defining some notation. For the present, it is sufficient to know that if K depends on only one parameter then the derivative $dK/d\psi$ is a single, signed number. The sign specifies which direction is up, and the magnitude of the number specifies the steepness of the gradient.

In order to examine how this works for a simple example, let us suppose that K is related to the square of ψ, as follows:

$$K = -(\psi + 1)^2 + 25. \tag{9.1}$$

The relationship between K and ψ is shown in figure 9.1. The value of the gradient is indicated by an arrow for different values of ψ. The length of each arrow specifies the magnitude of the gradient at the root of the arrow, and the direction (i.e., sign) of the gradient (i.e., left (-) or right (+)) is implicit in the direction of each arrow. Note that, in general, the value of the gradient at the maximum (or minimum) value of a function is zero.

It is easy to see from figure 9.1 that the magnitude of the gradient decreases and then increases as ψ increases from -4 to 4, and has a value of zero at $\psi = -1$, which corresponds to a maximum in K. This is consistent with the gradient obtained from differential calculus,

$$\frac{dK}{d\psi} = -2(\psi + 1), \tag{9.2}$$

because

$$-2(\psi + 1) = 0. \tag{9.3}$$

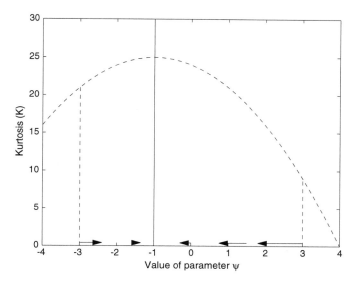

Figure 9.1

Graph showing how kurtosis K would vary in relation to a single unmixing coefficient ψ, if kurtosis were defined by equation (9.1) (which it isn't). The value of the gradient is indicated by an arrow at a number of points. The length of each arrow specifies the magnitude of the gradient at the root of the arrow, and the direction of the gradient (i.e., left or right) is given by the direction of each arrow.

We can now use this gradient to follow the gradient ascent strategy outlined above. Suppose we begin with a value of $\psi = -3$, where (from equation 9.2) the gradient is

$$\frac{dK}{d\psi} = -2(\psi + 1) \qquad (9.4)$$

$$= -2(-3 + 1) \qquad (9.5)$$

$$= +4. \qquad (9.6)$$

The gradient ascent strategy suggests that ψ should be incremented in proportion to the gradient.

$$\psi_{new} = \psi_{old} + \eta \frac{dK}{d\psi}, \qquad (9.7)$$

where η^1 is a small constant, typically $\eta = 1/1000$. In this case we have

$$\psi_{new} = \psi_{old} + \eta(+4). \qquad (9.8)$$

1. The Greek letter eta.

This update rule *increases* ψ by a small amount, which results in an increase in K. This can be seen from figure 9.1, where a small move to the right from $\psi = -3$ (which increases ψ) can be seen to increase K.

Similarly, if we begin at $\psi = +3$, where the gradient is $dK/d\psi = -8$ then, using the same gradient ascent strategy as above, we have

$$\psi_{new} = \psi_{old} + \eta(-8). \tag{9.9}$$

In this case, the gradient ascent update rule *decreases* ψ by a small amount, which, as above, results in an increase in K. This can be seen from figure 9.1, where a small move to the left from $\psi = +3$ (which decreases ψ) can be seen to increase K.

Note that, as the value $\psi = -1$ is approached the magnitude of the gradient decreases, and at $\psi = -1$ the gradient is zero. This correctly implies that the change in ψ should be zero if $\psi = -1$,

$$\psi_{new} = \psi_{old} + \eta(0), \tag{9.10}$$

so that at $\psi = -1$ no more changes are made. At this point the method of gradient ascent is said to have converged to the solution $\psi = -1$. Most importantly, this is the value of the unmixing parameter ψ which maximizes the kurtosis K of extracted signals.

9.3   Gradient Ascent on a Hill

The method described above for finding the maximum point along a single curve can be generalised to finding the maximum point on a hill. In this case, drawing a vertical line from the hill top to the ground plane defines values for two unmixing coefficients.

This three-dimensional (3D) hill can be generalised to n-dimensional hills which correspond to $n - 1$ unmixing coefficients ... but we will begin with a conventional 3D hill.

Figure 9.2 shows a hypothetical graph of how kurtosis might vary as a function of two unmixing coefficients (α, β). Each pair of coefficient values defines a point on the ground plane, and the corresponding height of the function f_K above the ground plane specifies the kurtosis K associated with (α, β). Formally, kurtosis is defined by the function f_K

$$K = f_K(\alpha, \beta). \tag{9.11}$$

In this case, we cheat a little by defining kurtosis as a quadratic function

$$f_K(\alpha, \beta) = -(\alpha^2 + \beta^2) + 25. \tag{9.12}$$

To reiterate, for every pair of values (α, β) the corresponding kurtosis of the signal extracted by these coefficients is given by the height of the surface depicted in figure 9.2, which is given by equation (9.11).

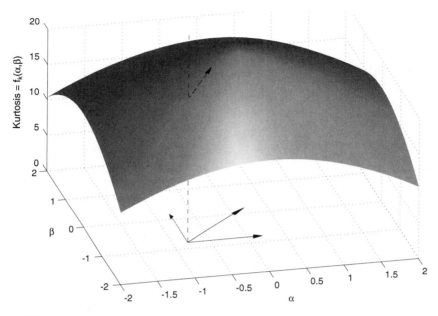

Figure 9.2
Graph showing how kurtosis K would vary in relation to two unmixing coefficients (α, β) if kurtosis were defined by equation (9.12) (which it isn't). Kurtosis varies as a function f_K of two unmixing coefficients (α, β), so that $K = f_K(\alpha, \beta)$. The values of (α, β) are represented by the two horizontal axes, which define a ground plane. The dashed vertical line connects the point $(\alpha, \beta, K) = (-0.8, -0.8, 0)$ on the ground plane with the point $(\alpha, \beta, K) = (-0.8, -0.8, 22.5)$, and therefore intersects the surface defined by the function f_K at $K = 22.5$. The gradient with respect to each of the coefficients (α, β) is indicated by the two axis-aligned arrows. The resultant of these two gradients specifies a vector-valued gradient $\nabla f_K = (\partial f_K / \partial \alpha, \partial f_K / \partial \beta)$, indicated by the horizontal diagonal arrow. This gradient points in the direction of steepest ascent of the function f_K, as indicated by the arrow on the surface defined by f_K. The function f_K is known as a *merit function*, and the surface it defines is often referred to as an *error surface*.

Finding the direction of steepest ascent can be decomposed into a number of subproblems. Specifically, if the direction of steepest ascent with respect to each unmixing coefficient is known then the the direction of steepest ascent on the ground plane can be obtained. Now the the direction of steepest ascent with respect to each coefficient is given by the example in the previous section.

In geometric terms, a vertical slice through the function f_K at a specific value $\beta = \beta_1$ yields a curve of the same form as that depicted in figure 9.1. This curve is defined by an equation of the form

$$K = -(\alpha^2 + \beta_1^2) + 25. \tag{9.13}$$

If we take the value $\beta_1 = -0.8$ as an example then the value of the gradient is a scalar which points in the direction indicated by the arrow parallel to the α axis in figure 9.2, and has a magnitude proportional to the length of that arrow. This gradient is given by the *partial derivative*

$$\frac{\partial f_K(\alpha, \beta)}{\partial \alpha} = -2\alpha. \tag{9.14}$$

The term *partial* derivative implies that the gradient with respect to one of many possible parameters is being evaluated (in this case, "many" equals two), while ignoring the derivatives with respect to these other parameters. Note that partial derivatives are defined with the symbol ∂ (e.g., $\partial y/\partial x$), in contrast to the derivative of a scalar function which is defined with the symbol d (e.g., dy/dx).

Similarly, a vertical slice through the function f_K at a specific value $\alpha = \alpha_1$ also yields a curve of the same form as that depicted in figure 9.1. This curve is defined by an equation of the form

$$K = -(\alpha_1^2 + \beta^2) + 25. \tag{9.15}$$

If we take the value $\alpha_1 = -0.8$ as an example then the value of the gradient is a scalar which points in the direction indicated by the arrow parallel to the β axis in figure 9.2, and has a magnitude proportional to the length of that arrow. In mathematical terms, this gradient is given by the partial derivative

$$\frac{\partial f_K(\alpha, \beta)}{\partial \beta} = -2\beta. \tag{9.16}$$

The direction of steepest ascent can be obtained by combining these two partial derivatives. Specifically, in the context of the function f_K, each partial derivative defines an axis-aligned vector

$$\left(\frac{\partial f_K(\alpha, \beta)}{\partial \beta}, 0 \right) = (-2\alpha, 0) \tag{9.17}$$

$$\left(0, \frac{\partial f_K(\alpha, \beta)}{\partial \alpha} \right) = (0, -2\beta). \tag{9.18}$$

The *vector sum* or *resultant* of these vectors points in the direction of steepest ascent, as indicated by the diagonal arrow on the ground plane in figure 9.2. The resultant of two vectors is given by their sum, which is obtained by scalar addition of corresponding elements of each vector

$$\left(\frac{\partial f_K}{\partial \alpha}, 0\right) + \left(0, \frac{\partial f_K}{\partial \beta}\right) = \left(0 + \frac{\partial f_K}{\partial \alpha}, 0 + \frac{\partial f_K}{\partial \beta}\right) \quad (9.19)$$

$$= \left(\frac{\partial f_K}{\partial \alpha}, \frac{\partial f_K}{\partial \beta}\right), \quad (9.20)$$

where the (α, β) arguments of the function f_K have been omitted for clarity.

This vector-valued derivative is known as *grad* f_K, and is denoted[2] ∇f_K. Thus the derivative ∇K of f_K with respect to the coefficients (α, β) is exactly

$$\nabla f_K = \left(\frac{\partial f_K}{\partial \alpha}, \frac{\partial f_K}{\partial \beta}\right). \quad (9.21)$$

To reiterate, $\partial f_K / \partial \alpha$ is a scalar (number) which gives the gradient in the direction corresponding to α (i.e., the horizontal direction $(\alpha, 0)$), and $\partial f_K / \partial \beta$ gives the gradient in the direction corresponding to β (i.e., the horizontal direction $(0, \beta)$). Thus, ∇K is a two-element vector which points in a direction on the ground plane, such that a small move along this direction is guaranteed to increase the value of K.

As in the one-dimensional case, the rule for performing gradient ascent with respect to the unmixing parameters is

$$\mathbf{w}_{new} = \mathbf{w}_{old} + \eta \nabla f_K^T, \quad (9.22)$$

so that, provided η is sufficiently small, $\mathbf{w}_{new}$ is guaranteed to extract a signal with a higher kurtosis that $\mathbf{w}_{old}$.

The equation (9.22) is a recipe for gradient ascent with respect to any number of unmixing parameters. Whilst such a recipe is hard to visualize, the logic of gradient ascent for two parameters applies equally well to $n > 2$ parameters.

Note that if the constant η is large then it is possible to step right past or right over the desired maximum in f_K, which is why it is important to set η to a small value and then re-evaluate ∇f_K for each successive step.

We will refer to the above method as *simple gradient ascent* in order to distinguish it from those described below.

A Caveat   While the preceding discussion applies to a problem that depends on two parameters, we already know that the unmixing problem depends on the orientation ψ of the weight vector $\mathbf{w} = (\alpha, \beta)^T$, and not on its length $|\mathbf{w}|$. So even though the unmixing problem *appears* to depend on $n = 2$ parameters α and β, it actually depends on only

---

2. The symbol ∇ is called *nabla* or *del*.

one parameter ψ which is a function of both α and β, where the orientation of $\mathbf{w}$ is given by $\psi = \arctan(\alpha/\beta)$. In general, an unmixing problem with n coefficients only depends on $n - 1$ angles. This just means that the apparent problem of estimating optimal values for two parameters (α, β) is actually a problem that requires estimation of one implicit parameter, the orientation ψ of the vector $\mathbf{w}$. More generally, as the number of mixtures is increased, the number of parameters to be estimated is one less than the number of unmixing coefficients. In practice, this is usually ignored during gradient ascent without any ill effects.

9.4   Second Order Methods

While the gradient ascent method described in the previous section is adequate, it has to contend with two fundamental problems.

First, the direction of steepest descent does not necessarily point directly at the maximum, so that the path length (or number of steps) to the maximum is longer than is necessary.

Second, and probably more importantly, the gradient *magnitude* of any function decreases as its maximum is approached. This, in turn, ensures that successive step sizes decrease as the distance to the maximum decreases, because the step size is proportional to the magnitude of the gradient. Thus, in principle, the maximum can only be reached after an infinite number of steps (this is analogous to Zeno's paradox). Despite this, simple gradient ascent provides good estimates of optimal parameter values.

Both the problems specified above can be alleviated to a large extent using *second order methods*. Such methods depend on estimating the local *curvature* of the function (as opposed to its gradient) and using this to jump to the estimated maximum. The curvature is simply the *gradient of the gradient*, and in the case of two parameters, is defined by a 2×2 matrix of second derivatives, known as a *Hessian matrix*. More generally, an n parameter problem defines a function whose curvature is given by an $n \times n$ Hessian matrix. In the case of a 2×2 unmixing matrix the number of parameters (unmixing coefficients) is four, which defines a 4×4 Hessian matrix. Second order methods such as Broyden-Fletcher-Goldfarb-Shanno (BFGS)[3] and the simpler conjugate gradient technique are beyond the scope of this book; it suffices to say that second order methods and simple gradient ascent arrive at the same solution for estimated parameter values, but second order methods tend to arrive at this solution sooner. A practical introduction to these methods can be found in (Press et al., 1989).

Note that second order methods have substantial advantages only as the maximum is approached. This is the because the "jump" to the estimated maximum will be accurate in terms of its direction and magnitude only if the function is well approximated by a

---

3. BFGS is a standard quasi-Newton search method.

quadratic function at the point from which the jump is made. Fortunately, in principle, "reasonable" functions do approximate a quadratic close to their maxima, as can be seen both in terms of the *Taylor expansion* of a function and in geometric terms.

In order to see why, we will explore a geometric version of the Taylor expansion by working back from the maximum of a function. At its maximum any function $K = f(\psi)$ can be locally approximated by a plane, albeit a very small plane. This is fine for our purposes as we are considering *local* approximations. As we move away from the maximum the local curvature of the function makes it untenable to continue to pretend that the function is locally approximately planar. At this point, we can approximate the function locally with a low-order curved surface, specifically a surface defined by a *quadratic function* (as depicted in figure 9.2). As we progress further from the maximum, the quadratic approximation also begins to look a bit shaky, and we are forced to employ increasingly high order approximating functions. In fact, the Taylor expansion can be used to approximate a function with a linear combination of successively high order functions, such as linear (e.g., 2ψ), quadratic (e.g., $\psi^2 + \psi$), and cubic (e.g., $\psi^3 + \psi^2 + \psi$) functions. The main point is that any "reasonable" function is well approximated by a quadratic function within a small region around any chosen location, although functions are often especially "well-behaved" for this purpose around a maximum. This ensures that the second order methods, and the natural gradient method described below, provide considerable speed advantages over simple gradient ascent.

9.5   The Natural Gradient

One twist on simple gradient ascent methods that has caused some excitement within the independent component analysis (ICA) community is the *natural gradient* (Amari et al., 1996, Amari, 1998, Cichocki & Amari, 2002). Essentially, the natural gradient method induces a local warping of the function f_K such that the natural gradient points directly at the maximum of f_K, provided f_K is locally well approximated by a quadratic function, which it always is close to a maximum (see above).

However, using the natural gradient method is likely to be no more efficient that employing a standard second order method (e.g., conjugate gradient), and the time complexities of the two methods may not be substantially different (although these speculations have yet to be tested empirically).

9.6   Global and Local Maxima

Each of the different gradient-based search methods described above for finding parameter values (e.g., ψ) that maximize a given merit function (e.g., f_K) yield the same solution (i.e. final parameter values). Thus, the *only* difference between these search methods is the speed with which solutions are obtained, and not the nature of those solutions. Additionally, the *time complexity*, (i.e. how the time required to find a solution scales with the number of parameters) of these different gradient-based methods can be very similar, e.g., see (Stone & Lister, 1994).

Given an initial set of parameter values and a merit function f, most search methods (and all of the gradient-based methods described above) adjust the parameter values in order to move (more or less efficiently) toward the *nearest* maximum in f. If f has only one maximum then moving toward the nearest maximum represents a good strategy. However, problems often have functions with many maxima. Rather than the single hill considered earlier, the function f is then analogous to a mountain range. The highest maximum of f is known as the *global maximum* of f, and each of the other maxima is known as a *local maximum*. A major disadvantage of the gradient-based search methods is that they tend to find local maxima.

In the case of ICA with an $M \times M$ unmixing matrix, there are at least M maxima of equal height, each of which is associated with a permutation of columns in $\mathbf{W}$. There also appear to be other sets of M equivalent maxima, which are of a similar height to those just described. However, this is an under-researched area, and it remains something of mystery as to why ICA, and also projection pursuit, performs as well as they do on most problems.

The particular complexity pursuit method described in chapter 8 has a merit function such that the optimal unmixing matrix $\mathbf{W}$ has one weight vector (row of $\mathbf{W}$) associated with the only global maximum, and all other weight vectors are associated with saddle points (i.e., regions of f that look like a saddle). The details of this need not concern us here, suffice to say that such a merit function behaves as if it has a single global maximum with respect to the unmixing matrix $\mathbf{W}$. Details of such merit functions can be found in standard texts on linear algebra, e.g., (Borga, 1998).

9.7 Summary

Given a merit function of a set of parameters, gradient ascent was described as a method for finding parameter values that maximize that merit function. This was introduced in terms of finding the highest point on a hill, in one or more dimensions, where each point on the ground plane corresponds to a specific set of parameter values, and height corresponds to the function value. Optimal parameter values are obtained by iteratively gaining height until there is no more height to be gained. At this point, the top of the hill is reached, and the corresponding parameter values are optimal parameter values. It was shown that the gradient ascent method requires an expression for the derivative of the merit function with respect to its parameters. Second order methods were introduced as a more efficient gradient-based method than simple gradient ascent for finding optimal parameter values. The natural gradient was briefly described as a method that was also more efficient than simple gradient ascent. Finally, the problem of finding a global maximum was discussed.

10 Principal Component Analysis and Factor Analysis

10.1   Introduction

ICA is not the only game in town. Historically, principal component analysis (PCA) and factor analysis (FA) have been widely used for the same types of problems currently being investigated with ICA. The main difference between ICA and PCA/FA is that ICA finds non-gaussian and independent source signals, whereas PCA/FA finds source signals which are (merely) gaussian and *uncorrelated*.[1] This subtle distinction has far reaching consequences for the power of ICA methods relative to PCA/FA methods.

This chapter provides a brief overview of PCA and FA in relation to ICA. For more detailed accounts of PCA and FA, consult (Everitt, 1984, Chatfield & Collins, 2000). We compare ICA to PCA first, and consider FA in a later section.

10.2   ICA and PCA

PCA can be interpreted in terms of blind source separation methods inasmuch as PCA is like a version of ICA in which the source signals are assumed to be gaussian. However, the essential difference between ICA and PCA is that PCA decomposes a set of signal mixtures into a set of uncorrelated signals, whereas ICA decomposes a set of signal mixtures into a set of independent signals.

In terms of moments, this implies that PCA finds a matrix which transforms the signal mixtures $\mathbf{x} = (x_1, x_2)$ with joint probability density function (pdf) $p_\mathbf{x}(x_1, x_2)$ into a new set of uncorrelated signals $\mathbf{y} = (y_1, y_2)$. Recall that uncorrelated signals have a joint pdf $p_\mathbf{y}(\mathbf{y})$ such that

$$E[y_1 y_2] = E[y_1]E[y_2]. \tag{10.1}$$

In contrast, ICA seeks an unmixing matrix which transforms the signal mixtures $\mathbf{x} = (x_1, x_2)$ with joint pdf $p_\mathbf{x}(x_1, x_2)$ into a new set of independent signals $\mathbf{y} = (y_1, y_2)$. Recall that independent signals have a joint pdf $p_\mathbf{y}(\mathbf{y})$ such that

$$E[y_1^p, y_2^q] = E[y_1^p]E[y_2^q], \tag{10.2}$$

for *every* positive integer value of p and q.

Actually, PCA does more than simply find a transformation of the signal mixtures such that the new signals are uncorrelated. PCA orders the extracted signals according to their variances (variance can be equated with power or amplitude), so that signals associated

---

1. Strictly speaking, in order to make *gaussian* signals independent it is sufficient to make uncorrelated, so uncorrelated gaussian signals are also independent. However, the fact remains that independent gaussian signals are merely uncorrelated, and do not therefore correspond to any physically meaningful sources, such as different voices.

with high variance are deemed more important than those with low variance. In contrast, ICA is essentially blind to the variance associated with each extracted signal.

It is worth noting that if the signals extracted by PCA are gaussian then the condition specified in equation (10.1) implies that such signals are not only uncorrelated, they are also independent. This is because gaussian signals have pdfs which are determined entirely by their second moments. Once these are fixed, all higher-order moments are determined. So, technically speaking, PCA does provide a set of independent signals, but only if these signals are gaussian.

Specifying that a set of uncorrelated gaussian signals is required places very few constraints on the signals obtained. So few that an infinite number of sets of independent gaussian signals can be obtained from any set of signal mixtures (recall that signal mixtures tend to be gaussian). For example, a relatively simple procedure such as Gram-Schmidt orthogonalisation (GSO) can be used to obtain a set of uncorrelated signals, and the set so obtained depends entirely on the signal used to initialize the GSO procedure (see appendix C). This is why any procedure which obtains a unique set of signals requires more constraints than simple decorrelation can provide. In the case of ICA, these extra constraints involve high order moments of the joint pdf of the set of mixtures. In the case of PCA, these extra constraints involve an ordering of the gaussian signals obtained. Specifically, PCA finds an ordered set of uncorrelated gaussian signals such that each signal accounts for a decreasing proportion of the variability of the set of signal mixtures. The uncorrelated nature of the signal obtained ensures that different signals account for non-overlapping or *disjoint* amounts of the variability in the set of signal mixtures, where this variability is formalized as *variance*.

10.3   Eigenvectors and Eigenvalues

As with ICA, the transformation from a set of zero-mean signal mixtures $\mathbf{x} = (x_1, x_2)^T$ to a set of extracted signals $\mathbf{y} = (y_1, y_2)^T$ is implemented as a matrix $\mathbf{W}_{pca}$,

$$\mathbf{y} = \mathbf{W}_{pca}\mathbf{x}, \tag{10.3}$$

where each row of the matrix $\mathbf{W}_{pca}$ is a vector, which is known as an *eigenvector*, so that

$$\mathbf{W}_{pca} = (\mathbf{w}_1, \mathbf{w}_2)^T. \tag{10.4}$$

Each eigenvector has unit length (i.e., $|\mathbf{w}_i| = 1$) and extracts exactly one signal y_i, or *principal component* (PC),[2] from the mixtures $\mathbf{x}$. The variance of each PC is known as

---

2. Although this distinction between eigenvectors and principal components is not always acknowledged.

its *eigenvalue*, which is usually denoted by the symbol[3] λ. Unlike the weight vectors of ICA, eigenvectors are mutually orthogonal, a property which ensures that they extract uncorrelated signals.[4]

More formally, an eigenvector is defined with respect to the symmetric $M \times M$ *covariance matrix* $\mathbf{S} = \mathbf{xx}^T$ of the $M \times N$ data array of zero-mean variables $\mathbf{x}$. The ijth element of $\mathbf{S}$ is the covariance between the variables x_i and x_j, defined as the central moment

$$\mathbf{S}_{ij} = \mathrm{E}[x_i x_j]. \tag{10.5}$$

A vector $\mathbf{w}_i$ is an eigenvector of $\mathbf{S}$ if

$$\lambda_i \mathbf{w}_i^T = \mathbf{S}\mathbf{w}_i. \tag{10.6}$$

Thus, if $\mathbf{w}_i$ is an eigenvector of the matrix $\mathbf{S}$ then using $\mathbf{S}$ to transform $\mathbf{w}_i$ has no effect on the orientation of $\mathbf{w}_i$, but the length or magnitude of $|\mathbf{w}_i|$ is altered by a factor λ_i. In other words, if $\mathbf{w}_i$ is a eigenvector of the matrix $\mathbf{S}$ then $\mathbf{S}$ simply scales $\mathbf{w}_i$ by a factor λ_i. For an $M \times M$ matrix $\mathbf{S}$ there are M eigenvectors.

10.4 PCA Applied to Speech Signal Mixtures

By definition, one eigenvector $\mathbf{w}_1$ found by PCA has an orientation such that the orthogonal projection defined by the inner product

$$y_1 = \mathbf{w}_1^T \mathbf{x} \tag{10.7}$$

extracts a signal y_1 with a variance σ_1^2 that cannot be exceeded by a vector $\mathbf{w}_1$ with any other orientation.

This can be seen graphically by rotating a unit length vector around in a two-dimensional space defined by two signal mixtures x_1 and x_2, as shown in figure 10.1. In this case, the mixtures consist of speech signals. The variance of the extracted signal at each orientation of a vector $\mathbf{w}$ is plotted as a smooth curve. When PCA is applied to such a set of mixtures it PCA fails to extract source signals. The first eigenvector yields a maximum variance signal (PC) with an orientation roughly mid-way between the two transformed axes S_1' and S_2'. We know from chapter 4 that in order to extract one source an eigenvector must be orthogonal to one of these transformed axes. Otherwise the signal obtained by an eigenvector is simply a new mixture of the source signals, as is the case here.

---

3. Lambda.

4. Eigenvectors are not orthogonal in general, but they are for the type of source separation problem considered here. This is because the *covariance matrix* of a set of signal mixtures is symmetric, and this, in turn, guarantees that its eigenvectors are orthogonal.

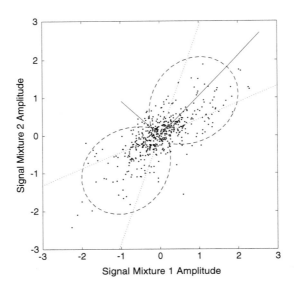

Figure 10.1
PCA of two speech signals. Each solid line defines one eigenvector, which corresponds to a weight
vector in ICA. Each eigenvector has a length proportional to its eigenvalue. In contrast to ICA,
eigenvectors are always orthogonal, which ensures that they extract signals which are uncorrelated.
Note that neither of the eigenvectors are orthogonal to the transformed axes S_1' or S_2' (drawn as dotted
lines), and that an eigenvector can only extract a speech signal if it is orthogonal to one of these
transformed axes. Each eigenvector therefore extracts an essentially arbitrary linear combination of
speech source signals.

The second eigenvector yields a minimum variance signal (PC), and it is true in general
that the final PC has minimum variance. For example, if we had considered a three-
dimensional (3D) space of mixtures then the third eigenvector would extract a minimum
variance signal (PC). Moreover, the PCs extracted by intermediate eigenvectors do not have
any physical interpretation, and do not therefore capture any specific physical properties;
they are simply determined by virtue of being orthogonal to all previous eigenvectors. In
fact, this is the defining feature of such intermediate eigenvectors. They are thus highly
constrained by the orientation of the first eigenvector, which, in turn, is determined by the
orientation associated with a maximum variance PC. The reason for emphasising this is
that the first PC, and therefore other PCs, can be altered simply by changing the amplitude
of a single mixture. For example, in the case of speech, if one voice signal s_1 output is
doubled in amplitude then the first eigenvector will move toward the orientation associated
with that signal (i.e., the transformed axis S_1'). There is no limit to this process, inasmuch

as a massively amplified signal s_1 will align the first eigenvector progressively closer to the orientation of S'_1, and would extract a mixture of voice signals. This would have a large effect on the set of eigenvectors obtained by PCA. Thus, PCA is at the mercy of the raw power of source signals. This can be useful if it is desired to identify high variance signals, but it is generally undesirable.

As PCA provides a set of orthogonal PCs that are ordered according to their variance, it is often used to reduce a large number of measured variables to a smaller set of variables consisting of the first few PCs. As the PCs with the lowest variances are discarded, this usually ensures that the retained PCs capture the main statistical structure of the original signal mixtures.

This ordering of extracted signals according to their variance is often used to reduce the size of a given data set (see appendix F). For example, the number of mixtures might be six, and PCA could be used to find six signals ordered by variance. If the variances of the first three extracted signals are high, and the variances of the last three extracted signals are close to zero then these could be discarded. This effectively halves the size of data set whilst retaining most of the variance associated with the original data set. In this case the reduced data set $(y_1, y_2, y_3)^T$ is given by

$$
\begin{pmatrix} y_1^1, y_1^2, \ldots, y_1^N \\ y_2^1, y_2^2, \ldots, y_2^N \\ y_3^1, y_3^2, \ldots, y_3^N \end{pmatrix} = \begin{pmatrix} w_{11}, w_{12}, \ldots, w_{16} \\ w_{21}, w_{22}, \ldots, w_{26} \\ w_{31}, w_{32}, \ldots, w_{36} \end{pmatrix} \begin{pmatrix} x_1^1, x_1^2, \ldots, x_1^N \\ x_2^1, x_2^2, \ldots, x_2^N \\ \vdots \\ x_6^1, x_6^2, \ldots, x_6^N \end{pmatrix}
$$

$$
= (\mathbf{w}_1, \mathbf{w}_2, \mathbf{w}_3)^T (x_1, x_2, x_3, x_4, x_5, x_6)^T, \tag{10.8}
$$

where the eigenvectors $\mathbf{w}_4$, $\mathbf{w}_5$ and $\mathbf{w}_6^T$ associated with low variance PCs have been discarded. This can be written more succinctly as

$$
\mathbf{y} = \mathbf{W}_{pca}\mathbf{x}. \tag{10.9}
$$

An example of how PCA finds a first PC which does not correspond to any particular source signal is given in figure 10.2.

10.5 Factor Analysis

Factor analysis (FA) is essentially a form of PCA with the addition of extra terms for modeling the sensor noise associated with each signal mixture. In contrast, both ICA and PCA are based on the assumption that such noise is zero.

In terms of a set of physical measurements, for instance using a set of microphones in a room with different sound sources, FA incorporates a model of the noise associated with

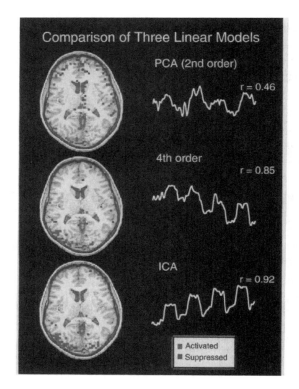

Figure 10.2

PCA, projection pursuit (PP) and ICA applied to fMRI data.

PCA, PP (labelled as "4th order") and ICA were used to extract spatial signals from fMRI brain data. A sequence of fMRI brain images were recorded (not shown), and the image recorded at each point in time is treated as a signal mixture of underlying prototypical brain images. PCA, PP, and ICA were used to estimate these prototypical images. These prototypical images reveal brain activity in primary visual areas (shaded areas) using only PP and ICA, consistent with the visual stimuli presented to the subject. Moreover the temporal sequence (right) associated with the prototypical images extracted by ICA and (to a less extent) PP reflects the on-off sequence of visual stimuli. In contrast, the temporal sequence identified by PCA bears little relation to the sequence of visual stimulation. The correlations between the extracted temporal sequences (right) and the time course of the on-off visual stimulation (PCA=0.46, PP=0.85, ICA=0.92). From (McKeown et al., 1998).

each mixture (microphone). As FA is often applied to psychological data this makes good sense, because two different psychological tests for the same underlying psychological competence can have very different variances, which is correctly modeled as noise by FA.

The model implied by FA for a given mixture x_i has the form

$$x_i = \lambda_1 s_{1i} + \lambda_{2i} s_2 + e_i, \tag{10.10}$$

where s_1 and s_2 are source signals, or *factors*, λ_1 and λ_2 are mixing coefficients, or *factor loadings*, and e_i is the noise associated with the ith measuring device (e.g., psychological test, microphone). Note that the symbol λ (lambda) is, by convention, used to denote factor loadings in FA, and eigenvalues in PCA.

Using FA, the number of mixtures and source signals does not have to be the same. Indeed, it is usually assumed that there is a small number of underlying factors for a given set of observed mixtures.

In the case of $M = 3$ mixtures and $K = 2$ sources this can be written as

$$\begin{pmatrix} x_1^1, x_1^2, \ldots, x_1^N \\ x_2^1, x_2^2, \ldots, x_2^N \\ x_3^1, x_3^2, \ldots, x_3^N \end{pmatrix} = \begin{pmatrix} \lambda_{11}, \lambda_{12} \\ \lambda_{21}, \lambda_{22} \\ \lambda_{31}, \lambda_{32} \end{pmatrix} \begin{pmatrix} s_1^1, s_1^2, \ldots, s_1^N \\ s_2^1, s_2^2, \ldots, s_2^N \end{pmatrix} + \begin{pmatrix} e_1^1, e_1^2, \ldots, e_1^N \\ e_2^1, e_2^2, \ldots, e_2^N \\ e_3^1, e_3^2, \ldots, e_3^N \end{pmatrix},$$

or more succinctly as

$$\begin{pmatrix} x_1 \\ x_2 \\ x_3 \end{pmatrix} = \begin{pmatrix} \lambda_1 \\ \lambda_2 \\ \lambda_3 \end{pmatrix} \begin{pmatrix} s_1 \\ s_2 \end{pmatrix} + \begin{pmatrix} e_1 \\ e_2 \\ e_3 \end{pmatrix}, \tag{10.11}$$

where $\lambda_i = (\lambda_{i1}, \lambda_{i2})$. This can be re-written as

$$\mathbf{x} = \Lambda \mathbf{s} + \mathbf{e}, \tag{10.12}$$

where the matrix of factor loadings Λ[5] corresponds to the mixing matrix $\mathbf{A}$ of ICA.

10.6 Summary

The essential difference between ICA and PCA is that PCA decomposes a set of signal mixtures into a set of uncorrelated signals, whereas ICA decomposes a set of signal mixtures into a set of independent signals. It was shown that this difference is critical because the signals extracted by PCA are under-constrained relative to those extracted by ICA and related methods. It was shown, for example, that given a set of speech mixtures PCA merely extracts a new set of speech mixtures which embody the weak constraint that the set of mixtures are uncorrelated.

---

5. Λ is a capital lambda λ.

IV APPLICATIONS

11 Applications of ICA

11.1 Introduction

ICA has been applied to a number of different problems, most strikingly in the field of neuroimaging. A brief overview of the results from ICA is provided in order to demonstrate the range of applicability of ICA implemented as either spatial (sICA) or temporal ICA (tICA).

Of the many ICA applications not included here are

- optical imaging of neurons (Brown et al., 2001);

- neuronal spike sorting (Lewicki, 1998);

- face recognition (Bartlett, 2001) (see chapter 1);

- modeling receptive fields of primary visual neurons (Bell & Sejnowski, 1997, Hyvärinen et al., 2001b);

- predicting stock market prices (Back & Weigend, 1997);

- mobile phone communications (see (Hyvärinen et al., 2001a) for an overview);

- color-based detection of the ripeness of tomatoes (Polder & van der Heijden, 2003).

11.2 Temporal ICA of Voice Mixtures

An example frequently cited in this book is the application of ICA to speech data. A simple but effective demonstration of this is given the now classic paper by Bell and Sejnowski (Bell & Sejnowski, 1995), see figure 11.1.

This example emulates five people speaking simultaneously in a room in five microphones are placed at different locations, so that each microphone records a different mixture of the set of five voices. In this example the five voice source signals $\mathbf{s} = (s_1, s_2, s_3, s_4, s_5)^T$ are known which permits the signals extracted by ICA to be compared to the original source signals. A set of five signal mixtures $\mathbf{x} = (x_1, x_2, x_3, x_4, x_5)^T$ were obtained using a randomly generated 5×5 mixing matrix $\mathbf{A}$, where $\mathbf{x} = \mathbf{As}$. Each mixture emulates the sound recorded by one of five microphones. As speech signals have high kurtosis, ICA was applied to these mixtures using a high-kurtosis model cumulative denisty function (cdf) for the source signals. The unmixing matrix $\mathbf{W}$ estimated by ICA was used to extract five signals $\mathbf{y} = \mathbf{Wx}$, corresponding to the five original source signals.

This example demonstrates the general utility of ICA, and precludes many of the problems associated with extracting speech signals from mixtures recorded in a room. For

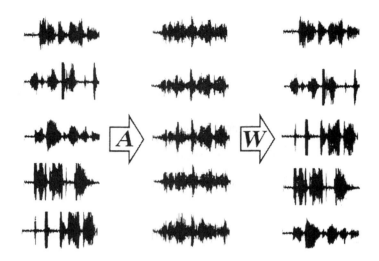

Figure 11.1

Speech Separation.

Example of ICA applied to speech data. This synthetic example emulates five people speaking simultaneously in a room where five microphones are placed at different locations, so that each microphone records a different mixture of the set of five voices. The five known source signals $\mathbf{s} = (s_1, s_2, s_3, s_4, s_5)^T$ are shown on the left. The signal mixtures $\mathbf{x} = (x_1, x_2, x_3, x_4, x_5)^T$ were obtained using a 5×5 mixing matrix $\mathbf{A}$, where $\mathbf{x} = \mathbf{As}$. Independent component analysis extracts five independent components each of which is taken to be an estimate of one of the original source signals (i.e., single voices). (Note that independent component analysis re-orders signals, so that an extracted signal y_i and its source signal s_i are not necessarily on the same row). From (Bell & Sejnowski, 1995).

example, the different distance of each speaker from each microphone would introduce a small lag between each voice at different microphones. Additionally, the walls introduce echoes into each mixture. These effects can be modeled and removed, but they require non-trivial extensions to ICA (Lee et al., 1997, Lee, 2001). For data where transmission time is essentially zero (e.g., electrical signals as in electroencephalography (EEG)) such problems do not arise.

11.3 Temporal ICA of Electroencephalograms

Every neuron in the human brain acts like a small electric generator when it is active. If large numbers of neurons become simultaneously active then it is possible to measure the resultant electrical effects at the scalp using an array of electrodes. The resultant set of temporal series of signals is called an *electroencephalogram*, or *EEG*. If the measured signals result from a specific stimulus event, such as as flash of light, then the result is known as an *event-related potential* or *ERP*.

The signal measured at each of up to 128 electrodes is known to be a mixture of underlying source signals. One major problem confronted by EEG researchers is to extract such source signals and to estimate where in the brain each source signal arises.

EEG data is in many ways ideally suited for ICA because there is a negligible amount of transmission delay between the source and each electrode, and because the assumption that each measured signal is a linear mixture of source signals is quite plausible for electrical signals traveling through human tissue. Moreover, the inverse of the unmixing matrix provides a spatial map of the associated scalp location of each source signal extracted by ICA.

A classic application of ICA to ERP data was reported in (Makeig et al., 1997), see figures 11.2 and 11.3. In this study, subjects were required to press a button whenever a weak, slow-onset noise burst was detected. These noise bursts were called targets, to distinguish them from non-target pure tones. The study compared ERPs of detected and undetected targets. A tICA decomposition of the output of the 14 electrodes for ERPs of detected and non-detected targets yielded two sets of quite distinct estimated temporal source signals. Additionally, the spatial image (map) associated with each source signal had a peak which differed in location and sign for detected and non-detected targets.

11.4   Spatial ICA of fMRI Data

Functional magnetic resonance imaging (*fMRI*) is sensitive to minute changes in the magnetic properties of brain tissue associated with brain activity, and can be used to record three-dimensional (3D) images of the brain at a rate of one 3D whole-brain image every 1–3 seconds.

When a set of neurons in one part of the brain become active they induce a localized influx of fresh, oxygenated blood cells. This has the effect of altering the local ratio of oxygenated to deoxygenated blood cells. This, in turn, alters the local magnetic susceptibility, because oxygen is carried on hemoglobin within red blood cells, and hemoglobin contains a small amount of iron, which alters its magnetic properties if it is bound to oxygen. It is these changes in local magnetic properties that are detected with fMRI.

In a classic paper on ICA of fMRI data, McKeown et al. (McKeown et al., 1998) scanned each subject for 6 minutes, which resulted in a temporal sequence of 144 whole-brain 3D images. Each subject was required to alternately perform a Stroop task for 40 seconds followed by 40 seconds of a control task. The Stroop task consists of naming the color of the ink of a printed a word such as "red" when the ink color and the printed word refer to different colors. For example, the word "red" might be printed in green ink, and the subject is required to name the color of the ink. As might be imagined attending to

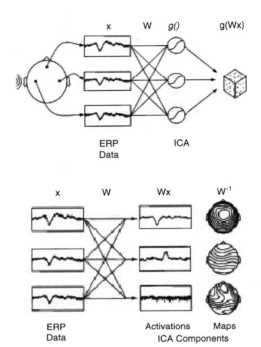

Figure 11.2
Schematic overview of temporal ICA (tICA) for ERP data.
Top: tICA transforms electrode outputs into a maximum entropy (uniform) distribution (joint pdf). Three out of 14 electrodes are shown. Their outputs form the signal mixtures $\mathbf{x} = (x_1, x_2, x_3)^T$. tICA finds an unmixing matrix $\mathbf{W}$ which transforms the mixtures $\mathbf{x}$ into maximally independent signals $\mathbf{y} = \mathbf{Wx}$, where $\mathbf{y} = (y_1, y_2, y_3)^T$. The unmixing matrix $\mathbf{W}$ is adjusted so that a function $\mathbf{Y} = g(\mathbf{y})$ of the extracted signals $\mathbf{y}$ has a maximum entropy (uniform) joint pdf. The joint pdf of the signals $\mathbf{Y}$ is represented by points in a cube, where each point represents the value of $\mathbf{Y}^t = (Y_1^t, Y_2^t, Y_3^t)^T$ at time t.
Bottom: Having obtained the unmixing matrix $\mathbf{W}$ with tICA, the estimated source signals $\mathbf{y} = \mathbf{Wx}$ can be computed. The spatial distribution or map of each source signal defines the relative amplitude of that source signal at each point on the scalp. The spatial map associated with the ith temporal source signal is obtained as the ith column of the the inverse $\mathbf{W}^{-1}$ of the unmixing matrix $\mathbf{W}$. From (Makeig et al., 1997).

the ink color while ignoring the color implied by the meaning of the word requires some mental effort, so that the Stroop task makes an ideal experiment for fMRI.

McKeown and colleagues applied spatial ICA (sICA) to the fMRI data obtained from the Stroop task. The sequence of 144 images yielded 144 estimated spatial source signals

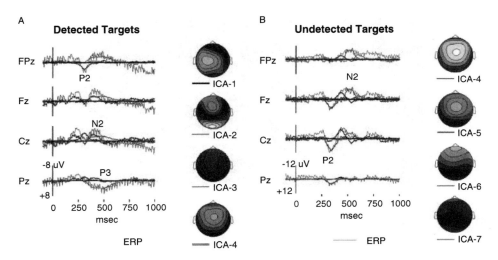

Figure 11.3
Temporal ICA (tICA) of ERP data for detected and undetected sounds (targets). A tICA decomposition of the output of the 14 electrodes for ERPs of detected and non-detected targets yielded two sets of quite distinct estimated temporal source signals. The spatial image (map) associated with each source signal had a peak which differed in location and sign for detected and non-detected targets. The symbols to the left of each trace denote the spatial position on the scalp of the electrode used to record that trace. The symbols P2, P3, and N2 refer to positive (P) or negative (N) ERP excursions which occur at 200ms (e.g., P2) or 300ms (e.g., P3).

(3D images). When the time course associated with each estimated source image was computed from the inverse of the unmixing matrix, several interesting findings emerged. The most striking finding was that one source image had a time course which almost exactly matched the time course of the experimental protocol. Specifically, the alternating 40 seconds of Stroop task and control task were clearly indicated in the time course of one source image, as shown in figure 11.4. Moreover, active brain regions of this source image included the Brodmann's area (a classic speech area) and the frontal cortex, a region activated by complex tasks. Other estimated source images were associated with temporal signals which suggested transient task related or head movement artifacts.

11.5 Spatial ICA for Color MRI Data

Accurate diagnosis based on magnetic resonance imaging *MRI* depends critically on being able to distinguish between different brain tissues, such as white matter tracts and gray matter. Unfortunately, standard MRI images are rendered in monochrome and do not show

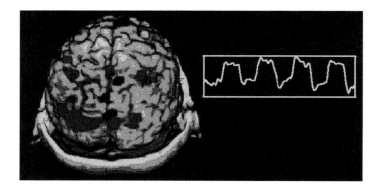

Figure 11.4
Spatial ICA (sICA) of fMRI data. sICA was applied to a temporal sequence of 144 whole-brain
three-dimensional (3D) images. Regions of significant activation are shaded light gray and regions
of significant deactivation are shaded dark gray. The figure shows a whole brain as viewed from the
back, with the associated time course of activations shown as an inset. This shows a temporal profile
which almost exactly matches the experimental protocol, which consisted of alternating 40 seconds
periods of the Stroop and control task (see text). This figure is a three-dimensional version of a figure
in (McKeown et al., 1998).

different tissues in detail. However, it is possible to use different MRI settings such that
each setting captures a different mixture of the source signals associated with different
tissues of interest (see figures 11.5 and 11.6). For example, a proton density weighted
MRI image reflects the local density of water molecules, which varies between tissues.
The resultant image therefore constitutes a *mixture* of signals associated with the tissues
of interest, such that the relative influence in the image of one tissue type is related to
its water concentration. As each MRI setting detects different raw signals, each setting
provides a different mixture of the different tissue types. Spatial ICA can therefore be used
to decompose a set of these image mixtures into their underlying spatial source signals.
After calibration with respect to an actual colored image of a human brain, the extracted
MRI source images can be recombined to provide an accurate high contrast colored image
of a brain in which white matter, gray matter and cerebrospinal fluid (the fluid around the
brain) are clearly demarcated. Even though the image in the lower right of figure 11.6 is
rendered in monochrome, the high contrast between different tissues is apparent.

11.6   Complexity Pursuit for Fetal Heart Monitoring

Non-invasive methods for monitoring fetal heart rhythm inevitably yield signals that are a
mixture of maternal and fetal heart signals. Fetal magnetocardiography (FMCG) relies on

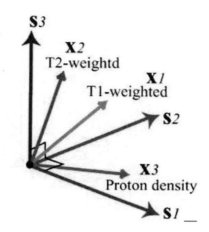

Figure 11.5
Theoretical model for high contrast colored MRI. Each different MRI setting (i.e., T1, T2, proton density) provides an image which in which different tissue types are more or less apparent. Thus each MRI setting provides a different image mixture $(x_1, x_2, x_3)^T$ of underlying independent source images $(s_1, s_2, s_3)^T$, where each source image may be associated with only one tissue type. sICA can be used to identify these spatial source images, which can then be recombined to yield an accurate high contrast color image of the brain.

the magnetic field generated by electrical activity in the heart to measure the cardiac signal (see figure 11.7). In (Araujo et al., 2003) it was shown that a simple form of complexity pursuit (augmented with autoregressive modeling of temporal structure) could be used to separate maternal and fetal signals from the 37 simultaneous signal mixtures measured using FMCG. Ten of these signals are shown in figure 11.7 (left bottom panel), and the results of applying the method to the full set of 37 mixtures are shown in the right bottom panel where the maternal and fetal heart signals are clearly defined.

11.7   Complexity Pursuit for Learning Stereo Disparity

When looking at an object, each eye sees a slightly different image, due to the fact that the eyes view the world from slightly different positions. The resultant small differences between the *stereo pair* of images in the left and right eyes are known as *stereo disparities*, and are used by the brain to estimate 3D depth. In its most rarefied form, stereo disparity can be presented to the visual system in the form of a *random dot stereogram* (RDS), as shown at the top of figure 11.8. In an RDS, each image is based on the same set of randomly positioned dots, but small differences in the positions of certain dots between the images of a stereo pair simulate the effects of depth on the disparity of those dots. If each image

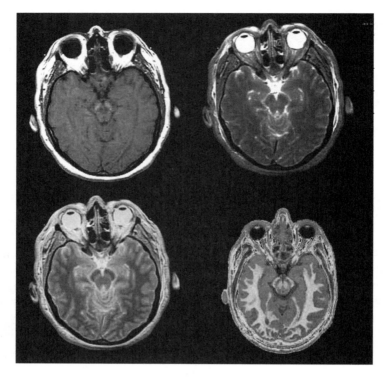

Figure 11.6
Using spatial ICA (sICA) to obtain high contrast color MRI images of the brain. Each panel shows a horizontal slice through a head, with the eyes at the top of the panel. Three different MRI settings (i.e., T1, T2, and proton density) each yield a different image (top left, top right, and bottom left, respectively). Each MRI setting provides a different mixture of underlying source images, where each source image is associated with only one tissue type. sICA can be used to identify these source images, which can then be recombined to yield an accurate high contrast image of the brain, rendered in monochrome here.

of a RDS is presented to one eye by viewing through a stereoscope then a compelling 3D structure is perceived.

Complexity pursuit has been used to learn to extract these stereo disparities from stereo pairs of images. This was achieved using an *artificial neural network* to learn a *non-linear* mapping from mixtures to source signals. Each input (i.e., mixture) to the network was a pair of small corresponding regions from a stereo pair of images (e.g., a small region from the stereo pair in figure 11.8), and the value of the source signal

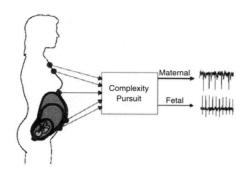

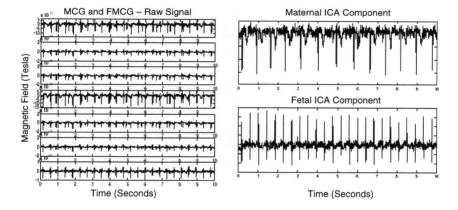

Figure 11.7

Fetal heart monitoring.

Top: The magnetic field generated by electrical activity in the heart is measured at 37 different locations using fetal magnetocardiography (FMCG). Each measured signal is a different mixture of fetal and maternal cardiac signals. Using an augmented form of complexity pursuit (Araujo et al., 2003), the set of 37 signal mixtures was decomposed to yield two estimated source signals corresponding to the maternal and fetal cardiac signals.

Bottom: Detail of 10/37 measured signals (left), and separated fetal and maternal cardiac signals (right). From (Araujo et al., 2003).

was the amount of stereo disparity implicit in each input pair of image regions. The network was not informed of the correct output source signal (i.e., stereo disparity). The network effectively "discovered" the notion of stereo disparity in the process of adjusting its unmixing coefficients (weights) in order to maximise the function F defined in equation (8.2) (Stone, 1999, Stone, 1996a, Stone, 1996b).

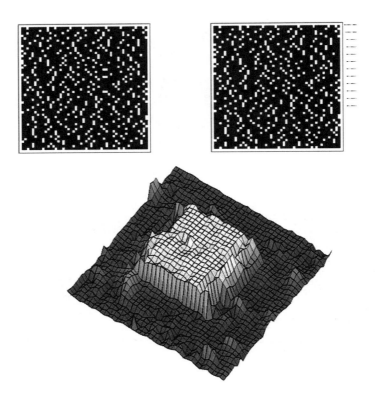

Figure 11.8

Learning stereo disparity from a pair of stereo images.

Top: Random dot stereogram. If these images are visually fused then a three dimensional image containing a small planar surface above a background planar surface is observed.

Bottom: Network output. Corresponding patches of the stereo images were used as input to an artificial neural network which learned by minimizing the complexity of its outputs (specifically, by maximizing the function F). This figure represents the resultant network outputs, which correspond to the correct three dimensional depth implied by the stereogram.

This demonstrates the general utility of the complexity pursuit strategy. Here, a non-linear artificial neural network learned to extract stereo disparity by maximizing the function F. In contrast, the unmixing coefficients of a linear transformation (i.e., the unmixing matrix **W**) were learned in order to extract multiple signals from a set of signal mixtures by maximizing the same function F that was used in chapter 8 (Stone, 2001).

V APPENDICES

A A Vector Matrix Tutorial

The single key fact about vectors and matrices is that each vector represents a point located in space and a matrix moves that point to a different location. Everything else is just details. Some of those details are described here.

A good pragmatic introduction to linear algebra is (Lay, 1997).

Vectors A number, such as 1.234, is known as a *scalar*, and a *vector* is an ordered list of scalars. Here is an example of a vector with two components α and β:

$$\mathbf{w} = (\alpha, \beta). \tag{A.1}$$

Note that vectors are written in bold type. The vector $\mathbf{w}$ can be represented as a single point in a graph, where the location of this point is by convention a distance of α from the origin along the horizontal axis and a distance of β from the origin along the vertical axis.

This notation for ordered lists of two scalars can be extended to any number of scalars, or components. For example, a vector with three components defines a point in a three-dimensional (3D) space (e.g., a point inside a cube):

$$\mathbf{w}_3 = (\alpha, \beta, \gamma). \tag{A.2}$$

The only tricky issue is how to visualize vectors once the number of vector components exceeds three. In fact, it is almost impossible to do so. Fortunately, the formal properties of vectors with three components are pretty much the same as those with any number of components, so any vector properties which can be visualized in three dimensions usually hold good for spaces with more than three dimensions.

Adding Vectors The *vector sum* of two vectors is the addition of their corresponding elements. Consider the addition of two pairs of scalars (x_1, x_2) and (α, β)

$$(\alpha + x_1), (\beta + x_2). \tag{A.3}$$

Clearly, (x_1, x_2) and (α, β) can be written as vectors:

$$
\begin{aligned}
\mathbf{z} &= (\alpha + x_1), (\beta + x_2) & \text{(A.4)} \\
&= (x_1, x_2) + (\alpha, \beta) & \text{(A.5)} \\
&= \mathbf{x} + \mathbf{w}. & \text{(A.6)}
\end{aligned}
$$

Thus the sum of two vectors is another vector which is known as the *resultant* of those two vectors.

Subtracting Vectors Subtracting vectors is similarly implemented by the subtraction of corresponding elements so that

$$\mathbf{z} = \mathbf{x} - \mathbf{w} \tag{A.7}$$

$$= (x_1 - \alpha), (x_2 - \beta). \tag{A.8}$$

Multiplying Vectors Consider the sum given by the multiplication of two pairs of scalars (x_1, x_2) and (α, β)

$$y = \alpha x_1 + \beta x_2. \tag{A.9}$$

Clearly, (x_1, x_2) and (α, β) can be written as vectors

$$y = (x_1, x_2).(\alpha, \beta), \tag{A.10}$$

$$= \mathbf{x}.\mathbf{w}_1, \tag{A.11}$$

where equation (A.11) is to be interpreted as equation (A.9). This multiplication of corresponding vector elements is known as the *inner*, *scalar* or *dot* product, and is often denoted with a dot, as here. The subscript "1" is used in $\mathbf{w}_1 = (\alpha, \beta)$ because we will need to define more $\mathbf{w}$ vectors soon.

Note that if $\mathbf{x}$ is a vector variable then we should denote the single tth pair of values as $\mathbf{x}^t = (x_1^t, x_2^t)$. However, the superscript t is omitted for now because we are considering a single pair of values.

Vector Length First, as each vector represents a point in space it must have a distance from the origin, and this distance is known as the vector's length, denoted as $|\mathbf{x}|$ for a vector $\mathbf{x}$. For a vector $\mathbf{x} = (x_1, x_2)$ with two components this distance is given by the length of the hypotenuse of a triangle with sides x_1 and x_2, so that

$$|\mathbf{x}| = \sqrt{x_1^2 + x_2^2}. \tag{A.12}$$

This generalizes to vectors with any number M of components so that

$$|\mathbf{x}| = \sqrt{x_1^2 + x_2^2, \ldots, x_M^2}. \tag{A.13}$$

Angle between Vectors Given any two vectors the angle between them is defined by

$$\cos\theta = \frac{\mathbf{x}.\mathbf{w}}{|\mathbf{x}||\mathbf{w}|}. \tag{A.14}$$

Note that the definition of angle vectors contains the inner product. If we rearrange equation (A.14) then we can obtain an expression for the inner product in terms of vector lengths and the angle between $\mathbf{x}$ and $\mathbf{w}$:

$$\mathbf{x}.\mathbf{w} = |\mathbf{x}||\mathbf{w}| \cos \theta. \tag{A.15}$$

If the lengths $|\mathbf{x}|$ and $|\mathbf{w}|$ are unity then it follows that

$$\mathbf{x}.\mathbf{w} = \cos \theta. \tag{A.16}$$

Thus, for unit length vectors, their inner product depends only on the angle between them.

Critically, if $\theta = 90$ degrees ($\pi/2$ radians) then the inner product is zero, because $\cos 90 = 0$, irrespective of the lengths of the vectors. Vectors at 90 degrees to each other are known as *orthogonal vectors*, and in general *the inner product of any two orthogonal vectors is zero*.

Row and Column Vectors Vectors come in two basic flavors, *row vectors* and *column vectors*. There are sound reasons for this apparently trivial distinction.

As might be surmised, the components of a row vector are written across the page,

$$(x_1, x_2), \tag{A.17}$$

whereas the components of a column vector are written down the page,

$$\begin{pmatrix} x_1 \\ x_2 \end{pmatrix}. \tag{A.18}$$

A simple notational device to transform a row vector (x_1, x_2) into a column vector (or vice versa) is the *transpose operator*, demonstrated here

$$(x_1, x_2)^T = \begin{pmatrix} x_1 \\ x_2 \end{pmatrix}. \tag{A.19}$$

The transpose operator is denoted with a superscript T here, but this can vary between texts.

The reason for having row and column vectors is because it is often necessary to combine several vectors into a single *matrix* which is then used to multiply a single vector $\mathbf{x}$, defined here as

$$\mathbf{x} = (x_1, x_2)^T. \tag{A.20}$$

In such cases it is necessary to keep track of which vectors are row vectors and which are column vectors. If we redefine $\mathbf{w}$ as a column vector,

$$\mathbf{w} \;=\; \begin{pmatrix} \alpha \\ \beta \end{pmatrix} \tag{A.21}$$

$$=\; (\alpha, \beta)^T \tag{A.22}$$

then the inner product $\mathbf{w}.\mathbf{x}$ can be written as

$$y \;=\; \mathbf{w}^T \mathbf{x} \tag{A.23}$$

$$=\; (\alpha, \beta) \begin{pmatrix} x_1 \\ x_2 \end{pmatrix} \tag{A.24}$$

$$=\; x_1 w_1 + x_2 w_2. \tag{A.25}$$

Here, each element of the row vector $\mathbf{w}^T$ is multiplied by the corresponding element of the column $\mathbf{x}$, and the results are summed. Writing the inner product in this way allows us to specify many pairs of such products as a vector-matrix product.

If $\mathbf{x}$ is a vector variable such that x_1 and x_2 have been measured N times (e.g., at N time consecutive time steps) then y is a variable with N values

$$(y^1, y^2, \ldots, y^N) \;=\; (\alpha, \beta) \begin{pmatrix} x_1^1, & x_1^2, & \ldots, & x_1^N \\ x_2^1, & x_2^2, & \ldots, & x_2^N \end{pmatrix} \tag{A.26}$$

$$=\; (\alpha, \beta) \begin{pmatrix} x_1 \\ x_2 \end{pmatrix} \tag{A.27}$$

$$=\; (\alpha, \beta)(x_1, x_2)^T \tag{A.28}$$

$$=\; \mathbf{w}^T \mathbf{x}. \tag{A.29}$$

Here, each (single element) column y_1^i is given by the inner product of the corresponding column in $\mathbf{x}$ with the row vector $\mathbf{w}$. This can now be rewritten succinctly as

$$y = \mathbf{w}^T \mathbf{x}. \tag{A.30}$$

Notice that the vector $\mathbf{w}$ essentially extracts y from $\mathbf{x}$.

Vector Matrix Multiplication If we reset the number of times $\mathbf{x}$ has been measured to $N = 1$ for now then we can consider the simple case of how two scalar values y_1 and y_2 are given by the inner products

$$y_1 \;=\; \mathbf{w}_1^T \mathbf{x} \tag{A.31}$$

$$y_2 \;=\; \mathbf{w}_2^T \mathbf{x}, \tag{A.32}$$

where $\mathbf{w}_1 = (\alpha, \beta)^T$ and $\mathbf{w}_2 = (\gamma, \delta)^T$. If we consider the pair of values y_1 and y_2 as a vector $\mathbf{y} = (y_1, y_2)^T$ then we can rewrite equations (A.31) and (A.32) as

$$(y_1, y_2)^T = (\mathbf{w}_1^T \mathbf{x}, \mathbf{w}_2^T \mathbf{x})^T. \tag{A.33}$$

If we combine the column vectors $\mathbf{w}_1$ and $\mathbf{w}_2$ then we can define a *matrix* $\mathbf{W}$

$$\mathbf{W} = (\mathbf{w}_1, \mathbf{w}_2)^T \tag{A.34}$$

$$= \begin{pmatrix} \alpha & \beta \\ \gamma & \delta \end{pmatrix}. \tag{A.35}$$

We can now rewrite equation (A.33) as

$$(y_1, y_2)^T = \begin{pmatrix} \alpha & \beta \\ \gamma & \delta \end{pmatrix} (x_1, x_2)^T. \tag{A.36}$$

This can be written more succinctly as

$$\mathbf{y} = \mathbf{W}\mathbf{x}. \tag{A.37}$$

This defines the standard syntax for vector-matrix multiplication. Note that the column vector $(x_1, x_2)^T$ is multiplied by the first row in $\mathbf{W}$ to obtain y_1 and is multiplied by the second row in $\mathbf{W}$ to obtain y_2.

Just as the vector $\mathbf{x}$ represents a point on a plane, so the point $\mathbf{y}$ represents a (usually different) point on the plane. Thus *the matrix $\mathbf{W}$ implements a* linear *geometric transformation of points from $\mathbf{x}$ to $\mathbf{y}$*. Essentially, the linear geometric transformation implemented by a matrix maps straight lines to straight lines (but usually with different lengths and orientations).

More generally, for $N > 1$ the tth column $(y_1^t, y_2^t)^T$ in $\mathbf{y}$ is obtained as the product of tth column $(x_1^t, x_2^t)^T$ in $\mathbf{x}$ with the row vectors in $\mathbf{W}$.

$$\begin{pmatrix} y_1^1, & y_1^2, & \cdots, & y_1^N \\ y_2^1, & y_2^2, & \cdots, & y_2^N \end{pmatrix} = \begin{pmatrix} \alpha & \beta \\ \gamma & \delta \end{pmatrix} \begin{pmatrix} x_1^1, & x_1^2, & \cdots, & x_1^N \\ x_2^1, & x_2^2, & \cdots, & x_2^N \end{pmatrix}$$

$$= (\mathbf{w}_1, \mathbf{w}_2)^T (x_1, x_2)^T \tag{A.38}$$

$$= \mathbf{W}\mathbf{x}. \tag{A.39}$$

The first term on the left is the pair of source signals $\mathbf{y} = (y_1, y_2)^T$, so that this can be rewritten as

$$\mathbf{y} = \mathbf{W}\mathbf{x}. \tag{A.40}$$

Given that $y_1^t = \alpha x_1^t + \beta x_2^t$ the correct way to read equation (A.39) is as follows.

Each (single element) column in y_1 is a scalar value which is obtained by taking the inner product of the corresponding column in $\mathbf{x}$ with the first row vector $\mathbf{w}_1^T$ in $\mathbf{W}$. Similarly, each column in y_2 is obtained by taking the inner product of the corresponding column in $\mathbf{x}$ with the second row vector $\mathbf{w}_2^T$ in $\mathbf{W}$.

This defines the basic syntax for vector-matrix multiplication, and demonstrates that the matrix $\mathbf{W}$ defines a spatial transformation of data points $\mathbf{x}$ to $\mathbf{y}$.

Transpose of Vector-Matrix Product: It is useful to note that if

$$\mathbf{y} = \mathbf{W}\mathbf{x} \qquad (A.41)$$

then the transpose $\mathbf{y}^T$ of this vector-matrix product is

$$\mathbf{y}^T = (\mathbf{W}\mathbf{x})^T = \mathbf{x}^T \mathbf{W}^T, \qquad (A.42)$$

where the transpose of a matrix is defined by

$$\mathbf{W}^T = \begin{pmatrix} \alpha & \beta \\ \gamma & \delta \end{pmatrix}^T = \begin{pmatrix} \alpha & \gamma \\ \beta & \delta \end{pmatrix}. \qquad (A.43)$$

B Projection Pursuit Gradient Ascent

Given a set of signal mixtures $\mathbf{x}$ and a signal $y = \mathbf{w}^T \mathbf{x}$ extracted from that set by an unmixing vector $\mathbf{w}$, the kurtosis of the extracted signal is

$$K = \frac{\mathrm{E}[(\bar{y} - y)^4]}{(\mathrm{E}[(\bar{y} - y)^2])^2} - 3. \tag{B.1}$$

In order to perform gradient ascent, we require the gradient of equation (B.1) with respect to $\mathbf{w}$.

While we could find the gradient of kurtosis with respect to $\mathbf{w}$ using the observed set of signal mixtures $\mathbf{x}$, matters are greatly simplified if we first transform $\mathbf{x}$ into another set of mixtures $\mathbf{z}$ that are uncorrelated with each other, where each new mixture z_i has unit variance (Hyvärinen et al., 2001a). This process is known as *whitening* or *sphering*.

Sphering Sphering is essentially decorrelation followed by scaling of each decorrelated mixture, and can be achieved using either Gram-Schmidt orthogonalisation (GSO) or principal component analysis (PCA). One useful form of PCA is *singular value decomposition* (SVD) (Press et al., 1989, Lay, 1997) (see appendix F). Given a set mixtures $\mathbf{x} = (x_1, x_2, \ldots, x_M)^T$ in the form of an $M \times N$ array of M mixtures measured over N time steps (for example), SVD provides a decomposition of the form

$$\mathbf{x} = UDV^T, \tag{B.2}$$

where $U = (U_1, U_2, \ldots, U_M)$ is an $M \times N$ matrix of eigenvectors, $V = (V_1, V_2, \ldots, V_M)$ is an $N \times N$ array of eigenvectors, and D is an $N \times N$ diagonal matrix of singular values (where each singular value is related to the power of corresponding eigenvectors in U and V).

Note that the eigenvectors in the columns of U and V are orthogonal and are therefore uncorrelated. For our purposes, only U is required because each column vector in U is a combination of column vectors in $\mathbf{x}$ such that all columns in U are mutually orthogonal. Thus the column vectors in U are new signal mixtures, but they are now orthogonal and therefore uncorrelated signal mixtures. By convention SVD provides unit length eigenvectors in U, and we require unit variance vectors (signal mixtures). This is achieved by rescaling each vector $U_i = U_i / \mathrm{E}(U_i^2)$. For notational convenience we define $\mathbf{z} = U$, where $\mathbf{z} = (z_1, z_2, \ldots, z_M)^T$ is a set of M *sphered* mixtures.

The signal extracted by a weight vector $\mathbf{w}$ is $y = \mathbf{w}^T \mathbf{z}$, and the kurtosis of y can be written

$$K = \frac{\mathrm{E}[y^4]}{(\mathrm{E}[y^2])^2} - 3. \tag{B.3}$$

If the weight vector $\mathbf{w}$ has unit length then $E[(\mathbf{w}^T\mathbf{z})^2] = 1$, so that kurtosis can be written as

$$K = E[(\mathbf{w}^T\mathbf{z})^4] - 3. \tag{B.4}$$

The gradient of kurtosis for an extracted signal $y = \mathbf{w}^T\mathbf{z}$ can then be shown to be

$$\frac{\partial K(\mathbf{w}^T\mathbf{z})}{\partial \mathbf{w}} = c\, E[\mathbf{z}(\mathbf{w}^T\mathbf{z})^3], \tag{B.5}$$

where c is a constant of proportionality, which we set to unity for convenience. Note that this gradient changes the length as well as the angle of $\mathbf{w}$, and we know that changes in length do not affect the form of the extracted signal (see section 4.2.1). If we restrict the length of $\mathbf{w}$ to unity then the rule for updating $\mathbf{w}$ is

$$\mathbf{w}_{new} = \mathbf{w}_{old} + \eta\, E[\mathbf{z}(\mathbf{w}_{old}^T\mathbf{z})^3\mathbf{z}], \tag{B.6}$$

where $\mathbf{w}_{new}$ is normalised to unit length after each update specified by equation (B.6)

$$\mathbf{w}_{new} = \mathbf{w}_{new}/|\mathbf{w}_{new}|. \tag{B.7}$$

We then set

$$\mathbf{w}_{old} = \mathbf{w}_{new}, \tag{B.8}$$

before repeating the update in equation (B.6).

Projection Pursuit MatLab Code

This is the core projection pursuit algorithm in MatLab. The results of running this code are given in figure B.1. This code extracts one source signal only, and is intended to demonstrate how projection pursuit works on a simple problem. In order to extract source signals sequentially, a form of GSO would be required. See appendix C and (Hyvärinen et al., 2001a).

The following code can be downloaded from http://www.shef.ac.uk/~pc1jvs/.

```
% Basic projection pursuit algorithm demonstrated on 2 sound signals,
% only one signal is extracted here.
% The default value of each parameter is given in [] brackets.

% [0] Set to 1 to hear signals.
listen=0; % set to 1 if have audio.

% [1] Set random number seed.
seed=99; rand('seed',seed);  randn('seed',seed);
```

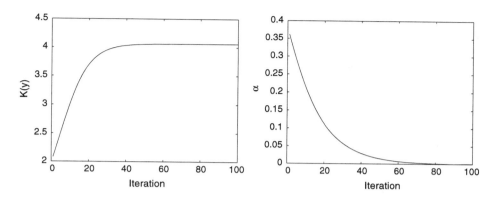

Figure B.1

Results of running projection pursuit (PP) MatLab code listed in text on two mixtures of two sound sources.

Left: Graph of kurtosis function K during gradient ascent.

Right: Graph of angle between optimal weight vector and gradient vector during gradient ascent. The initial correlations between the extracted signal and the two source signals are 0.8241 0.5679, and the final correlations are 1.0000 and 0.0086.

```
% [2] M = number of source signals and signal mixtures.
M = 2;
% [1e4] N = number of data points per signal.
N = 1e4;

% Load data, each of M=2 rows contains a different source signal.
% Each row has N columns (signal values).

% Load standard matlab sounds (from MatLab's datafun directory)
% Set variance of each source to unity.
load chirp; s1=y(1:N); s1=s1-mean(s1); s1=s1'/std(s1);
load gong;  s2=y(1:N); s2=s2-mean(s2); s2=s2'/std(s2);

% Combine sources into vector variable s.
s=[s1; s2];

% Make mixing matrix.
A=randn(M,M)';

% Listen to source signals ...
% [10000] Fs Sample rate of sound.
Fs=10000;
if listen  soundsc(s(1,:),Fs); soundsc(s(2,:),Fs);end;

% Plot histogram of each source signal -
% this approximates pdf of each source.
figure(3);hist(s(1,:),50); drawnow;
figure(4);hist(s(2,:),50); drawnow;
```

```
% Make M mixures x from M source signals s.
x = A*s;

% Listen to signal mixtures signals ...
if listen soundsc(x(1,:),Fs); soundsc(x(2,:),Fs); end;

% Sphere mixtures using SVD.
[U D V]=svd(x',0);
% Set new x to be left singular vectors of old x.
z=U;
% Each eigenvector has unit length,
% but we want unit variance mixtures ...
z=z./repmat(std(z,1),N,1);
z=z';

% Initialise unmixing vector to random vector ...
w = randn(1,M)';
% ... with unit length.
w=w/norm(w);

% Initialise y, the estimated source signal.
y = w'*z;

% Print out initial correlations between
% each estimated source y and every source signal s.
fprintf('Initial correlations of source and extracted signals\n');
%rinitial=abs(r(M+1:2*M,1:M))
r1=corrcoef([y; s1]');
r2=corrcoef([y; s2]');
rinitial=abs([r1(1,2) r2(1,2)])

maxiter=100;  % [100] Maximum number of iterations.
eta=2e-2; % [1e-2 /2] Step size for gradient ascent.

% Make array hs to store values of function and gradient magnitude.
Ks=zeros(maxiter,1);
gs=zeros(maxiter,1);

% Begin gradient ascent on K ...
% Define known optimal weight vector ...
wopt=[-0.6125    0.7904];
for iter=1:maxiter
% Get estimated source signal, y.
y = w'*z;

% Get estimated kurtosis.
K = mean(y.^4)-3;

% Find gradient @K/@w ...
y3=y.^3;
yy3 = repmat(y3,2,1);
g = mean( (z.*yy3)' )';
```

```
% Update w to increase K ...
w = w + eta*g;
% Set length of w to unity ...
w = w/norm(w);
% Record h and angle between wopt and gradient ...
Ks(iter)=K; gs(iter)=subspace(g,wopt');
end;

% Plot change in K and gradient/wopt angle during optimisation.
jfig(1);plot(Ks,'k');
title('Function values - Kurtosis');
xlabel('Iteration');ylabel('K(y)');
jfig(2);plot(gs,'k');
title('Angle \alpha Between Gradient g and Final Weight Vector w');
xlabel('Iteration');ylabel('\alpha');

% Print out final correlations ...
r=corrcoef([y; s]');
fprintf('FInal correlations between source and extracted signals ...\n');
r1=corrcoef([y; s1]');
r2=corrcoef([y; s2]');
rfinal=abs([r1(1,2) r2(1,2)])

% Listen to extracted signal ...
if listen soundsc(y,Fs); end;
%%%%%%%%%%%%%%%%%%%%%%%%%%%%%%%%%%%%%%%%%%%%%%%%%%%%%%%%%%%%%%%%
```

C Projection Pursuit: Stepwise Separation of Sources

With projection pursuit, we can extract estimated source signals $\mathbf{y} = (y_1, \ldots, y_M)^T$ in a stepwise manner from M signal mixtures $\mathbf{x} = (x_1, \ldots, x_M)^T$ using *Gram-Schmidt orthogonalisation* (GSO). This involves repeated cycles of extraction of a *single* signal y_i, followed by subtraction of that signal from the remaining set of signal mixtures. This operation is repeated until all the estimated source signals have been extracted.

If projection pursuit is applied to the original set of signal mixtures $\mathbf{x}(0) = (x_1(0), \ldots, x_M(0))^T$ then a weight vector $\mathbf{w}_1$ is obtained which extracts a signal $y_1 = \mathbf{w}_1^T \mathbf{x}(0)$, where the number in parentheses (0) denotes the original set of mixtures. We can effectively subtract y_1 from each signal mixture $x_i(0)$,

$$x_i(1) = x_i(0) - \frac{E[y_1 x_i(0)] y_1}{E[y_1^2]}, \tag{C.1}$$

where E denotes expected value, and the number in parentheses indexes how many recovered signals have been subtracted from the original mixture $x_i(0)$. Thus after one signal y_1 has been extracted GSO yields a new set of mixtures $\mathbf{x}(1)$ from which y_1 has been subtracted.

GSO ensures that each extracted signal y_1 is orthogonal to every mixture of signals yet to be extracted, so that $E[x_i(1) y_1] = 0$ for $i = \{1, \ldots, M\}$.

If projection pursuit is now applied to the modified mixtures $\mathbf{x}(1) = (x_1(1), \ldots, x_M(1))^T$ then the recovered signal $y_2 = \mathbf{w}_2^T \mathbf{x}(1)$ can be subtracted from each mixture $x_i(1)$

$$x_i(2) = x_i(1) - \frac{E[y_2 x_i(1)] y_2}{E[y_2^2]}. \tag{C.2}$$

This stepwise extract-and-subtract procedure can be repeated until M estimated source signals have been extracted.

D ICA Gradient Ascent

If M unknown source signals $\mathbf{s} = (s_1, s_2, \ldots, s_M)^T$ have a common cumulative density function (cdf) g and pdf p_s then given an unmixing matrix $\mathbf{W}$ which extracts M signals $\mathbf{y} = (y_1, y_2, \ldots, y_M)^T$ from a set of observed signal mixtures $\mathbf{x}$, the entropy of the signals $\mathbf{Y} = g(\mathbf{y})$ is

$$H(\mathbf{Y}) \quad = \quad H(\mathbf{x}) + \mathrm{E}\left[\sum_{i=1}^{M} \ln p_s(y_i)\right] + \ln |\mathbf{W}|, \tag{D.1}$$

where $y_i = \mathbf{w}_i^T \mathbf{x}$ is the ith signal, which is extracted by the ith row of the unmixing matrix $\mathbf{W}$. This expected value will be computed using N sampled values of the mixtures $\mathbf{x}$.

By definition, the pdf p_s of a variable is the derivative of that variable's cdf g

$$p_s(y) = dg(y)/dy, \tag{D.2}$$

where this derivative is denoted $g'(y) = p_s(y)$, so that we can write

$$H(\mathbf{Y}) \quad = \quad H(\mathbf{x}) + \mathrm{E}\left[\sum_{i=1}^{M} \ln g'(y_i)\right] + \ln |\mathbf{W}|. \tag{D.3}$$

We seek an unmixing matrix $\mathbf{W}$ that maximizes the entropy of $\mathbf{Y}$. As the entropy $H(\mathbf{x})$ of the signal mixtures $\mathbf{x}$ is unaffected by $\mathbf{W}$ its contribution to $H(\mathbf{Y})$ is constant, and can therefore be ignored. We can therefore proceed by finding that matrix $\mathbf{W}$ that maximizes the function

$$h(\mathbf{Y}) \quad = \quad \mathrm{E}\left[\sum_{i=1}^{M} \ln g'(y_i)\right] + \ln |\mathbf{W}|, \tag{D.4}$$

which is the change in entropy associated with the mapping from $\mathbf{x}$ to $\mathbf{Y}$. We can find the optimal matrix $\mathbf{W}^*$ using gradient ascent on h by iteratively adjusting $\mathbf{W}$ in order to maximize the function h. In order to perform gradient ascent efficiently, we require an expression for the gradient of h with respect to the matrix $\mathbf{W}$.

Evaluating the Gradient of Entropy: General Case

We proceed by finding the *partial derivative*[1] of h with respect one scalar element $\mathbf{W}_{ij}$ of $\mathbf{W}$, where $\mathbf{W}_{ij}$ is the element of the ith row and jth column of $\mathbf{W}$. The weight $\mathbf{W}_{ij}$ determines the proportion[2] of the jth mixture in the ith extracted signal y_i.

---

1. See chapter 9 for a brief account of partial derivatives.

2. Strictly speaking, $\mathbf{W}_{ij}$ determines the proportion only if the weights that contribute to y_i sum to unity, but this is of no consequence for our purposes.

Given that $\mathbf{y} = \mathbf{Wx}$, and that every source signal has the same pdf g', the partial derivative of h with respect to the ijth element in $\mathbf{W}$ is

$$\frac{\partial h}{\partial \mathbf{W}_{ij}} = \mathrm{E}\left[\sum_{i=1}^{M} \frac{\partial \ln g'(y_i)}{\partial \mathbf{W}_{ij}}\right] + \frac{\partial \ln |\mathbf{W}|}{\partial \mathbf{W}_{ij}}. \tag{D.5}$$

We will evaluate each of the two derivatives on the right hand side of equation (D.5) in turn. From the summation in

$$\mathrm{E}\left[\sum_{i=1}^{M} \frac{\partial \ln g'(y_i)}{\partial \mathbf{W}_{ij}}\right], \tag{D.6}$$

we can rewrite the term

$$\frac{\partial \ln g'(y_i)}{\partial \mathbf{W}_{ij}} = \frac{1}{g'(y_i)} \frac{\partial g'(y_i)}{\partial \mathbf{W}_{ij}}. \tag{D.7}$$

Using the chain rule

$$\frac{\partial g'(y_i)}{\partial \mathbf{W}_{ij}} = \frac{dg'(y_i)}{dy_i} \frac{\partial y_i}{\partial \mathbf{W}_{ij}}. \tag{D.8}$$

The derivatives on the right hand side can be rewritten as

$$\frac{dg'(y_i)}{dy_i} = g''(y_i), \tag{D.9}$$

where $g''(y_i)$ is the second derivative of g with respect to y_i, and

$$\frac{\partial y_i}{\partial \mathbf{W}_{ij}} = x_j. \tag{D.10}$$

Substituting equations (D.9) and (D.10) into equation (D.8) yields

$$\frac{\partial g'(y_i)}{\partial \mathbf{W}_{ij}} = g''(y_i)x_j. \tag{D.11}$$

Substituting equation (D.11) into equation (D.7) yields

$$\frac{\partial \ln g'(y_i)}{\partial \mathbf{W}_{ij}} = \frac{1}{g'(y_i)} g''(y_i)x_j. \tag{D.12}$$

Substituting equation (D.12) into equation (D.6) yields

$$\mathrm{E}\left[\sum_{i=1}^{M} \frac{\partial \ln g'(y_i)}{\partial \mathbf{W}_{ij}}\right] = \mathrm{E}\left[\sum_{i=1}^{M} \frac{g''(y_i)}{g'(y_i)} x_j\right]. \tag{D.13}$$

For notational convenience we can define

$$\psi(y_i) = \frac{g''(y_i)}{g'(y_i)},$$

(D.14)

which yields

$$E\left[\sum_{i=1}^{M} \frac{\partial \ln g'(y_i)}{\partial \mathbf{W}_{ij}}\right] = E\left[\sum_{i=1}^{M} \psi(y_i) x_j\right].$$

(D.15)

Now, turning our attention to the second term on the right hand side of equation (D.5), we state without proof

$$\frac{\partial \ln |\mathbf{W}|}{\partial \mathbf{W}_{ij}} = [\mathbf{W}^{-T}]_{ij},$$

(D.16)

where we define a special notation for the inverse of the transposed unmixing matrix $\mathbf{W}$

$$\mathbf{W}^{-T} = [\mathbf{W}^T]^{-1}.$$

(D.17)

Thus $[\mathbf{W}^{-T}]_{ij}$ is the ijth element of the inverse of the transposed unmixing matrix $\mathbf{W}$. Substituting equation (D.16) and equation (D.13) into equation (D.5) yields

$$\frac{\partial h}{\partial \mathbf{W}_{ij}} = [\mathbf{W}^{-T}]_{ij} + E\left[\sum_{i=1}^{M} \psi(y_i) x_j\right].$$

(D.18)

If we consider all elements of $\mathbf{W}$ then we have

$$\nabla h = \mathbf{W}^{-T} + E\left[\psi(\mathbf{y})\,\mathbf{x}^T\right],$$

(D.19)

where[3] ∇h is an $M \times M$ (Jacobian) matrix of derivatives in which the ijth element is $\partial h/\partial \mathbf{W}_{ij}$ (D.19).[4]

Given a finite sample of N observed mixture values of $\mathbf{x}^t$ for $t = 1, \ldots, N$ and a putative unmixing matrix $\mathbf{W}$, the expectation $E[.]$ can be estimated as the mean

$$E\left[\psi(\mathbf{y})\,\mathbf{x}^T\right] = \frac{1}{N}\sum_{t=1}^{N} \psi(\mathbf{y}^t)\,[\mathbf{x}^t]^T,$$

(D.20)

where $\mathbf{y}^t = \mathbf{W}\mathbf{x}^t$.

Thus the gradient ascent rule, which in its most general form is

$$\mathbf{W}_{new} = \mathbf{W}_{old} + \eta\nabla h,$$

(D.21)

---

3. The symbol ∇ is pronounced *nabla* and terms such as ∇h are often referred to as *grad h*.

4. The product of an M-element column vector with an M-element row vector (e.g., $\psi(\mathbf{y})\,\mathbf{x}^T$) yields an $M \times M$ matrix, known as the *outer product*.

can be written as

$$\mathbf{W}_{new} = \mathbf{W}_{old} + \eta \left(\mathbf{W}^{-T} + \frac{1}{N} \sum_{t=1}^{N} \psi(\mathbf{y}^T) \, [\mathbf{x}^t]^T \right), \tag{D.22}$$

where η is a small constant. This rule for updating $\mathbf{W}$ maximizes the entropy of $\mathbf{Y} = g(\mathbf{y})$.

Evaluating the Gradient For Super-Gaussian Signals

We will now derive an expression for ∇h for a specific cdf of the source signals. A commonly used cdf to extract super-gaussian source signals is the tanh function. Given the cdf

$$g(\mathbf{y}^t) = \tanh(\mathbf{y}^t), \tag{D.23}$$

this implies that the pdf g' is given by the first derivative of tanh is

$$g'(\mathbf{y}^t) = 1 - \tanh^2(\mathbf{y}^t), \tag{D.24}$$

and that the second derivative of tanh is

$$\begin{align}
g''(\mathbf{y}^t) &= dg'(\mathbf{y}^t)/d\mathbf{y}^t \tag{D.25} \\
&= \frac{d(1 - \tanh^2(\mathbf{y}^t))}{d\mathbf{y}^t} \tag{D.26} \\
&= -2\tanh(\mathbf{y}^t) \, \frac{d\tanh(\mathbf{y}^t)}{d\mathbf{y}^t} \tag{D.27} \\
&= -2\tanh(\mathbf{y}^t) \, g'(\mathbf{y}^t), \tag{D.28}
\end{align}$$

so that

$$\begin{align}
\psi(\mathbf{y}^t) &= \frac{g''(\mathbf{y}^t)}{g'(\mathbf{y}^t)} \tag{D.29} \\
&= \frac{-2\tanh(\mathbf{y}^t) \, g'(\mathbf{y}^t)}{g'(\mathbf{y}^t)} \tag{D.30} \\
&= -2\tanh(\mathbf{y}^t). \tag{D.31}
\end{align}$$

Substituting equation (D.31) into equation (D.19) yields

$$\nabla h = \mathbf{W}^{-T} + \mathrm{E}\left[-2\,\tanh(\mathbf{y}^t) \, [\mathbf{x}^t]^T\right]. \tag{D.32}$$

Given a finite sample of N observed mixture values of $\mathbf{x}^t$ for $t = 1, \ldots, N$ and a putative unmixing matrix $\mathbf{W}$ such that $\mathbf{y} = \mathbf{W}\mathbf{x}$, the expectation $E[.]$ can be estimated as the mean

$$\mathrm{E}\left[-2\,\tanh(\mathbf{y}) \, \mathbf{x}^T\right] = \frac{-2}{N} \sum_{t=1}^{N} \tanh(\mathbf{y}^t) \, [\mathbf{x}^t]^T. \tag{D.33}$$

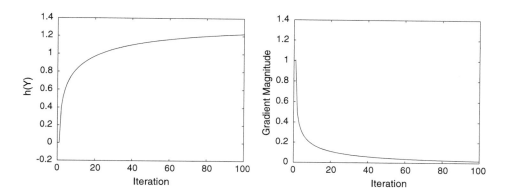

Figure D.1

Results of running ICA MatLab code listed in text on two mixtures of two sound sources.

Left: Graph of function h during gradient ascent. This approximates the entropy of the signals $\mathbf{Y} = g(\mathbf{y})$, where $\mathbf{y} = \mathbf{xW}$.

Right: Graph of magnitude of gradient of function h during gradient ascent. At a maximum in h the gradient magnitude should be zero. As can be seen the gradient magnitude converges toward zero, suggesting that a maximum has been reached.

The rule for updating $\mathbf{W}$ in order to maximize the entropy of $\mathbf{Y} = g(\mathbf{y})$ is therefore

$$\mathbf{W}_{new} = \mathbf{W}_{old} + \eta \left(\mathbf{W}^{-T} - \frac{2}{N} \sum_{t=1}^{N} \tanh(\mathbf{y}^t) \, [\mathbf{x}^t]^T \right), \tag{D.34}$$

where η is a small constant.

ICA MatLab Code

This is the core ICA algorithm in MatLab, and is based on the ICA algorithm described in (Bell & Sejnowski, 1995). The results of running this code are given in figure D.1, and the final correlation between the original source signals and the extracted signals is > 0.99, even on this relatively short run of 100 iterations. This code can be downloaded from http://www.shef.ac.uk/˜pc1jvs/.

```
% Basic Bell-Sejnowski ICA algorithm demonstrated on 2 speech signals.
% The default value of each parameter is given in [] brackets.

% [0] Set to 1 to hear signals.
listen=0; % set to 1 if have audio.

% [1] Set random number seed.
seed=9; rand('seed',seed); randn('seed',seed);
```

```
% [2] M = number of source signals and signal mixtures.
M = 2;
% [1e4] N = number of data points per signal.
N = 1e4;

% Load data, each of M=2 rows contains a different source signal.
% Each row has N columns (signal values).

% Load standard matlab sounds (from MatLab's datafun directory)
% Set variance of each source to unity.
load chirp; s1=y(1:N); s1=s1/std(s1);
load gong;  s2=y(1:N); s2=s2/std(s2);

% Combine sources into vector variable s.
s=[s1,s2]';

% Make new mixing matrix.
A=randn(M,M)';

% Listen to speech signals ...
% [10000] Fs Sample rate of speech.
Fs=10000;
if listen  soundsc(s(:,1),Fs); soundsc(s(:,2),Fs);end;

% Plot histogram of each source signal -
% this approximates pdf of each source.
figure(1);hist(s(1,:),50); drawnow;
figure(2);hist(s(2,:),50); drawnow;

% Make M mixures x from M source signals s.
x = A*s;

% Listen to signal mixtures signals ...
if listen soundsc(x(1,:),Fs); soundsc(x(2,:),Fs); end;

% Initialise unmixing matrix W to identity matrix.
W = eye(M,M);

% Initialise y, the estimated source signals.
y = W*x;

% Print out initial correlations between
% each estimated source y and every source signal s.
r=corrcoef([y; s]');
fprintf('Initial correlations of source and extracted signals\n');
rinitial=abs(r(M+1:2*M,1:M))

maxiter=100;  % [100] Maximum number of iterations.
eta=1; % [0.25] Step size for gradient ascent.

% Make array hs to store values of function and gradient magnitude.
hs=zeros(maxiter,1);
gs=zeros(maxiter,1);
```

```
% Begin gradient ascent on h ...
for iter=1:maxiter
% Get estimated source signals, y.
y = W*x; % wt vec in col of W.
% Get estimated maximum entropy signals Y=cdf(y).
Y = tanh(y);
% Find value of function h.
detW = abs(det(W));
h = ( (1/N)*sum(sum(Y)) + 0.5*log(detW) );
% Find matrix of gradients @h/@W_ij ...
g = inv(W') - (2/N)*Y*x';
% Update W to increase h ...
W = W + eta*g;
% Record h and magnitude of gradient ...
hs(iter)=h; gs(iter)=norm(g(:));
end;

% Plot change in h and gradient magnitude during optimization.
jfig(1);plot(hs);title('Function values - Entropy');
xlabel('Iteration');ylabel('h(Y)');
jfig(2);plot(gs);title('Magnitude of Entropy Gradient');
bookxlabel('Iteration');ylabel('Gradient Magnitude');

% Print out final correlations ...
r=corrcoef([y s]');
fprintf('FInal correlations between source and extracted signals ...\n');
rfinal=abs(r(M+1:2*M,1:M))

% Listen to extracted signals ...
if listen soundsc(y(1,:),Fs); soundsc(y(2,:),Fs);end;
%%%%%%%%%%%%%%%%%%%%%%%%%%%%%%%%%%%%%%%%%%%%%%%%%%%%%%%%%%%%%%%%
```

E Complexity Pursuit Gradient Ascent

Extracting a Single Signal[1]

Consider a scalar signal mixture y_i formed by the application of a weight vector $\mathbf{w}_i$ to a set of M signals $\mathbf{x} = (x_1, x_2, \ldots, x_M)^T$. Given that $y_i = \mathbf{w}_i^T \mathbf{x}$, equation (8.2) can be rewritten as

$$F = \ln \frac{\mathbf{w}_i \overline{C} \mathbf{w}_i^T}{\mathbf{w}_i \hat{C} \mathbf{w}_i^T}, \qquad (E.1)$$

where $\overline{C}$ is an $M \times M$ matrix of long-term covariances between signal mixtures, and $\hat{C}$ is a corresponding matrix of short-term covariances (see chapter 8). The long-term covariance $\overline{C}_{ij}$ and the short-term covariance $\hat{C}_{ij}$ between the ith and jth mixtures are defined as

$$\hat{C}_{ij} = \sum_{\tau}^{n} (x_{i\tau} - \hat{x}_{i\tau})(x_{j\tau} - \hat{x}_{j\tau}) \qquad (E.2)$$

$$\overline{C}_{ij} = \sum_{\tau}^{n} (x_{i\tau} - \overline{x}_{i\tau})(x_{j\tau} - \overline{x}_{j\tau}). \qquad (E.3)$$

Note that $\hat{C}$ and $\overline{C}$ need only be computed once for a given set of signal mixtures, and that the terms $(x_{i\tau} - \overline{x}_{i\tau})$ and $(x_{i\tau} - \hat{x}_{i\tau})$, can be precomputed using fast filtering operations, as described in (Eglen et al., 1997) (also see the MatLab code at the end of this appendix).

Gradient ascent on F with respect to $\mathbf{w}_i$ could be used to maximize F, thereby maximising the predictability of y_i. The derivative of F with respect to $\mathbf{w}_i$ is

$$\nabla_{\mathbf{w}_i} F = \frac{2\mathbf{w}_i}{V_i} \overline{C} - \frac{2\mathbf{w}_i}{U_i} \hat{C}. \qquad (E.4)$$

The function F could be maximized using gradient ascent to iteratively update $\mathbf{w}_i$ until a maximum of F is located

$$\mathbf{w}_i = \mathbf{w}_i + \eta \nabla_{\mathbf{w}_i} F, \qquad (E.5)$$

where η is a small constant (typically, $\eta = 0.001$).

Unfortunately, repeated application of the above procedure to a single set of mixtures extracts the same (most predictable) source signal. Whilst this can be prevented by using deflation procedures (e.g., Gram-Schmidt orthonormalisation (GSO), see appendix C), a more elegant method for extracting all of the sources simultaneously exists, as described next.

---

1. This appendix is based on the analysis presented in (Stone, 2001).

Simultaneous Extraction of Signals

The gradient of F is zero at a solution where, from equation (E.4)

$$\mathbf{w}_i \overline{C} = \frac{V_i}{U_i} \mathbf{w}_i \hat{C}. \tag{E.6}$$

Extrema in F correspond to values of $\mathbf{w}_i$ that satisfy equation (E.6), which has the form of a generalized eigenproblem (Borga, 1998). Solutions for $\mathbf{w}_i$ can therefore be obtained as eigenvectors of the matrix $(\hat{C}^{-1}\overline{C})$, with corresponding eigenvalues $\gamma_i = V_i/U_i$. The first such eigenvector defines a maximum in F, and each of the remaining eigenvectors define saddle points in F.

The matrix $\mathbf{W} = (\mathbf{w}_1, \mathbf{w}_2, \ldots, \mathbf{w}_M)^T$ can be obtained using a generalized eigenvalue routine. Results presented in chapter 8 were obtained using the MatLab eigenvalue function $\mathbf{W}^T = eig(\overline{C}, \tilde{C})$. All M signals can then be recovered,

$$\mathbf{y} = \mathbf{W}\mathbf{x}, \tag{E.7}$$

where each row of $\mathbf{y}$ is one extracted signal y_i. See (Borga, 1998) for a review of generalized eigenproblems.

If the number M of mixtures is greater than the number of source signals then a standard procedure for reducing M consists of using principal component analysis (PCA). PCA is used to reduce the dimensionality of the signal mixtures by discarding eigenvectors of $\mathbf{x}$ which have eigenvalues close to zero (see appendix F).

Complexity Pursuit MatLab Code

This is the core complexity pursuit algorithm in MatLab. The results of running this code are given in figure E.1. The first part of the code extracts one source signal only, and is intended to demonstrate how complexity pursuit works on a simple problem. In order to extract source signals sequentially a form of Gram-Schmidt orthogonalisation would be required (e.g., see appendix C). The second part of the code extracts all three signals simultaneously, as described above. The code below can be downloaded from http://www.shef.ac.uk/˜pc1jvs.

```
%%%%%%%%%%%%%%%%%%%%%%%%%%%%%%%%%%%%%%%%%%%%%%%%%%%%%%%%%%%%%%%%%%%%%%%%%%%%%
% Complexity pursuit: Gradient ascent code to extract one signal, and
% code for parallel extraction of all source signals using eig function.
%%%%%%%%%%%%%%%%%%%%%%%%%%%%%%%%%%%%%%%%%%%%%%%%%%%%%%%%%%%%%%%%%%%%%%%%%%%%%

% Set rand number seeds.
seed=1;randn('state',seed);rand('state',seed);
```

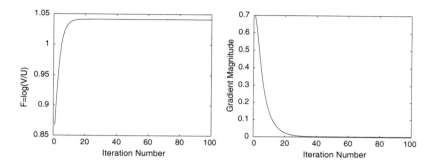

Figure E.1

Results of running complexity pursuit (CP) MatLab code listed in text on three mixtures of three sound sources.

Left: Graph of predictability function F of extracted signal y during gradient ascent, where F is inversely related to complexity.

Right: Graph of weight vector magnitude during gradient ascent. The initial correlations between the extracted signal and the three source signals are [0.597 0.724 0.409], and the final correlations are [0.075 0.972 0.252], indicating that the gradient ascent method has extracted source signal 2. Corresponding results for the parallel method are superior with correlations for this extracted signal of [0.015 0.999 0.004].

```
num_sources = 3;
num_mixtures = num_sources;
num_samples  = 5000;


%%%%%%%%%%%%%%%%%%%%%%%%%%%%%%%%%%%%%
% GET DATA.
%%%%%%%%%%%%%%%%%%%%%%%%%%%%%%%%%%%%%

% Define max mask len for convolution.
max_mask_len= 500;
% [8] n = num half lives to be used to make mask.
n = 8;

% Make source signals as set of increasingly smooth signals.

% Make mask.
% h= half-life of exponential in mask which is then convolved with random signal.
h=2; t = n*h; lambda = 2^(-1/h); temp = [0:t-1]'; lambdas = ones(t,1)*lambda;
mask = lambda.^temp;
mask1 = mask/sum(abs(mask));
h=4; t = n*h; lambda = 2^(-1/h); temp = [0:t-1]'; lambdas = ones(t,1)*lambda;
mask = lambda.^temp;
mask2 = mask/sum(abs(mask));
h=8; t = n*h; lambda = 2^(-1/h); temp = [0:t-1]'; lambdas = ones(t,1)*lambda;
mask = lambda.^temp;
mask3 = mask/sum(abs(mask));
```

```
sources = randn(num_samples,num_sources);
sources(:,1)=filter(mask1,1,sources(:,1));
sources(:,2)=filter(mask2,1,sources(:,2));
sources(:,3)=filter(mask3,1,sources(:,3));

% Transpose data.
mixtures=mixtures';
sources=sources';

% Make mixing matrix.
A = randn(num_sources,num_sources)';

% Make mixtures.
mixtures = A*sources;

%%%%%%%%%%%%%%%%%%%%%%%%%%%%%%%%%%%%%%
% COMPUTE V AND U.
%%%%%%%%%%%%%%%%%%%%%%%%%%%%%%%%%%%%%%
% Set short and long half-lives.
shf  = 1;
lhf  = 900000;

%%%%%%%%%%%%%%%%%%%%%%%%%%%%%%%%%%%%%%%%%%%%
% Get masks to be used to find (x_tilde-x) and (x_bar-x)
% Set mask to have -1 as first element, and remaining elements must sum to unity.

% Short-term mask.
h=shf; t = n*h; lambda = 2^(-1/h); temp = [0:t-1]';
lambdas = ones(t,1)*lambda; mask = lambda.^temp;
mask(1) = 0; mask = mask/sum(abs(mask));  mask(1) = -1;
s_mask=mask; s_mask_len = length(s_mask);

% Long-term mask.
h=lhf;t = n*h; t = min(t,max_mask_len); t=max(t,1);
lambda = 2^(-1/h); temp = [0:t-1]';
lambdas = ones(t,1)*lambda; mask = lambda.^temp;
mask(1) = 0; mask = mask/sum(abs(mask));  mask(1) = -1;
l_mask=mask; l_mask_len = length(l_mask);
%%%%%%%%%%%%%%%%%%%%%%%%%%%%%%%%%%%%%%%%%%%%%%

% Filter each column of mixtures array.
S=filter(s_mask,1,mixtures')';
L=filter(l_mask,1,mixtures')';

% Find short-term and long-term covariance matrices.
U=cov(S',1);
V=cov(L',1);

%%%%%%%%%%%%%%%%%%%%%%%%%%%%%%%%%%%%%%%%%%%%%%%%%%%%%%%%%%%%%%%%%%%%%%%%%%%%%%%%%%%%%%
% FIND **SINGLE** SOURCE SIGNAL USING GRADIENT ASCENT.
%%%%%%%%%%%%%%%%%%%%%%%%%%%%%%%%%%%%%%%%%%%%%%%%%%%%%%%%%%%%%%%%%%%%%%%%%%%%%%%%%%%%%%
cl=V;
cs=U;
```

```
% Make initial weight vector.
w=randn(1,num_sources);
w=w/norm(w);
w0=w;

% Use initial w0 to extract source
y0=w0*mixtures;

% Find correlation of y0 with sources
rs0=corrcoef([y0; sources]');
fprintf('Using Grad ascent: \n');
fprintf('Correlation of signal with sources extracted by initial w ...\n');
abs(rs0(1,2:4))

% Set learning rate ...
eta=1e-1;
% Set max number of iterations ...
maxiter=100;

% Make arrays to store results.
gs=zeros(maxiter,1); % gradient magnitude |g|
Fs=zeros(maxiter,1); % function value F

%%%%%%%%%%%%%%%%%%%%%%%%%%%%%%
% Do gradient ascent ...
for i=1:maxiter

% Get value of function F
Vi = w*cl*w';
Ui = w*cs*w';
F = log(Vi/Ui);

% Get gradient
g = 2*w*cl./Vi - 2*w*cs./Ui;

% Update w
w = w + eta*g;

% Record results ...
Fs(i)=F;
gs(i)=norm(g);

end;
%%%%%%%%%%%%%%%%%%%%%%%%%%%%%%%%

% Plot results ...
figure(1); plot(Fs); xlabel('Iteration Number'); ylabel('F=log(V/U)');
figure(2); plot(gs); xlabel('Iteration Number'); ylabel('Gradient Magnitude');

% Use w to extract source
y1=w*mixtures;
```

```
% Find correlation of y1 with sources
rs=corrcoef([y1; sources]');
fprintf('Using Grad ascent:\n');
fprintf(' Correlation of signal with sources extracted by initial w\n');
abs(rs(1,2:4))

%%%%%%%%%%%%%%%%%%%%%%%%%%%%%%%%%%%%%%%%%%%%%%%%%%%%%%%%%%%%%%%%%%%%%%%%%%%%%%%%
% NOW USE W MATRIX FROM EIG FUNCTION TO EXTRACT **ALL** SOURCES.
%%%%%%%%%%%%%%%%%%%%%%%%%%%%%%%%%%%%%%%%%%%%%%%%%%%%%%%%%%%%%%%%%%%%%%%%%%%%%%%%
%%%%%%%%%%%%%%%%%%%%%%%%%%%%%%%%%%%%%%%%%%
% Find optimal solution as eigenvectors W.
%%%%%%%%%%%%%%%%%%%%%%%%%%%%%%%%%%%%%%%%%%
[Wtemp d]=eig(V,U);
W=Wtemp'; W=real(W);

ys = W*mixtures;
a=[sources; ys]'; c=corrcoef(a);
rs=c(1:num_sources,num_sources+1:num_sources*2);
fprintf('Using EIG: Correlations between sources and all recovered signals\n');
abs(rs)
%%%%%%%%%%%%%%%%%%%%%%%%%%%%%%%%%%%%%%%%%%%%%%%%%%%%%%%%%%%%%%%%%%%%%%%%%%%%%%%%%
```

The printed output of the above code is as follows.

```
Using Grad ascent: Correlation of single with sources extracted by initial w ...
      0.5974    0.7237    0.4092

Using Grad ascent: Correlation of single with sources extracted by initial w ...
      0.0750    0.9720    0.2521

Using EIG: Correlations between sources and all recovered signals ...
      0.1334    0.9919    0.0153
      0.0396    0.0026    0.9995
      0.9988    0.0397    0.0044
```

F Principal Component Analysis for Preprocessing Data

Most implementations of ICA require a square $M \times M$ unmixing matrix $\mathbf{W}$, where M is the number of signal mixtures. However, this can involve very large matrices. Principal component analysis (PCA) can be used to to reduce the size of $\mathbf{W}$, e.g., see (Stone et al., 2002). This is achieved by finding an approximation to the M signal mixtures in terms of $K < M$ new signal mixtures, where these K new mixtures are *principal components*. As the data are now approximated by K principal components (PCs), a smaller $K \times K$ unmixing matrix is required. Note that ICA would work equally well on the full set of M new mixtures (PCs) as it would on the M observed mixtures $\mathbf{x}$, but that representing $\mathbf{x}$ as a set of principal components permits "irrelevant" aspects of the data to be discarded.

Given an $M \times N$ data array $\mathbf{x}$, each of the M N-element row vectors in $\mathbf{x}$ defines a single point in an N-dimensional space. If most of these points lie in a K-dimensional subspace (where $K \ll N$) then we can use K judiciously chosen *basis vectors* to represent the M rows of $\mathbf{x}$. For example, if all N points in a cube (i.e., an $M = 3$ dimensional space) lie on one face of the cube then we can describe the points in terms of only two basis vectors defined by $K = 2$ edges of that face. Such a set of K N-element basis vectors can be obtained as *eigenvectors* using PCA.

A very general and useful form of PCA is *singular value decomposition* (SVD) (Press et al., 1989, Lay, 1997).

In order to deal with a concrete example we assume that the columns of $\mathbf{x}$ contain a temporal sequence of images, such that each column contains an image associated with time t, as in chapter 7. Given that each column of $\mathbf{x}$ is an image vector of M pixels, this implies that each column of U is a spatial eigenvector or *eigenimage*, and each column of V is a temporal eigenvector or *eigensequence*.

Singular Value Decomposition

Given a set of signal mixtures $\mathbf{x} = (x_1, x_2, \ldots, x_N)^T$ in the form of an $M \times N$ array of N temporal mixtures, each measured over M time steps, SVD provides a decomposition of the form

$$\mathbf{x} = UDV^T, \tag{F.1}$$

where $U = (U_1, U_2, \ldots, U_N)$ is an $M \times N$ matrix of N (spatial) column eigenvectors, $V = (V_1, V_2, \ldots, V_N)$ is an $N \times N$ array of N (temporal) column eigenvectors, and D is an $N \times N$ diagonal matrix of N ordered *singular values*. Each singular value is equal to $\lambda^{1/2}$, where λ is an *eigenvalue* of one eigenvector in U and V. More formally, the columns in U are the *left singular vectors* and the columns in V are the *right singular vectors* of $\mathbf{x}$. The eigenvectors in the columns of U and V are orthogonal and are therefore uncorrelated.

By convention SVD provides unit length eigenvectors in U and V. See section 10.3 for a formal definition of eigenvectors.

Each eigenvalue specifies the amount of variance associated with the direction defined by a corresponding eigenvector in U and V. We can therefore discard eigenvectors with small eigenvalues because these account for trivial variations in the data set. If we discard all data associated with eigenvalues below some value then we are left with K eigenvectors which provide a reasonable approximation $\tilde{\mathbf{x}}$ to the original data $\mathbf{x}$:

$$\mathbf{x} \approx \tilde{\mathbf{x}} = \tilde{U}\tilde{D}\tilde{V}^T. \tag{F.2}$$

Note that $\tilde{U}$ is an $M \times K$ matrix of K column eigenvectors, $\tilde{V}^T$ is a $K \times M$ matrix of K row eigenvectors, and $\tilde{D}$ is a diagonal $K \times K$ matrix of K singular values.

We could perform ICA on U in order to extract independent components. However the results would be the same as performing ICA on $\mathbf{x}$. This is because U is a linear transformation of $\mathbf{x}$, so that each column in U is a linear combination of columns in $\mathbf{x}$. Therefore each column of U is simply a new mixture of source signals. However, performing ICA on U would not reduce the size of $\mathbf{W}$.

Given that we require a small unmixing matrix $\mathbf{W}$, it is desirable to use $\tilde{U}$ instead of $\mathbf{x}$ (or equivalently U) for spatial ICA (sICA), and $\tilde{V}$ instead of $\mathbf{x}^T$ (or equivalently V) for temporal ICA (tICA). The basic method consists of performing ICA on $\tilde{U}$ or $\tilde{V}$ to obtain K signals, and then using the relation $\tilde{\mathbf{x}} = \tilde{U}\tilde{D}\tilde{V}^T$ to recover the unknown mixing matrix A.

tICA Using SVD

Using tICA, each row of $\mathbf{x}$ is considered to be a temporal signal mixture

$$\mathbf{y} = \mathbf{W}\mathbf{x}, \tag{F.3}$$

where each N-element row of $\mathbf{y}$ is an extracted signal and $\mathbf{W}$ is an $N \times N$ matrix. Replacing the $M \times N$ data array $\mathbf{x}$ with the $K \times N$ matrix $\tilde{V}^T$ in Equation F.3 yields

$$\mathbf{y} = \mathbf{W}\tilde{V}^T, \tag{F.4}$$

where $\mathbf{W}$ is now a $K \times K$ matrix, and each row of the $K \times N$ matrix $\tilde{V}^T$ is an eigensequence. In this case, ICA extracts K N-element sequences $\mathbf{y}$.

The set of dual images would normally be found in the matrix $\mathbf{A} = \mathbf{W}^{-1}$, where each image corresponds to one of the K extracted temporal signals. However, because $\mathbf{W}$ is a $K \times K$ matrix (and its inverse is the same size) $\mathbf{A} = \mathbf{W}^{-1}$ each image vector in $\mathbf{A}$ has only K pixels. We can estimate the M-pixel images as follows.

Assuming that $\mathbf{y} = \mathbf{s}$,

$$\tilde{V}^T = \mathbf{A}\mathbf{y} \tag{F.5}$$

$$= \mathbf{W}^{-1}\mathbf{y}, \tag{F.6}$$

and given that

$$\tilde{\mathbf{x}} = \tilde{U}\tilde{D}\tilde{V}^T \tag{F.7}$$

we have

$$\tilde{\mathbf{x}} = \tilde{U}\tilde{D}\mathbf{W}^{-1}\mathbf{y} \tag{F.8}$$

$$= \mathbf{A}\mathbf{y}, \tag{F.9}$$

from which it follows that

$$\mathbf{A} = \tilde{U}\tilde{D}\mathbf{W}^{-1}, \tag{F.10}$$

where $\mathbf{A}$ is an $M \times K$ matrix in which each column is an image. Thus, we have extracted K independent N-element sequences and their corresponding dual M-element images using a $K \times K$ unmixing matrix $\mathbf{W}$.

sICA Using SVD

Using sICA, each row of $\mathbf{x}^T$ is considered to be a spatial signal mixture, or image. We can use SVD to find K independent images and their corresponding dual time courses, as follows.

Replacing $\mathbf{x}^T$ with $\tilde{U}^T$ in $\mathbf{y} = \mathbf{W}\mathbf{x}^T$ yields

$$\mathbf{y} = \mathbf{W}\tilde{U}^T, \tag{F.11}$$

where each row of the $K \times M$ matrix $\tilde{U}^T$ is an eigenimage, and $\mathbf{W}$ is a $K \times K$ matrix. In this case, ICA recovers K M-element images.

The set of dual temporal sequences corresponding to the K extracted spatial signals can be obtained as follows. If the extracted signals $\mathbf{y}$ are equal to the K source signals $\mathbf{s}$ then $\mathbf{A} = \mathbf{W}^{-1}$ so that

$$\tilde{U}^T = \mathbf{A}\mathbf{y} \tag{F.12}$$

$$= \mathbf{W}^{-1}\mathbf{y}. \tag{F.13}$$

Given that

$$\tilde{\mathbf{x}}^T = \tilde{V}\tilde{D}\tilde{U}^T, \tag{F.14}$$

we can substitute Equation F.6 in Equation F.14

$$\tilde{\mathbf{x}} = \tilde{V}\tilde{D}\mathbf{W}^{-1}\mathbf{y} \qquad (\text{F}.15)$$

$$= \mathbf{Ay}, \qquad (\text{F}.16)$$

from which it follows that

$$\mathbf{A} = \tilde{V}\tilde{D}\mathbf{W}^{-1}, \qquad (\text{F}.17)$$

where $\mathbf{A}$ is a matrix in which each column is a temporal sequence. Thus, we have extracted K M-pixel images and their corresponding dual N-element time courses using a $K \times K$ unmixing matrix $\mathbf{W}$.

Note that using SVD in this manner requires an assumption that the source signals are not distributed amongst the "smaller" eigenvectors, which are usually discarded. The validity of this assumption is by no means guaranteed, e.g., (Green et al., 2002). For this reason, it may be preferable to specify the exact number K (where K is no larger than the number M of signal mixtures) of signals to be extracted by ICA from the original data set using a non-square $M \times K$ unmixing matrix (Porrill & Stone, 1997, Amari, 1999, Penny et al., 2001).

G Independent Component Analysis Resources

Books

Bartlett, M. S., (2001), Face Image Analysis by Unsupervised Learning. Kluwer Academic Publishers; International Series on Engineering and Computer Science, Boston.

Cichocki, A., and Amari, S-I., (2002), Adaptive Blind Signal and Image Processing—Learning Algorithms and Applications. New York, John Wiley and Sons.

Girolami, M., (1999), Self-Organising Neural Networks: Independent Component Analysis and Blind Source Separation. London, Springer-Verlag.

Girolami, M, editor, (2000), Advances in Independent Component Analysis, (Perspectives in Neural Computing). London, Springer-Verlag.

Haykin, S., editor, (2000), Unsupervised Adaptive Filtering: Blind Source Separation. John Wiley and Sons.

Hyvärinen, A., Karhunen, J., and Oja, E., (2001), Independent Component Analysis. London, John Wiley and Sons.

Lee, T. W., (1999), Independent Component Analysis: Theory and Applications. Kluwer Academic Publishers.

Roberts S., and Everson, R., editors, (2001), Independent component analysis: principles and practice. Cambridge UK, Cambridge University Press.

Mailing List

http://tsi.enst.fr/˜cardoso/icacentral/mailinglist.html

Annual Conference

Papers presented at ICA2004, the fifth international meeting in the series, can be found at http://ica2004.ugr.es. This includes links to papers presented at previous conference meetings.

Demonstrations and Software on the Web

A good place to start is http://www.cnl.salk.edu/˜tony/ica.html

ICA MatLab code for two-dimensional images, which includes skew-pdf model for image analysis and spatiotemporal ICA options. Uses second order (conjugate gradient) method: http://www.shef.ac.uk/˜pc1jvs

ICA MatLab code: http://mole.imm.dtu.dk/toolbox/

A comprehensive ICA MatLab package (the fastICA algorithm is included): http://www.bsp.brain.riken.go.jp/ICALAB/

MatLab code for EEG analysis: http://sccn.ucsd.edu/˜scott/ica.html

FastICA MatLab package for projection pursuit: http://www.cis.hut.fi/projects/ica/fastica/

Complexity Pursuit: Blind source separation using temporal predictability. MatLab code available from: http://www.shef.ac.uk/˜pc1jvs

Relative Newton Method for Blind Source Separation: MatLab code and paper available from: http://iew3.technion.ac.il/˜mcib

H Recommended Reading

Introductory Texts

Abbot, P., (1977). Calculus. Teach Yourself Series, London, Hodder and Stoughton.
Originally published in 1940, this remains an excellent tutorial introduction to calculus.

Ballard, D., (1997). An Introduction to Natural Computation. MIT Press, Cambrdige, MA.
Expansive tutorial introduction to several core methods, such as vector matrix algebra, and principal component analysis.

Bishop C.M., (1996). Neural Networks for Pattern Recognition. Oxford UK, Oxford University Press.
Although this is principally a book on artificial neural networks, it is an excellent and thorough introduction to maximum likelihood estimation and Bayesian methods.

Cowan, G., (1998). Statistical Data Analysis. Oxford, UK, Clarendon Press.
Sivia, D.S., (1996). Data Analysis: A Bayesian Tutorial. Oxford, UK, Clarendon Press.
Both of these slim volumes provide excellent tutorial accounts of Bayesian methods, maximum likelihood estimation and probability density functions.

Lay, D.C., (1997). Linear Algebra and its Applications. New York, Addison-Wesley.
A thorough geometric introduction to vector matrix algebra and principal component analysis.

Reference Texts

Cover, T.M., and Thomas, J.A., (1991). Elements of Information Theory. New York, John Wiley and Sons.
The modern reference book on information theory.

DeGroot, M.H., (1986). Probability and Statistics, 2nd Edition, Addison-Wesley, London.
A very thorough, although demanding, account of probability and probability density functions.

Everitt, B.S., and Dunn, G., (2001). Applied Multivariate Analysis. New York, Oxford University Press.
Includes a thorough account of principal component analysis and factor analysis.

Everitt, B.S., (1984). An Introduction to Latent Variable Methods, London, Chapman and Hall.
The modern standard on factor analysis.

Press, W.H., and Flannery, B.P., and Teukolsky, S.A., and Vetterling, W.T., (1989). Numerical Recipes in C. Cambridge UK, Cambrdige University Press.
Originally intended as a set of practical computer programs in various languages, the text accompanying each program is so lucid that this book is an excellent reference for topics such as gradient ascent optimisation, conjugate gradients.

Reza, F.M., (1961). Information Theory, McGraw-Hill Inc. Reprint, New York, Dover Publications, 1994.
An old book (originally published in 1961), but still a good substitute for Cover and Thomas.

References

Amari, A, Cichocki, A, & Yang, HH. 1996. A new learning algorithm for blind signal separation. *Pages 757–763 of:* Touretzky, DS, Mozer, MC, & Hasslemo, ME (eds), *Advances in neural information processing systems 8.* Cambridge, MA, MIT Press.

Amari, S. 1998. Natural gradient works efficiently in learning. *Neural computation*, **10**, 251–276.

Amari, S. 1999. Natural gradient learning for over- and under-complete bases in ica. *Neural computation*, **11**, 1875–1883.

Araujo, D., Barros, A. K., Baffa, O., Wakai, R., Zhao, H., & Ohnishi, N. 2003 (April). Fetal magnetocardiographic source separation using the poles of the autocorrelation function. *Pages 833–836 of: Ica03: Fourth international symposium on ica and blind signal separation.*

Attias, H. 2000. Independent factor analysis with temporally structured factors. *In:* Solla, SA, Leen, TK, & Mller, KR (eds), *Advances in neural information processing systems 12.* Cambridge, MA, MIT Press.

Back, AD, & Weigend, AS. 1997. A first application of independent component analysis to extracting structure from stock returns. *International journal of neural systems*, **8**(4), 473–484.

Barlow, HB. 1981. Cortical limiting factors in the design of the eye and the visual cortex. *Proceedings royal society london b*, **212**, 1–34.

Bartlett, MS. 2001. *Face image analysis by unsupervised learning.* Boston, Kluwer Academic Publishers.: Kluwer International Series on Engineering and Computer Science.

Bell, AJ, & Sejnowski, TJ. 1995. An information-maximization approach to blind separation and blind deconvolution. *Neural computation*, **7**, 1129–1159.

Bell, AJ, & Sejnowski, TJ. 1997. The independent components of natural scenes are edge filters. *Vision research*, **37**(23), 3327–3338.

Borga, M. 1998. Learning multidimensional signal processing. *Linkoping university, sweden.*

Brown, GD, Yamada, S, & Sejnowski, TJ. 2001. Independent components analysis (ica) at the neural cocktail party. *Trends in neuroscience*, **24**(1), 54–63.

Cardoso, J. 2000. On the stability of source separation algorithms. *Journal of vlsi signal processing systems*, **26**(1/2), 7–14.

Cardoso, J-F. 1997. Infomax and maximum likelihood for blind source separation. *Ieee signal processing letters*, **4**(4), 112–114.

Chatfield, C, & Collins, AJ. 2000. *Introduction to multivariate analysis*. London, Chapmanand Hall/CRC.

Cichocki, A, & Amari, S. 2002. *Adaptive blind signal and image processing - learning algorithms and applications*. London, John Wiley and Sons.

Cover, TM, & Thomas, JA. 1991. *Elements of information theory*. New York, John Wiley and Sons.

DeGroot, MH. 1986. *Probability and statistics, 2nd edition*. UK, Addison-Wesley.

Eglen, S, Bray, A, & Stone, JV. 1997. Unsupervised discovery of invariances. *Network*, **8**, 441–452.

Everitt, BS. 1984. *An introduction to latent variable methods*. London, Chapman and Hall.

Friedman, JH, , & JW, Tukey. 1974. A projection pursuit algorithm for exploratory data analysis. *Ieee transactions on computers*, **23**(9), 881–890.

Fyfe, C, & Baddeley, R. 1995. Non-linear data structure extraction using simple hebbian networks. *Biological cybernetics*, **72**, 533–541.

Green, CG, Nandy, RR, & Cordes, D. 2002. Pca-preprocessing of fmri data adversely affects the results of ica. *Proceedings of international society of magnetic resonance in medicine*, **10**.

Hyvärinen, A. 2001. Complexity pursuit: Separating interesting components from time series. *Neural computation*, **13**, 883–898.

Hyvärinen, A, & Oja, E. 1997. A fast fixed-point algorithm for independent component analysis. *Neural computation*, **9**(7), 1483–1492.

Hyvärinen, A, Karhunen, J, & Oja, E. 2001a. *Independent component analysis*. New York, John Wiley and Sons.

Hyvärinen, A, Hoyer, PO, & Inki, M. 2001b. Topographic independent component analysis. *Neural computation*, **13**(7), 1527–1574.

Jessop, A. 1995. *Informed assessment: An introduction to information, entropy and statistics*. London, Ellis Horwood.

Kruskal, JB. 1969. Toward a practical method which helps uncover the structure of a set of observations by finding the line transformation which optimizes a new "index of condensation". *Pages 427–440 of:* Milton, RC, & Nelder, JA (eds), *Statistical computation*. New York, Academic Press.

Lay, DC. 1997. *Linear algebra and its applications*. New York, Addison-Wesley.

Lee, T-W. 2001. *Independent component analysis*. London, Kluwer Academic Press.

Lee, T-W, Bell, AJ, & Lambert, R. 1997. Blind separation of delayed and convolved sources. *Pages 758–764 of: Neural information processing systems 9*. Cambridge, MA, MIT Press.

Lewicki, MS. 1998. A review of methods for spike sorting: the detection and classification of neural action potentials. *Network: Computation in neural systems*, **9**(4), 53–78.

Lewicki, MS, & Sejnowski, TJ. 2000. Learning overcomplete representations. *Neural computation*, **12**, 337–365.

Makeig, S, Jung, T, Bell, AJ, Ghahremani, D, & Sejnowski, TJ. 1997. Blind separation of auditory event-related brain responses into independent components. *Proceedings national academy of sciences of the united states of america*, **94**, 10979–10984.

McKeown, MJ, Makeig, S, Brown, GG, Jung, TP, Kindermann, SS, & Sejnowski, TJ. 1998. Spatially independent activity patterns in functional magnetic resonance imaging data during the stroop color-naming task. *Proceedings national academy of sciences of the united states of america*, **95**(Feburary), 803–810.

Molgedey, L, & Schuster, HG. 1994. Separation of a mixture of independent signals using time delayed correlations. *Physical review letters*, **72**(23), 3634–3637.

Pearlmutter, BA, & Parra, LC. 1996. A context-sensitive generalization of ica. *In: International conference on neural information processing, hong kong*. Available from http://www.cs.unm.edu/b̃ap/publications.html#journal.

Penny, WD, Roberts, SJ, & Everson, RM. 2001. Ica: Model order selection and dynamic source models. *Pages 299–314 of:* Roberts, S, & Everson, R (eds), *Independent component analysis : principles and practice*. Cambridge, UK, Cambridge University Press.

Polder, G, & van der Heijden, GWAM. 2003. Estimation of compound distribution in spectral images of tomatoes using independent component analysis. *Pages 57–64 of:* Leitner, R. (ed), *Spectral imaging, international workshop of the carinthian tech research.* Austrian Computer Society.

Porrill, J, & Stone, JV. 1997 (August). *Independent components analysis for signal separation and dimension reduction.* Tech. rept. 124. Psychology Department, Sheffield University, Sheffield, UK, available from http://www.shef.ac.uk/˜pc1jvs.

Press, WH, Flannery, BP, Teukolsky, SA, & Vetterling, WT. 1989. *Numerical recipes in c.* Cambridge, UK, Cambridge University Press.

Reza, FM. 1961. *Information theory.* New York, McGraw-Hill.

Sivia, DS. 1996. *Data analysis: A bayesian tutorial.* Oxford, UK, Clarendon Press.

Stone, J V. 1996a. A canonical microfunction for learning perceptual invariances. *Perception*, **25**(2), 207–220.

Stone, J V. 1996b. Learning perceptually salient visual parameters through spatiotemporal smoothness constraints. *Neural computation*, **8**(7), 1463–1492.

Stone, J V, & Lister, R. 1994. On the relative time complexities of standard and conjugate gradient back-propagation. *Pages 84–87 of: Proceedings of the ieee international conference on neural networks, orlando, fl.*

Stone, JV. 1999. Learning perceptually salient visual parameters using spatiotemporal smoothness constraints. *Pages 71–100 of:* Hinton, G, & Sejnowski, T (eds), *Unsupervised learning:foundations of neural computation.* London, MIT Press.

Stone, JV. 2001. Blind source separation using temporal predictability. *Neural computation*, **13**(7), 1559–1574.

Stone, JV, & Porrill, J. 1999. Regularisation using spatiotemporal independence and predictability. *Sheffield university technical report 201.*

Stone, JV, Porrill, J, Porter, NR, & Wilkinson, IW. 2002. Spatiotemporal independent component analysis of event-related fmri data using skewed probability density functions. *Neuroimage*, **15**(2), 407–421.

Xie, S, He, Z, & Fu, Y. (in press). A note on stone's conjecture of blind signal separation. *Neural computation.*

Index